Amethyst in Ashes

The Sezna Seer, Volume 1

Kiersten Lillis

Published by Kiersten Lillis, 2019.

This is a work of fiction. Similarities to real people, places, or events are entirely coincidental.

AMETHYST IN ASHES

First edition. March 28, 2019.

Copyright © 2019 Kiersten Lillis.

ISBN: 978-1-7336178-1-9

Written by Kiersten Lillis.

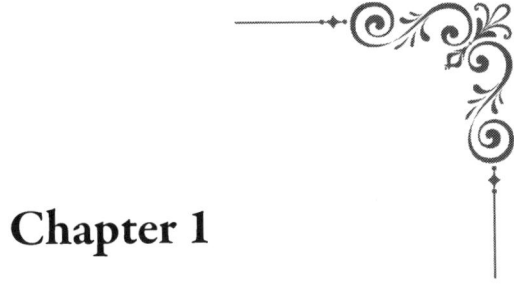

Chapter 1

Talullah slipped through the invisible magical barrier, wincing at the tingle that ran up her spine. No matter how many times she passed through her town's protection spell, she couldn't get used to it. She adjusted her cloth knapsack and shook her long black braid over her shoulder. This would have to be a quick trip. She had too much to do before the festival the next day. No distractions, she told herself, as she made her way to the edge of the forest, boots crunching in the first fallen leaves of autumn.

Counting the tree stumps in the middle of the clearing, she recited her list. Fabric for Penny's dress. Cinnamon, if the merchant had any. Though she doubted he would. It had been months since some Viltresorian noble had snatched up the last of his store.

That was it. Short list, today. She'd stocked up on the essentials at the last Hidden Market a few months ago. Lucky, too. They hadn't sold much at the family antique shop recently, so she didn't have much money to spend. She already planned to use her personal wages to buy the material for her youngest sister's new dress.

Pewter coins tinkled in the leather pouch at her waist as she stopped between the sixth and seventh stumps. Again, her body tingled as she stepped between them and through the cloaking spell.

The smell of freshly cut melon welcomed her to the Hidden Market. Already, merchants and buyers haggled in urgent tones, scanning the cobbled streets for spies from Terrapese or Viltresor. The two territories' rulers, though technically at peace, fought a silent war. Their citizens, however, put their differences aside in the name of trade. Where else could a Viltresorian mother acquire fresh greens for her family's dinner? Not the neglected farms in her own neighborhood, that was for sure. Rationed water and poor soil made it impossible to grow anything that didn't taste like sand. And if a Terrapesian man wanted to woo his wife with fine fabrics or sharp, clear stones, he had no choice but to purchase from Viltresorian craftspeople. As long as the spies from each territory received their quarterly bribes—and as long as the cloaking spell held—the system worked. The kings need not know their people cooperated.

Talullah smiled at the fruit stand's proprietor as she passed.

"Two pewters for a melon, dear," the portly woman said. She gestured to the halved fruit, their pink and orange and green flesh glistening.

"Sorry," said Talullah. "Not today." She moved on. Four Hidden Markets a year for the past eight years had taught her not to linger too long at the merchants' booths. Once, when she was twelve, she'd gotten stuck talking to a jeweler for an hour. She'd made the mistake of asking why he'd become a jeweler. Too polite. At fifteen, she finally understood surviving the Hidden Market with money in her pocket and time still on the clock meant sticking to business. *What is it? Where'd it come from? How much?* It wasn't rude. On the contrary, merchants appreciated efficiency. More eyes on their wares meant more food in their children's mouths and fewer holes in their shoes.

Gem-toned fabric draped on wooden poles shaded the marketgoers from the morning sun and separated the stalls. She passed tables of dried game and fruits, rice and beans, nut flours and baked goods until she reached her first stop. Pulling aside the yellow gauze of the spice seller's tent, she poked her head through the gap.

"Anything today?" she asked, not daring to get her hopes up.

The man's rich dark skin glowed. A conspiratorial smile spread across his weathered face, revealing a mouthful of bone white teeth.

"Come in," he whispered, dropping from the woven rainbow hammock where he swayed in the corner. He dipped behind a table and pulled out a glass jar the size of Talullah's little finger.

Dark red powder filled it to the cork cap. Talullah's mouth dropped open.

"Others have asked me, and I told them no, not today, maybe next time," he whispered. He offered the jar to her with a wink. "I lied."

"You saved it for me? Thank you, Baako." Talullah offered him five pewter coins.

Baako shook his head. "I did not give you a birthday present last market day. Accept this instead. Freshly ground this morning with my own hands."

"Baako, this is too much for a gift. Especially from you."

The man waved at her as if shooing a fly. "Fifteen is an important year. You have chosen your trade?"

Talullah nodded. "To stay at my father's shop." The antique trade had more or less chosen her, but that was beside the point. Baako knew that already, but she appreciated the pretense of choice. She did enjoy her job, at least.

He sighed, each of his seventy years of age etched as a line in his face. "You have been a loyal customer, Talullah. And a good friend to an old man. Please, take it."

She smiled. Respect for him prevented her arguing. She slipped the container of cinnamon in an interior pocket of her bag. Baako was the one exception to Talullah's no-dallying rule. She'd ended many of her Hidden Market days in his tent learning about spices and listening to stories of his life before the First War. His wife had passed to the next life many years before, and his children had all moved away to pursue their trades. He'd been like a grandfather to Talullah, who'd never known her own.

"I wish I could stay…"

"Go, go." He waved her out, humor dimpling his cheeks. "I have many customers to disappoint today."

"I'll stay longer next time. Promise." She swished out through the opening in the fabric and headed for the textile tents.

After much deliberation, she settled on yellow silk for Penny's dress. Golden as her sister's hair and bright as the sun. Penny would love it.

Check and check. The two items on her list were complete. And she still had time to research some of the new items at the shop. She'd turned onto the main road when a dark blue tent caught her eye. Embroidered with silver stars, the fabric swayed in the breeze like the night sky. She'd never seen that one before.

A woman about her father's age sat behind a table underneath the tent. Her rosy lips popped against her pale skin. "Oh, hello," she said as Talullah approached. "Can I interest you in a reading?" Shaking her long blond curls from her face, the woman shuffled a deck of cards and set them in front of Talullah. "Or perhaps a peek into the crystal fortune?" She gestured to a clear orb the size of a pomegranate which sat on a bronze base.

"You're a fortune teller?" Talullah asked. In early childhood, the idea of magic had thrilled her. Knowing her town appeared invisible to outsiders felt like living in a storybook. The Viltresorian magical community's artifacts had stolen hours of her daydreams, invented stories of witches and dragons and faeries waltzing through her imagination.

But the wonder had faded. Now, she avoided the Viltresorian tents when she could. Some effused an energy that made her hair stand on end, dark magic hiding among the sparkling crystals and brewed tonics. Disguised, of course. No one advertised cursed objects or poison. But it was there. Magic equaled deception, and Talullah preferred the truth.

"Yes," the woman sighed. "And no one cares in the slightest." She scrutinized Talullah's face, and then her gray eyes lit up. "I do have some other things, though. Trinkets. Non-magical, but still." She rummaged in a box and produced a handful of items, which she lay on the table.

A pair of gem-encrusted knitting needles. Five pocket-watches. Scraps of fabric stitched together to form a small blanket. And a heart-shaped compass.

"May I?" Talullah asked.

"Please," the woman said.

Talullah picked up the compass. Its golden shell warmed in her palm. "What's this say?" She ran her thumb over the engraved symbols encircling the navigation marks.

The corners of the woman's mouth turned upward. "I'm not sure. I've never been good at languages. Intriguing, though, aren't they?"

Talullah nodded, already imagining herself flipping through the thousands of pages of *Languages of the World* and comparing the etchings to the symbols within. "And the needle points south. I've never heard of such a thing."

The woman shrugged. "Might be broken. Might be that way on purpose. Again, not sure."

A buzz spread from Talullah's fingers to her heart. This was the kind of object that made her job worthwhile. It had a story, and she wanted to learn it. "How much?" Talullah pulled two pewter coins from her pouch, scraping the bottom with her fingertips. That was all she had left.

The woman glanced at her outstretched palm. "I think two pewters will suffice."

Talullah raised her brows. "Are you sure?" The compass shell alone was worth twice that if it truly was gold.

"Sure. Like I said, it might not even work. And you've been a gem talking to me. I think you'll find some use for it."

Before the woman could change her mind, Talullah handed over her money and stowed the compass in her bag. "Thanks. I hope you find someone to read for, so your whole day won't be wasted."

A smile lit the woman's face. "I can assure you, today has been anything but wasted."

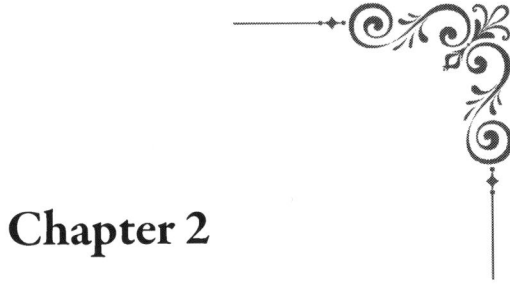

Chapter 2

Pinching the smooth fabric between her fingers, Talullah pulled it closer to her face. Early morning sun peeked through her window and its rays skipped off the canary yellow satin. She squinted at the light—it couldn't be morning already. The whole night had dissolved in a blur of cutting and pinning and stitching.

Weave and sew, weave and sew. Forever she would weave and sew.

She heaved a sigh and rubbed her dry eyes.

The song her mother used to sing during challenging times forced its way into her mind, its catchy cadence bobbing in her subconscious.

Through the fire blazing bright, trust yourself, harness your might. Inner struggle blinds your eyes, let it go and win the prize. Use your heart, keep your mind, and what you seek, you shall find.

As a child, Talullah had felt empowered by the song, like it could give her the strength to conquer her deepest fears, to extinguish her wildest fires. Now she gritted her teeth and cursed the rhyme that flowed through her head, despite the years she'd spent trying to forget it.

She'd stopped relying on her mother years ago. No need to start now.

Focus.

Just one more line of stitching on the hem and Penny's dress would be finished. As her practiced hands worked, weaving the needle in and out in a perfectly straight line, her mind wandered.

She tried not to grimace. Only a few hours until the Sunflower Festival. Each year, the people of River Hill celebrated the founding of their town by gorging themselves on food and wine and dancing until the sun came up.

But Talullah could only focus on the magic barrier cloaking River Hill. It shielded the town from outside threats, but it also held them hostage. Could an invisible cage truly be called freedom?

If only she could leave River Hill for real and travel the world, as few brave others had done over the years. Ten-minute walks to and from the Hidden Market didn't count. She imagined the vastness of the ocean whose waves were rumored to beat upon a snow-white beach on the edge of the continent. If she thought about it hard enough, she could almost smell the salt.

She flinched. A small bead of blood welled on her golden fingertip. She pressed it against her dark linen pants. Her heart jumped as she checked the fabric. A bloodstain on Penny's new dress was the last thing she needed. Talullah had promised her sister something new and beautiful, for once. She didn't want to let her down.

Exhale. Still clean, thank the Founders.

As she bandaged her finger, she scolded herself for letting her mind stray. When focused, she could sew a straight line with her eyes closed, relying only on the feel of the fabric and needle in her hands. She finished the hem as the sun broke past the horizon, bathing her room in light.

Yawning, she laid the dress across her bed, which was still made from the day before. As she twisted her long obsidian hair into a braid, she glanced out the window at the row of hazelnut trees in the yard.

Talullah was five when her mother planted them. She'd sat on the front porch as her mother dug the soil for the saplings and braced the new trees with string.

"Mother, how come you have to tie the string to the trees?" she had asked, rocking her newborn sister, Margot, in a basket while her mother worked.

"The trees need to grow their roots deep into the ground. That's how they stand so tall and strong for many years. Now the trees' roots are small. They need the string to help them fight against the harsh weather. But very soon the roots will be strong enough to hold up the tree all by themselves. That's when we will cut away the string."

Talullah had screwed up her face in confusion. "But, Mother, how will we know the roots are strong enough if they're buried under the ground?"

A sparkling grin reached all the way to her mother's chocolate eyes. It was the last time she'd seen her mother smile that way. "My dear, Talullah, we don't always see with our eyes."

Two years later, after Penny was born, Talullah's mother had walked out on them.

Talullah turned her gaze from the trees and secured her hair with a band. Every year on September first, her town celebrated the liberation of their ancestors. Instead, she suffocated under the memory of watching her mother walk away forever.

Side-stepping the creaky boards so as not to wake her father and sisters, she pushed open the front door to the porch and set her mug of tea—now hours cold—on the steps. The sweet smell of dew greeted her, and a cool breeze tickled her skin. She relished the freshness of morning, knowing it wouldn't last long.

She approached the line of hazelnut trees and lifted her hand to touch a branch.

Over the years, she'd considered cutting them down, but Margot and Penny loved them. They spent hours climbing as high as they could into the branches, pretending to be adventurers on a quest in the jungle.

Tears stung Talullah's eyes as she touched the branch. Blinking them back and setting her jaw, she tugged a leaf from the tree and let it flutter to the ground.

"Tuley! I get to be a Sunflower Princess today!" Penny said brightly, bouncing out the front door and onto the porch.

Talullah turned, swapping her frown for a smile. "I know! It's going to be the best day! But Penny, you shouldn't be wearing this dress now. It's for the festival, not for playing."

"I know, Tuley. But it's so pretty! I wanted to try it on. Just for a few minutes. I can't wait for the parade!" She closed her eyes and twirled with her arms held out to the sides, her two golden braids flapping against her shoulders and the dress billowing out around her. "I love it!"

Talullah headed for the porch, eyeing her mug of tea. Crystal ball or no, she could guess what was about to happen. "Careful."

"Whoa, I'm dizzy." Penny stumbled and fell, giggling. "It's okay, Tuley, I'm fine."

Dark tea crept up Penny's hem as Talullah reached her. "My dress! Oh, I've ruined it!" she shrieked. Her emerald eyes welled with tears.

"Are you hurt?" Talullah sat and checked Penny's arms and legs for bruises.

"No, but I'm sorry, Tuley. I didn't mean to. It was an accident." She hiccupped between sobs.

"It's okay, Penny." She'd spent all night making that dress, not to mention all her extra money. A calming breath filled her lungs. "Go inside and change, and I'll take care of it."

"Thank you, Tuley. I love you," Penny said, her voice barely audible, before disappearing inside.

"Love you, too, Penny."

Talullah picked up the mug, shaking her head. The dress *had* been new when Penny had first put it on. That had to count for something.

Half an hour later, Talullah had managed to scrub the dress clean—thank the Founders—and piled breakfast ingredients on the kitchen counter.

"Can we have cinnamon pancakes?" Penny squealed from the table. Talullah set the sack of flour on the counter. A cloud of white powder puffed in the air. "Tuley, can we have—"

"Already working on it." She rummaged through the cabinet and retrieved the jar of cinnamon she'd procured at the Hidden Market. Bless Baako and his kindness.

Cinnamon pancakes were Margot and Penny's favorite, and Talullah always made them on special occasions. Even when, like today, she didn't feel up to it.

"Did someone say cinnamon pancakes?" Margot yawned and shuffled into the kitchen still wearing her pajamas.

Talullah stirred the pancake batter in a wooden bowl.

"You're not going to wear that into town, are you?" Penny asked, giggling.

"Of course not, Pennilyn," Margot said, as if it were obvious. "I'll change after breakfast." She smoothed her hair, the same color and silky texture as Penny and their father's. Talullah had been the only one to inherit their mother's dark tresses, though they all had gotten her tanned skin.

Margot, at ten, was more pragmatic than the rest of the family. Talullah, for one, appreciated her foresight. It was doubtful the tea stain would be the only thing she'd have to scrub out of Penny's dress before the Sunflower Festival. She spooned batter into the pan and smiled when it sizzled.

Syncopated thudding echoed through the hall, followed closely by their father's warm voice. "Do I smell cinnamon?"

He rounded the corner. Talullah rolled her eyes at the sight of the cane he'd pulled from a closet last week. It had a garish carved fish on top, which looked like it had tried to swallow the rest of the cane. Its tail curved backward, making the body a suitable handle. Talullah shivered as the sunlight glinted off its one red eye.

"Morning, Father," the girls chorused.

"I don't know why you insist on using that thing. You already have a cane," Margot said, cracking a smile.

"Oh yes, but this one has more personality." Their father examined the cane, running his fingers over the carved scales.

"Father has always had unique taste. You just wait. I bet these fish canes are going to be the next big thing." Talullah winked at her father. She flipped the pancakes and a spicy warmth enveloped the kitchen.

He shrugged. "I'm an antiques man. How am I supposed to sell anything if I don't believe in the product myself? I'd forgotten all about this one. Had it for a long time." He brushed a stray hair out of his eyes and stared at the cane, looking wistful. "Now, what is on the agenda for today?" he asked, taking his place at the table.

"Dad, you didn't forget, did you?"

He laughed. "Of course not, Mar! How could we forget the Sunflower Festival?" He raised his mug of tea in cheers and stole a meaningful glance at Talullah. Margot and Penny were too young to remember, but her father would never forget the day's double meaning.

Talullah gave an imperceptible nod as she plopped full plates on the table and took her place in between Margot and Penny. The empty chair next to her father beckoned her gaze, but she refused.

Margot heaved a sigh of relief. "Tuley said she would take Pennilyn and me into town after she gets back from the library."

In her mind, Talullah scolded herself. She'd only said that to get her sisters to stop bothering her while she worked, but she should have realized they wouldn't forget. Margot, especially, remembered everything, no matter how insignificant.

"I think that's a fine idea," their father replied, wiping syrup off his chin. "And swallow your food before you speak, Margot. Working today, Talullah?"

She met his gaze for a brief second before returning to her breakfast. "Just a bit of cataloguing I want to get done before everything starts."

When Talullah had turned fifteen, she had officially begun her apprenticeship at her father's antique shop. She'd been helping out since she could hold a broom, but her responsibilities had grown after her mother left. Her father couldn't handle the shop alone while taking care of three children, so Talullah stepped up.

Her father met her eye. "Very well. But don't overdo it. There's plenty of time to work and not so much time to play."

Talullah nodded. She loved the history of the objects and the stories behind them, but she longed to find the treasures, not just read about them. Most nights she fell asleep with her face in a book about far off lands and the items that remained when the people disappeared.

But her father's legs were getting worse and Talullah feared the day would soon come when he'd be unable to walk at all. With her sisters still so young, Talullah couldn't leave River Hill. Not without a mother to help take care of them.

Talullah subconsciously traced her necklace, thinking. The small, gold and silver eye-shaped trinket was the only thing of value Talullah had ever owned, a family heirloom she received from her mother on her seventh birthday. She'd spent countless hours researching it in the books in the library, convinced it had belonged to a great queen. After eight years, she'd still found nothing.

Recently, when she found herself particularly upset, she considered putting the necklace in the store's inventory and letting someone take it away. But every time she touched the clasp, a warm tingling trickled across her collarbone and she'd remember everything she'd tried so hard to forget. The warmth of her mother's hug, the dulcet tone of her voice talking about trees, the sweet smell of lavender that clung to her clothes no matter how long she'd been hunting in the forest.

Every time, Talullah decided to keep it.

After breakfast, Talullah settled her father on the couch and was halfway out the front door, her bag full of books and trinkets, when her father called her back in.

"Talullah, dear, could you grab my cane for me? I left it against the wall in the kitchen."

She doubled back. Grimacing, she grabbed the handle.

As soon as her fingers grazed the carved scales, her vision went fuzzy.

Not again.

She blinked, trying to dissolve the developing scene. A moment later she stood in a forest that looked carved from rubies. A large wall of fire blazed in front of her.

A cloaked figure appeared out of nowhere, its chin-length hair blowing back as it crept toward the fire.

Talullah tried to yell out, but she choked on thick smoke. Heat pressed against her body like a solid, burning wall, and sweat trickled down the back of her neck.

The figure reached the flames. It covered its head with its hood, pushed its hands into the cloaks' sleeves, rolled back its shoulders, and walked into the fire.

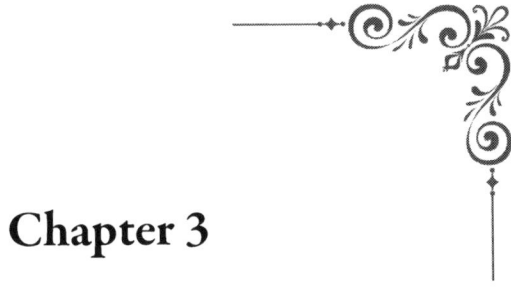

Chapter 3

Talullah barely made it to the sink before she heaved. Cold sweat beaded on her forehead as she expelled the contents of her stomach, the cinnamon burning the back of her throat. She closed her eyes and took three deep breaths. On the third exhale she opened her eyes, careful to focus on one, unmoving spot on the wall.

As the dizziness faded, she pieced together what she'd seen. No, what she'd *experienced*.

The wall of flames still flickered behind her eyes, and her skin held the memory of its warmth. The girl, too, lingered like smoke from an extinguished candle. Talullah hadn't seen her face, but something about the girl pulled a loose thread in Talullah's mind. Did she know the girl somehow?

Worry lines etched themselves in her forehead. Almost always the visions played with her senses, but never before had she lost track of herself. This one had absorbed her. And she had let it.

As she splashed cold water on her face and rinsed her mouth, she counted the number of visions she'd had last month. Sixteen, the most ever in such a short time.

The first vision she remembered had come on her seventh birthday, though now she couldn't recall what she'd seen. More memorable was the feeling that accompanied it—adrenaline rushing through her veins, and after it was over, the clenching in her stomach and the sour taste of bile. And a throbbing headache.

Talullah's mother had made her drink a mug of hot tea that tasted like charred wood and onions—despite Talullah's protests—and massaged her temples until the pain subsided. When Talullah had asked why it looked like the shadows in her dreams were hiding behind colored veils, hard lines had formed between her mother's eyebrows. Talullah had studied those eyes. Behind them, her mother's mind worked to find the right words. In the end, her mother had settled on the song about fire and water, challenge and strength. Despite Talullah's pressure for more explanation, her mother had given her none.

Her father had said the visions were just the result of so much reading. "Overstimulation of imagination," he'd called it. For so long she'd agreed they were nothing. But now she wasn't so sure. Something in her gut told her this one was different. Important. It challenged her to solve its riddle, whose words she didn't understand.

Swallowing the lump in her throat, she traced the eye-shaped amulet dangling from a thin chain around her neck. Immediately the tension in her shoulders melted away and the tightness in her chest faded.

"Talullah, have you found it?" her father called from the living room.

"I'm coming," she answered, bending down to retrieve the cane, which she'd dropped on her way to the sink. She hesitated, her hand hovering over the handle. Pursing her lips and bracing herself, she closed her fingers around the pole. This time, nothing happened.

"TULEY, CAN I GET A lemonade?"

"Mar, the festival parade is about to start." Talullah wiped her sweaty palms on her pants and fanned her face. Even though they'd managed to snag a spot on the shaded hill in the center of town, the heat was unbearable.

Almost as hot as a wall of fire.

Talullah shook her head, clearing the thought. The vision had plagued her all morning. She'd barely gotten any work done.

"I know. But it's hot, and I'm thirsty." Margot dragged a handkerchief across her brow. "And the cart is close. I'll be back before Father gets here."

"There are a lot of people, Mar. I don't think you should go alone."

The girl was alone. Why was she alone?

Talullah's gut churned. She was missing something. But what?

Margot placed a hand on her hip and pushed her chin forward. "Tuley, I'm ten. I'm not a baby."

Talullah licked her lips. Her mouth felt like cotton. Scanning the square, her eyes landed on the lemonade cart. Margot was right—it wasn't far at all. An ice-cold lemonade *was* tempting. "Okay," she said, handing Margot some pewter coins her father had given her. "Get two lemonades and come right back."

"And a pretzel?" Margot added, her eyebrows raised.

"Just the lemonades."

Margot sighed. "Fine. Just the lemonades." She pocketed the money and wove her way down the hill and into the crowd, her blond bun bobbing on top of her head.

Talullah wiped her brow and gazed down on the square. Vendors of all kinds stood at tented booths, selling food and drinks and trinkets. Each of them wore a sunflower pinned to his or her apron or hat and chatted with the townsfolk who stopped to peruse their wares. The smoky sweetness of roasted meat carried in the slight breeze.

The parade was only the beginning of the festival. After the evening feast, when the sun had slipped below the horizon, the townspeople would dance until the wee hours of the morning, their smiling faces lit by firelight.

Rolling her eyes at the large sunflower swaying atop his hat, she waved at her father. He headed straight for her, a wide grin plastered to his face. Despite the past, he still loved the Sunflower Festival.

A bow drew across a violin, releasing a single, smooth note into the crowd noise. Talullah sucked in a breath, her body suddenly tense. The townsfolk fell silent, but their excited energy pulsed through the crowd. The melody built, growing in speed and intensity until it reached the chorus. On the downbeat, other instruments joined in and the crowd erupted into cheers, their voices mingling with the fiddles and horns. The sting of tears surprised her, though it shouldn't have. They came every year. With each passing festival, she thought she'd be stronger, that it wouldn't matter as much. Yet again, she was wrong.

Maybe she was also wrong about the visions. Whether they were premonitions or memories or something else, she'd never been able to make sense of them. The rest had faded quickly, leaving only faint traces of its existence. But this vision had sunk in its claws and refused to release her.

She would figure it out. But not now. It was Penny's moment.

She dried her eyes and turned her attention to the Sunflower Princes and Princesses, lined up behind the band on the library lawn, dressed in their best and ready to march. She found Penny, radiant in her yellow dress, a crown of flowers decorating her hair. One of the braids Talullah had pinned to her head had already come loose. Watching Penny bounce in line, Talullah knew it was only a matter of time before the other braids broke free as well. She itched to cross the square and fix them.

The band marched and the children followed behind, scattering petals in their wake. Talullah searched the crowd for Margot. She spotted her next to the pretzel cart in front of the pond, lemonade in one hand and a pretzel in the other. Talullah's jaw clenched. Of course Margot had ignored her simple instructions. She narrowed her eyes on her sister and willed her to look toward the hill, but Margot stared straight ahead, as if she knew Talullah was watching her.

Grumbling to herself, she looked for her father, wondering what had prevented him from reaching her. She spotted him halfway up the hill, engrossed in conversation with Mabel Miller, who owned the teapot shop. Once Mabel started talking there was no stopping her.

The band wound through the square with the children in tow. Penny twirled in line, beaming as she showered the crowd in yellow petals. Despite herself, Talullah grinned.

Her eyes darted between her family members. Regardless of how she felt, they should be watching Penny's big moment together. Pursing her lips, Talullah held her breath against the sour smell of sweat and squeezed a path through the wall of bodies, heading toward her father. Halfway down the hill another sound cut through the music—hooves.

The crowd stirred in confusion, searching for the source. But they didn't have to wait long. From the west corner of the square galloped six horses, each topped by a rider wearing golden boots and an embroidered silk cloak.

Talullah's heart jumped into her throat. She tried to draw breath, but her lungs wouldn't work. *Soldiers from Terrapese.* Even from a distance the crest on their shoulders was unmistakable. As a child she'd been taught to avoid all contact with anyone bearing that mark. They were monsters and menaces. They were dangerous.

Someone screamed. A thousand questions ricocheted in her mind, but there wasn't time to ask how they'd gotten through the magic barrier or why they'd come. She needed to find her sisters. Adrenaline surged in her veins as she searched the crowd. She caught her father's eye and he mouthed, "Find Margot."

Gritting her teeth, she pushed against the mass of slick, salty bodies.

The meat vendors had abandoned their stations without extinguishing the fires. The square filled with clouds smelling of scorched lamb. Tightness crept into her chest as she passed through the smoke, barely aware of the screaming people around her.

She touched the eye through her tunic. *Please be there. Please be okay.*

With one powerful shove, she created a gap in the mob. Air filled her lungs as she broke free, stumbling off the hill and into the square.

Through the smoke, she saw three soldiers halt their horses next to the pretzel cart, swords glinting at their waists. Talullah's blood turned to ice in her veins.

"Margot!" she tried to shout, but her constricted throat stifled all sound.

A soldier dismounted. Pulled Margot, kicking and punching, from her hiding spot behind the cart.

Talullah's mind raced as she pushed her legs to move faster, dodging people and straining to see through the cloud of smoke. *I can't lose them, too.*

She skidded to a stop behind an abandoned cart and crouched down, trying to catch her breath and form a plan. Bare hands would be no match for their steel swords, but she had to do something. She was close enough to see a soldier hoist Margot, hands and feet bound, onto a horse. Silver-capped teeth arranged in a crooked smile glinted from under his dark hood. Talullah heard the word "necklace" but couldn't make out the rest of the soldier's question.

Margot pushed her chin forward and lifted her head, staying silent.

"You little brat. Think you can defy the guards of Terrapese, do you? I'll show you what that gets you." The venom in his thick brogue made Talullah's muscles tense. He lifted his gloved hand as if to strike Margot. Talullah's eyes widened, her heart pounding so loud she was convinced they could hear it from fifteen feet away. Before Talullah could call out, another soldier caught his arm.

"No need for that, Rantoul." The soldier's voice reminded Talullah of warm honey amid chaos. "We're not going to hurt you," he said to Margot. He turned to the other men and said, "It's not at the house, but we'll find it." Without warning, he slapped Margot's horse on the hind. It whinnied and took off across the now empty square toward the forest, flanked by the rest of the soldiers.

"Margot!" Talullah yelled.

Nonononono. She tore after them, hot air wheezing in her lungs, her limbs tingling with fear. "Come back!" Hoof beats thundered against the cobblestone, drowning out her desperate attempts to draw the soldiers' attention. Why hadn't she said something, anything?

At the edge of the forest, she clutched the stitch in her side, panting and peering through the trees for any sign of her quarry. The scent of pine and earth welcomed her to the place she'd spent much of her childhood, but today it didn't bring her comfort.

A sob escaped her quivering lips. The soldiers were gone, and so was her sister.

Chapter 4

Talullah's feet pounded the earth in even rhythm. She barely noticed the burning in her chest or the wetness on her cheeks as she crossed into the center of town, now deserted, and made her way to the back of the teapot shop. If her father and Penny were still in River Hill, they would have gone to their family safe-spot. They'd practiced the emergency plan so often Talullah's body carried out the steps automatically.

She glanced over her shoulder, though she knew the soldiers were long gone. Each of their six shrinking silhouettes had imprinted on her mind as they'd disappeared into the forest. Still, she couldn't shake the feeling she was being watched.

Someone had extinguished the fires in the square, but lingering smoke stung her eyes. Sharp thorns tore at her arms and face as she forced her body past the overgrown blackberry bush behind the shop. Without hesitation, she brushed aside enough gravel to reveal the smooth metal hoop in the cellar door and heaved it open.

Sunlight spilled into the small space. She jumped in, her boots sending a puff of dirt into the air. It took only a quick glance for her to see she was alone. A vice squeezed her heart.

But something in the far corner caught her eye. Her breath hitched in her chest as she approached Penny's stuffed rabbit, Artemis, whose crown of flowers still encircled its head.

Talullah picked up the toy with care and stared at it in disbelief. If Artemis was there, Penny had been, too. Had their father been there? Where had they gone? And why hadn't they waited for her?

She paced the cellar looking for another clue, ignoring the prickling of her skin. Almost immediately she saw them. Footprints. But instead of lifting her spirits, they made her stomach plummet. Three sets, not two. One pair the size of large riding boots.

GLASS SHARDS—the only remnants of her favorite mirror—crunched beneath her boots as she tore through her house, shoving things haphazardly into her knapsack. Rope, healing salve, dried meat and stale bread. She dodged pieces of splintered furniture which covered the floor. Papers and books peeked from beneath overturned tables and broken chairs. Their recent acquisitions—antiques they'd prepped to sell but hadn't yet moved to the shop—had been destroyed.

Fury fueled her movements, and its burn reached every inch of her. Not only had the soldiers kidnapped her family but also ransacked her home.

Her room was in a similar state. She spotted her compass on her bed and beelined for it. When she caught sight of her tabletop loom lying near it amongst the chaos, she paused, distracted. It had been years since she'd removed it from its box in her closet.

She fought the urge to grab the loom, though she could feel the threads beneath her fingers without making contact. Weaving had been her mother's idea. *A useful skill*, she'd called it. Talullah had obliged. Eventually she even grew to like it. Until she didn't.

Her hands tingled at the memory. But her heart knew she didn't want it. Didn't need it. Not anymore.

What she did need was her canteen.

If she stopped too long, she'd realize the danger she was about to face. Leaving home for the first time on her own, fighting an army with a four-inch hunting blade. She'd need a better weapon.

One step at a time. Find the canteen.

It wasn't in her room or the kitchen. Where else could it be? Her stomach rolled. Margot and Penny had been playing with it that morning in their bedroom. They'd been pretending to be adventurers.

Her body tense, Talullah pushed into her sisters' room. Dusty boot prints wove a path across the worn wooden floor. The thought of dirty soldiers rifling through her sisters' things made her queasy, but she tried to ignore it. She found the canteen tossed atop Margot's covers.

She picked it up and rushed back to the kitchen. Artemis seemed to watch her as she finished packing. An invisible force tugged at Talullah's heart. She grabbed the toy and hugged it to her chest, squeezing it as if by doing so she could make Penny appear in her arms. Something rough scratched against her collarbone. She hadn't noticed it before, but a thin piece of fishing line wrapped around Artemis' neck like a collar. Though the line was clear, the feel of it beneath her fingertips was unmistakable. Her fingers followed it across the rabbit's neck until she felt the familiar texture of parchment buried in the rabbit's fur.

Her mouth grew dry as she loosened the small roll from the fishing line.

Hands shaking, she unfurled the paper.

The handwriting was unfamiliar, but the words made her stomach drop to her toes.

Go see Mirella.

"Mirella." Talullah's great-aunt's name tasted foreign on her tongue. She couldn't remember the last time she'd spoken it aloud, or even thought it, for that matter.

Go see Mirella.

Talullah had vague memories of playing in Mirella's garden as a small child while her mother and great-aunt had tea in the large sunroom. That was before Margot and Penny were born, before the visions.

Her father had taken her and her sisters to visit Mirella only once, a few weeks after her mother left. It had been all hushed voices and closed doors and "not now, the adults are talking." When they'd left, Talullah had thought her father looked older somehow, even more pained than when they'd arrived.

That was the last time Talullah had seen her great-aunt.

Mirella had sent letters twice a year since. Talullah had seen her name written in loopy handwriting on the envelopes. But whenever she asked what they said, her father always responded, "Nothing important." Talullah suspected their contents had something to do with whatever Mirella had told her father during their last visit. Whatever had made his face look like despair.

The parchment crumpled in Talullah's clenched fist. Her aunt enjoyed a quiet, secluded life away from River Hill. She could only be found when she wanted to be. So, who had made the connection?

And why hide the note with a child's toy?

To make sure the right person found it.

They'd left the toy in her family's safe spot. Only Talullah's family would recognize the rabbit as Penny's and care enough to pick it up. But who knew enough to piece together that plan?

Her father. Why hadn't she thought of that first? Maybe it was his way of telling her where they'd gone.

She checked the note again. Her hand trembled. It wasn't his handwriting.

Destroyed furniture, Terrapesian soldiers, a secret note, three—no, *four*—missing family members. Pain pulsed against Talullah's temples.

She shoved the note in her knapsack. She simply couldn't trust that whomever had written the note had her best interests in mind. There were too many variables, too many possibilities, too many motives. Margot was in danger, Penny and her father were missing, and she wouldn't waste another second deliberating.

Talullah flung her knapsack over her shoulder, sheathed her knife on her boot, and strode back through the only place she'd ever called home. The front door weighed heavy in her hand, as if all her grief and confusion and fear flowed from her into its dark woodgrain.

She swallowed the lump lodged in her throat. The one made of the knowledge that she might never come home again and the burning fear she *would* return, but all alone.

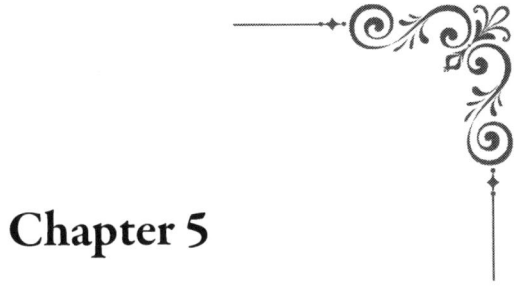

Chapter 5

As a child, Talullah had explored the woods bordering Nainehta Forest, but she'd never entered the forest itself. She hadn't been allowed. No one had. It had grown quickly and strangely in the first few years after the town's founding and acted as a natural border between River Hill and Terrapese. Merchants at the Hidden Market who hawked wares from Terrapese had all told her the same thing—they'd rather walk three extra days around Nainehta than take the shortcut through it. The risk of getting caught by Terrapesian soldiers was preferable to the forest. Others had entered, taunting it to do its worst. Most never came back out. And those who did never smiled again.

Shivers ran up Talullah's spine as she stood at the threshold. Never before had she considered passing through the line of ashy trunks that gave off smoke day and night, though they'd never—to her knowledge—caught flame. Even in the heaviest rain the trees effused their warning to keep out.

Flames. The wall of fire from her vision appeared again in her mind. The girl in the hooded cloak straightened her back and walked through it.

Not now.

She forced the scene away and rifled through her knapsack for her compass, hands shaking. Surely she'd packed it. Another image flashed behind her eyes—her compass lying on her bed next to the loom. Her stomach sank. How had she forgotten it? She buried her face in her hands and groaned into her palms. Hours wasted. And it would be dark by the time she made it back. She couldn't afford mistakes like this. *Her family* couldn't afford them.

Blood pumping hot, she flung the knapsack over her shoulder. Something small and golden popped out of the top pocket, which she hadn't bothered to close. The item landed at her feet, shining in the sun.

Talullah's eyes lit up. She picked up the item and dusted it off with her tunic. She'd forgotten all about the compass she'd purchased from the fortune teller at the Hidden Market. That morning she'd spent hours in the library researching it before the Sunflower Festival. Despite the daily humdrum, Talullah loved her job. She cherished the thrill of discovering a clue to an object's history and following it into the unknown. The chance to explore life in another time and another place.

The feel of the compass sent sparks through her body. Its heart-shaped shell fit perfectly in her palm, as if it were molded for her hand. It looked forged from gold, but its weight resembled silk more than metal.

With renewed confidence, she secured her knapsack pockets and focused on the compass's needle.

It quivered on the round face, then spun to point south, just as it had when she'd first examined it. She jiggled the compass and spun ninety degrees. The needle held fast at due south. Brows furrowed, she stole a glance at the smoky sentries guarding the entrance to the forest. There was no way she'd be able to navigate through the thick fog without something to guide her. For a second, she entertained the option of going around Nainehta, like the merchants had done. Her heart thundered in protest, the names of her family members reverberating through every inch of her veins.

She gripped the compass tighter. Stories she'd read about Terrapesian soldiers escaped the vault in her mind where she'd locked them. Their gory transgressions painted the trees with scenes of torture and malice, of prisoners beaten and starved. Her family members appeared amongst the chaos. Sweat trickled from her temple, racing the tears from her eyes. She swiped both with her sleeve and blinked the images away.

Three days would be too long. Going through Nainehta was her only choice.

She approached the entrance with measured steps, eyes and ears alert. Her thumb grazed the tiny symbols engraved around the circumference of the compass' navigational circle. She had spent that morning nestled in her favorite cushy wingback chair pouring over *Languages of the World: A Complete Anthology* and comparing the symbols within to the ones on the compass. Hours of squinting had been in vain; she hadn't discovered their meaning. Still, the feel of them brought her comfort.

Smoke billowed from the trees, but its scent was floral and familiar, not at all like burning wood. Somehow it encouraged her. She took a step forward. Tension melted from her shoulders and all the sudden she wondered why she'd ever been afraid. A soft breeze wafted the sweet smoke around her. More clarity. The forest was just a forest. She knew how to hunt and defend herself.

Another step forward and she came in line with the trees. She breathed deeply, filling her lungs to capacity with the wonderful smell. Lavender, she realized.

She entered Nainehta Forest with a casual confidence. She wasn't walking into danger, but simply returning home.

A few paces into Nainehta, doubt crept into her foggy mind. If anyone could just walk into Nainehta without a care, then what had befallen all of those men? Men who were bigger, stronger, and older than she. Goosebumps dotted her arms. She shook her head and clarity streamed in, like she'd dislodged whatever had been blocking her best judgment. The forest must be playing tricks on her already.

She drew her knife and spun in a slow circle, assessing her surroundings. Despite having walked only a few feet, she could no longer see the smoking trees. The entrance had disappeared. She swallowed hard and tried to squash the panic rising in her. Years of research had taught her everything eventually gave away its secret. The answer lay in the details. One simply had to pay attention.

With all senses on high alert, Talullah crept through the forest, glancing at the compass now and then. Using south as her reference point was strange, but she'd take unconventional help over none. Though the fog was less dense amidst the trees than it had been at the edge of the forest, it still distorted things. Shadows shaped like small animals moved across the ground, but the bodies which cast them somehow stayed hidden. Without the compass to confirm she was traveling almost due north, she would have sworn she was walking in circles. She saw nothing but trees, all of which looked the same, except one here or there which had a thin diagonal line scratched into its black bark. She tried not to picture what might have made them.

The marks weren't deep enough to expose the wood beneath, but Talullah thought she could see a bit of color seeping through. Warmth flowed into her palm from the tree's surprisingly smooth surface. Was it her imagination, or was the trunk pulsing?

She withdrew her hand and shook her head, regarding the tree warily. Her own pulse thrummed beneath her wrists. Trees didn't have hearts. It had to be *her* heartbeat she'd felt. She sucked in a deep breath and released it slowly, calming her nerves.

The air smelled stale, like opening a chest drawer and releasing years of trapped air and memories.

A glance at the sky made a knot twist in her chest. The faded pink sun sat on the horizon, barely visible. It was almost dark. The forest had stolen the whole day without her noticing. She'd expected to make more progress by nightfall.

Panic rubbed holes in her paper-thin confidence. Terrapese still lay miles ahead. To rest would lose her too much time. With each passing second her sister got further away.

But she'd always hated the dark. It played tricks on her eyes. What might the forest have in store once the sun disappeared completely?

All of those men before her, once cocky and carefree. The forest had liberated them of their happiness. What would become of her?

Margot's face appeared in her mind, jaw pushed forward and eyes narrowed. The way she'd stared down the soldier before he'd kidnapped her. Strong in the face of fear.

Talullah mirrored her sister's look. Her family needed her. Not even the terrors of night in Nainehta would stop her.

With a quivering hand she traced the eye charm at her collarbone and pressed on.

A movement in the near distance caught her attention. A pair of icy gray eyes peered at her. Her body trembled as she stared back. She should have grabbed her knife from its holster on her boot or something, *anything,* to defend herself in case the beast attacked. But her limbs were made of stone. She couldn't move. For five long seconds she held its gaze, wondering which of them would fold first.

Though adrenaline coursed through her veins, her mind slipped into a sleepy haze, like the last time she'd had a fever. Was she hallucinating? Was this another of the forest's illusions?

Her eyelids grew heavy. She willed them to stay open, to keep locked on the animal. If she lost sight of it, it could ambush her.

Breathe. Concentrate. Relax.

The invisible force trapping her limbs loosened just enough for her to grab hold of her knife and rise to her knees.

A twig snapped to her left. Without thinking, she whipped her head in that direction.

No one was there, and she'd lost sight of the creature. Squinting, she searched for it. But that little time had been enough. The gray eyes were gone.

Chapter 6

Every noise snagged in her heightened senses. She took notice of her surroundings but tried to project confidence. She'd hunted enough with her mother to know predators could smell fear. Though the creature's presence lingered in the back of her mind, she forced herself to keep moving toward Terrapese. Toward her sister.

A voice reached her ears from somewhere nearby. Low tones with a hint of brogue.

The hair on her arms prickled. She'd heard that voice before. At the Sunflower Festival. He'd hoisted Margot onto the horse that carried her away.

A raw desire rose in Talullah, to silence his crass tongue with a swipe of her knife. But where was he? Her hand moved to the holster as she peered around trees, ears perked. The voice grew louder, and she identified other pitches. Different voices with different cadences. Three voices, all male.

Her heart skipped. She crouched behind a large tree to think. Maybe she could still rescue her sister before she ever set foot in Castle Terrapese.

She peeked from behind the tree. The group of soldiers had split up. Margot wasn't there. But Talullah wouldn't give up that easily. These soldiers would return to Terrapese, and when they did, she'd follow them. For now, she listened, biding her time.

"Cap, can you explain why we're out here in this forsaken forest when we could be enjoying the finer things Terrapesian court has to offer?" The voice sounded young, probably a new cadet.

"Fallon, we told you already. No way you're getting yourself invited to the courtiers' ball. You haven't done anything of note, yet, to attract their attention. And you will address me as Captain or Captain Caprico." This voice sent chills down Talullah's spine. Caprico. He'd been the commanding officer at the raid.

"Oh, I don't know, Captain. Young Fallon here may have a chance yet," the man with the brogue crooned. "Lucinda has been giving this little kipper the heavy eyes since he arrived." There was a pause and then an eruption of laughter. Talullah could almost hear the tears squeeze from his eyes as he choked on his own joke.

"Aww, Rantoul, lay off the kid. You know he's a romantic. Fallon's not concerned with some of the things you hogs call fun," Caprico said, teasing. "And we're out here because Renevelda will have our heads if we don't find the necklace and the kid. And I happen to be quite attached to my head. Whatever you're about to say, Rantoul, swallow it."

The kid. Had Margot escaped, or were they looking for Talullah? She pressed her back against the tree trunk. Either way, she couldn't risk being spotted.

Stifled laughter wove through the crunch of the leaves. For soldiers, they seemed totally unconcerned with their task. They were close enough she could make out the Terrapesian insignia on their capes. Talullah's heart beat against her ribcage.

"Surprised the necklace wasn't at the house. That's where I woulda kept it. Somewhere safe," said Fallon.

"I bet it's with one of the other brats," Rantoul said. He spat. "We'll know soon enough, I suppose. If that spit-fire of a blonde knows where it is, it's only a matter of time before Renevelda breaks her."

Talullah's limbs tingled with rage, her hand poised over her knife.

"We'll all be subject to the she-devil sorceress's *methods* if we don't find that necklace, and the hostage, for that matter," said Caprico.

"Is it true what she said? That the necklace is from the Suditzas themselves?" Fallon asked, his voice shaking.

Rantoul snorted. "Sure, the authors of destiny put their divine power into a piece of jewelry and gave it to a human. If you believe that, you're more hopeless than I thought."

Talullah's collarbone warmed. Gears shifted in her head. They'd mentioned a necklace during the raid. She touched the eye charm through her tunic. Surely they didn't mean *her* necklace.

"No use arguing about it," Caprico said. "Renevelda wants to alter something in time. If we want to live long enough to continue this debate, we have to find Dunamai's Eye. And that kid."

The hair on the back of Talullah's neck stood on end. Alter time? Plenty of tradespeople at the Hidden Market claimed they could predict the future. Like the curly-haired woman who'd sold her the compass. But none of that compared with the feat the men had described. No one could *change* time.

"Wouldn't want to disappoint her, that's for sure. I just joined a few months ago." Fallon's voice shook.

"Then I wouldn't go back unless you've got something to show for your effort. Last cadet who showed up empty handed is now no-handed, if you catch my drift," Rantoul said, casually.

"Is that true, Captain?"

"Just keep looking, Fallon. The kid is in the forest somewhere, according to Cleo. Dumped a beak-full of this grass on the throne room floor. Convenient timing, actually. I'd rather not make this trip twice. Our query is young, probably untrained, and alone. The sooner we find what we came for, the sooner we all go home."

Talullah held her breath, afraid to move lest she announce her position. She kept her right hand poised over her knife. Her left traced the eye charm. The young soldier, Fallon, passed so close he must have heard her thinking. But his eyes scanned only what was in front of him. He didn't bother turning his head. She could have grabbed him around the neck and held her knife to his throat. Bartered his life for Margot's release and the lives of her other family members. She entertained the thought for a moment, weighing the possibility that he'd be worth enough to Renevelda to make a trade. Not to mention the other two men would bind her in seconds, before she'd even had the chance to make demands.

A hawk circled above, screeching at an obscene decibel. Talullah winced.

"Figures that damn bird is here to spy on us," Rantoul groaned, pointing up at the sky.

"Cleo serves the same authority we do," Caprico answered. "And suffers consequences."

The bird descended, hovering a few feet above the soldiers.

"Yeah, yeah, we know. We're looking." Rantoul swatted at the bird, who beat him in the face with its wing before rising again. "Disgusting fowl."

Fallon dragged his boot back and forth in the dirt. "I've heard stories about this place. It does weird things to people who stay too long. Do you reckon any of it's true?"

Rantoul snorted. "You mean all that horse shit about magic fairies and ghost animals that kidnap people to the underworld?" He arched a brow at Fallon, whose eyes widened.

"Ghosts?" Fallon gulped. "I was talking about the w-weather and the blinding d-darkness." He stole a look at Caprico. "What do you know about g-ghosts?"

"Kid, if you're gonna be a soldier, you're gonna have to buck up." He slapped Fallon on a shoulder so hard the kid stumbled.

Even fifty feet away, Talullah could see the horror on Fallon's face. Caprico hadn't answered his question, and her own stomach lurched as if she'd missed a step. She wasn't prepared for ghosts.

"Take it easy. We'll protect you," Rantoul jeered.

"Let's move," Caprico said. "Need to find better cover before nightfall." He mounted his horse.

"What happens at nightfall, Captain? Captain?"

But Fallon didn't get an answer. Caprico kicked his horse into a cantor, the other two following suit.

Not yet! I need more time.

Breaking into a run, Talullah dodged branches and brambles. No matter how fast she moved, her legs couldn't close the gap.

The soldiers' bodies dissolved into the distance, but she pushed forward. Caprico said they were going to find a place to camp. She'd catch up when they stopped. She had to.

Minutes later, though, true darkness settled over the forest like a black velvet cloak—heavy and impossible to see through.

Fumbling through her pack, she found a small lantern and a box of matches.

She dragged a match against her boot. A small flame danced on its end, but as she sucked in a breath it extinguished.

Damn it.

Hands shaking, she lit another and guided it toward the wick. Not even her fingers, inches from the lit end, illuminated in the flame's glow. Heat spread as the wick caught. Still, she could only see the lantern itself.

Grabbing the handle, she held it away from her body. And gasped.

Darkness remained where light should have pushed it aside.

She spun in a circle, extending her arm to full length. The night swallowed the lantern's glow.

The first few moments of night were always the darkest. Her eyes would adjust soon. She took a tentative step, lifting her legs higher than what was necessary to avoid any hidden tree roots.

Had the soldiers had gone that way? Or had she turned while lighting her lantern?

Impenetrable night smothered her in its embrace. She couldn't see two inches in front of her. Whispers floated through the trees, sending a tingle up her neck.

Ghosts?

She turned, searching for the source, not sure if she'd be able to see them, if they were ghosts.

A flicker of purple colored her peripheral vision. When she turned, it had already disappeared. Another of the forest's tricks. Making her see things that weren't there.

Another flicker a few feet away.

Or were they real? Would they attack? She gripped her knife and almost laughed to herself. How could she defend against something already dead?

More whispers surrounded her. Her veins buzzed.

"Keys," one of the voices said. Talullah jumped, surprised she could pick a real word out of the muttering.

"Guide the Keeper," whispered another.

A sudden gust of wind blew past her, pulling hairs from her braid.

All was quiet.

And then she could *see*. Not everything and not clearly. But a small arrow on the ground in front of her illuminated her boots. She almost cried with joy. When she took a step, the arrow moved with her.

With the arrow lighting her path, she could catch up to the soldiers. If she could remember which way they'd gone. Turning had disoriented her.

She took a step to her right. The arrow didn't move. She moved left, and it did.

The light—more likely the forest—had an agenda. It might guide her, but where? How could she trust it would lead where she wanted to go?

She couldn't. Her temporary rush of euphoria faded.

Which was worse: waiting until morning, or taking a chance on the forest's detour?

The soldiers faced the same crippling darkness. She'd experienced enough of the forest's magic to know she couldn't trust it.

Heart thumping, Talullah pulled a threadbare blanket from her pack—it was too dark to set up her tent—and leaned her back against the nearest tree. She kept her eyes open and her hand on her knife.

The soldiers weren't going anywhere tonight. And apparently, neither was she.

Chapter 7

The vision slid easily to the front of her mind. Dense violet fog filled the small stone room, its scent sweet like honey. Despite squinting, she couldn't quite bring the scene into focus. She parted the fog with her hands and noticed the blurry shape of a young man. He faced away from her, head turned toward an open window.

Her heart pattered with recognition, though she couldn't make out his features.

A plum-sized bird landed on the sill. The boy removed something from the bird's beak, and it flew away. He paused, watching it go before unfolding the parchment. The fog thickened until it obscured the boy from view.

Talullah touched the warm place near her collarbone.

Something small and solid dropped on top of her head.

She woke with a start, shaking the vision away. Her eyes shot back and forth, taking in her surroundings. Morning's first light reflected off the damp grass and a bird sang in the distance. Above her, a squirrel shook a tree branch, dislodging a handful more nuts.

Exhaling with relief, she shoved her blanket back into her pack and stood. A new surge of confidence flowed through her. She'd done something many others couldn't—survived a night in Nainehta Forest.

Her stomach sloshed and groaned, a mix of anxiety and hunger. Breakfast consisted of a handful of jerky, stale bread, and lukewarm water while she walked. It sated her hunger but the clenching in the pit of her stomach remained.

Please let them be near. Please let it not be too late.

The forest stayed quiet save for the occasional bird and the shuffle of her own boots in the grass.

The group couldn't have ridden long after she lost them. If they hadn't left yet, she should reach them soon. Hopefully it would be soon enough. A lump formed in her throat and she swallowed it. It had to be soon enough.

Now that the sun had risen, heat haze clung to the air. More than once she thought she saw small creatures peeking out from behind trees. An ear here, a tail there. But every time she got close, they vanished. Mirages, she told herself. That had to be it. Sweat dripped off the tip of Talullah's nose, evaporating before it hit the ground. She wiped her face with her sleeve.

Without thinking, she chugged the last of her water supply. She reveled in the lukewarm liquid washing over her parched tongue and slipping down her scratchy throat. Water had never tasted so good.

Relief came and went in an instant, her mouth suddenly dry at noticing the lightness of the canteen in her hand.

It was empty.

What was wrong with her?

There was no way she'd survive even a few hours in the heat without water. She needed to find a river.

Black spots dotted her vision. She leaned against a tree to keep her body upright. Instinctively, her fingers traced the eye charm and she closed her eyes to listen. The forest sounds muted, as if she'd plugged her ears with cotton. Minutes passed, or maybe only seconds.

Come on. Think. Where would a stream be?

Warmth spread from her collarbone through her shoulder blades. Then, the soft babble of a stream. The longer she focused, the louder and clearer it grew. Was it another of the forest's tricks, or could she trust her own senses?

The path would take her off course, but she had no choice. She was no good to her family if she died of heatstroke.

She set her jaw and forced her fatigued legs to move toward the stream. It wasn't close, but it wasn't too far either. She'd drink as much as she could, fill her canteen, and be on her way. Damned if she was going to let a bunch of trees get the best of her.

Head swimming and bleary-eyed, she stumbled through the forest.

Through the fire blazing bright, trust yourself, harness your might...

The song danced in her clouded head, almost taunting her. She didn't have the strength to push it away. As if sensing her weakness, the forest waged its own assault. Thousands of birds squawked. Hooves pawed the ground all around her. She whipped her head back and forth searching for the sources of the noise. She saw nothing but trees.

Sweat stung her eyes and soaked her tunic, but she pushed forward. Pressing her hands to her ears only amplified the sounds, as if they emanated from her mind and not the forest. She had to get to the river. Water would relieve her from the hallucinations.

Even through the cacophony, the faint trickle of water remained. She focused all her energy on that sound, and it carried her through the thickest trees yet.

Just a few more feet. A few more. Almost there.

Images of her sisters in manacles and her father bound and gagged swam before her eyes. Fury boiled her blood, hotter than the sun. Her family was her life. Founders help the soldiers if—no, *when*—she caught up. Her face might be the last they'd ever see.

She tripped as she crested a small hill, a mountain to her tired body. But her efforts were rewarded. On the other side ran two parallel streams, each haloed by a different color steam.

She crawled the last fifteen feet to the closest source, not caring that rocks ripped holes in her trousers and pine needles stabbed her exposed skin. The sounds of the forest still pounded in her head. Invisible fire singed her body. But she'd wash it all away in seconds.

On her stomach, she pulled herself to the edge of the water, reaching through the orange mist and leaning toward the surface. It smelled of fresh apricots. It would be heaven to dunk her face into its sweet reprieve.

A gravelly voice cut through the rest of the noise.

"Not that one, you Wrecker!"

Talullah hesitated, confused as to whether the voice was real or in her head like the rest. Water from nowhere rained down on her burning face. The temperature change shocked her mind and body awake. It smelled like blueberries.

She rolled onto her back and drew her knife, wiping the water from her eyes with her other hand. She didn't see anything.

"Don't be messin' with River Lethe, unless you want to end up like the rest of 'em."

Talullah scanned the ground for the voice's owner.

"We got work to do and we can't be doin' it with Wreckers about. Go on." It didn't sound like a threat, though the tone was clipped and harsh. It had to all be in her imagination.

Finally, Talullah found her voice, hoping if she acknowledged the figment it would go away. "I'm trying to go. I need water." Her throat was so dry the words came out in a whisper.

"Just fill your canteen, then, and get out of here. River Ketslane, not River Lethe, if you want to live."

She drew even, measured breaths. It wasn't real. It would stop soon. She just needed water.

"The blue river. Not the orange. And hurry up."

Maybe the voice was her own subconscious taking over, telling her how to survive. She fumbled through her knapsack for her canteen and dipped it into the blue stream, filling it until it overflowed. She drained it in one breath, the chilly tart water refreshing her from the inside out. Immediately, she felt whole again, in control. The sounds dissipated, and the forest quieted once again. Her skin cooled. She sighed deeply. The hallucinations vanished.

Something thudded on the ground. Talullah's head snapped up and she locked eyes with a wild-looking man no taller than Margot. She gasped. His round orange eyes glinted in the sunlight as he stalked toward her. "You've got your water. Now go back to where you came from and leave us be, Wrecker!"

Talullah blinked rapidly, but he didn't disappear. The voice hadn't been in her head at all. The stout creature moved silent as the wind and angry as a spring storm.

From the trees streaked a flash of white. It blazed around the gravel-voiced creature three times then stopped to stare at Talullah.

"Four Worlds, Kahu! What have you been doin' all this time?"

The beast was the size of a small horse with thick, powerful legs and a mischievous mouth full of dagger-sharp teeth. Talullah drew a sharp inhale, staring at the icy-eyed wolf. The eyes from the night before bored into hers, as if reading her mind. White-knuckled, Talullah held out her knife and assumed a defensive stance. The eye charm warmed against her collarbone. She held her breath as the short creature said something to the wolf in a foreign tongue.

The wolf cocked its head to the side, its eyes never leaving hers. And then it headed straight for her.

For a second, she stood frozen and wide-eyed. And then the switch in her brain flipped. She turned and ran into the thickest patch of trees she could find. She had a head start on the wolf, but not much. It was built for hunting. It was only a matter of time before it caught up. One labored breath at a time she tried to calm herself. What had she read about wolves? Adrenaline pounded out all logic and any information she'd once known. All she could think to do was run.

The gravelly voice shouted something after her, but she couldn't make it out for the blood pulsing in her ears. Probably egging the wolf on. Telling it to catch her. To kill her.

The deeper she moved into the forest, the larger the trees became, both in height and diameter. She circled behind one that had to be twelve feet across and paused, wheezing. Maybe she could climb the tree and wait there. The lowest branch hung five feet above her head; she'd have to scale the trunk to reach it. She ran her hands along the tree's bark. It was smoother than other trees, but it did have grooves.

Ears primed for snapping twigs and rustling leaves, she groped for holds. Her fingers slipped off the oddly-shaped ridges. The tree was too wide to wrap her limbs around.

The gravelly voice and pattering of paws in leaves raced towards her.

Two figures cleared the trees. The wolf spotted her and took off. It was too late to run. Desperately she clawed at the tree trunk and tried to pull herself up. Her necklace bobbed free of her tunic and grazed the tree's matte black bark.

The wolf closed in.

Talullah choked back a sob. This wasn't how she'd thought she'd die. Alone in the middle of nowhere. Her family would think she abandoned them. They'd never find her body. If there was one left to find.

Through her tears, she once again locked gazes with the gray eyes. Strange, she found no malice there, no hunger.

Thirty feet away.

She braced her back against the tree, drawing her knife more as a formality than a defense. The wolf's jaw could snap her neck in less than a second. But she wouldn't just give up.

Twenty feet.

The ridges in the tree pushed outward, shoving Talullah forward. Ten.

"Kahu, heel!" the gravelly voice yelled.

The wolf stopped in its tracks, cocking its head to the side like a pet dog. A groaning crack issued from the tree. Symbols embossed the trunk, pushing out from the inside the way grass grows up through dirt. Colored fibers shimmered around the edges of the symbols. They were familiar, but Talullah couldn't remember where she'd seen the markings before.

The ground quaked, pitching her into the tree. She hugged the trunk to steady herself, pressing her whole body against it. The metal eye dug into her flesh and she squeezed her eyes shut as tight as she could.

As soon as it had started, the shaking stopped.

Talullah fell to her knees, gaping. She was inside a circular enclosure twelve feet around. The wolf was nowhere to be seen. Her shoulders relaxed.

Millions of shimmering colored lines covered the walls and hung above her, as if infinite spools of silk had unraveled in every direction. They seemed to go on forever, woven together in a tapestry so she couldn't tell where one began and another ended. She stared, hypnotized. It was as if she had crawled inside a piece of fabric and could see and touch its individual fibers.

She approached the nearest wall. An overwhelming urge to touch the strands came over her. Were they as delicate as they looked? Her hand shook as it hovered. No, the threads themselves vibrated, not her hand. Their colors blurred until she could no longer discern the individual lines.

Exhaustion weighed down her eyelids. Her knees buckled, and she curled into a ball on the ground.

In her last moment of consciousness, she heard a hawk screech.

Chapter 8

Talullah awoke with a start, her stomach in knots. She'd seen the short-haired girl walking through flames again, the whole scene colored crimson. Familiarity tugged at the back of Talullah's mind. Did she know the girl somehow?

The first thing she noticed when she opened her eyes was a fire crackling in a stone fireplace. There hadn't been a fireplace before. In the tree. She sat up and blinked her surroundings into focus.

Her heart pumped faster as she analyzed her surroundings. Where in the Founders' names was she? She paused. Not in a tree, but in a room. Had Terrapesian soldiers captured her, too?

She reached for her knife but the holster on her boot was empty, as was the thigh strap. Hell and a half. She must have dropped the knife in the forest. Her only means of defense. Perfect.

Her eyes scanned for anything she could use as a weapon. A wooden table and two chairs sat near the fireplace, and just beyond, a small kitchen. Kitchens meant knives.

She pushed herself upright. Why couldn't she remember coming to this place? She had fallen asleep in a tree the previous night, hadn't she? Or maybe it was all part of the forest's magic. Another illusion.

Something white and fluffy flashed in the corner of her eye. A tail.

Eyes widening, she noticed the large white wolf attached to the tail. The animal slept, but Talullah's mouth went dry. She cursed under her breath.

She stood carefully, facing the animal, and backed into the kitchen. Its eye twitched and it dragged a large paw across its face. Talullah found a paring knife on the counter. It would have to do.

The weathered cabinets would make too much noise if she opened them, and she couldn't risk waking the beast. Holding the knife out in front of her, she eased toward the front door taking care to step light as a bird.

"Kahu!" grunted a gravelly voice. "Wake up you lazy thing!"

Talullah froze, her gaze locked on the wolf as it yawned and rolled onto its feet. It didn't look her way as it padded toward the voice, its nails clicking on the wooden floor and its tail swishing.

"Can't waste the whole day sleeping, my furry friend," said the voice again. The wild man from before.

She pressed her back to the front door and felt for a knob in the knotty wood. There was nothing to grab onto. By the Founders, who had a door with no way to open it? Her legs burned as she leaned backward with all her weight. The door didn't budge.

The short man ambled into the room, the wolf trotting at his heels. Bits of leaves and twigs protruded from his tangled red hair. She'd been too focused on not getting ripped to shreds the night before to notice the man's appearance, but now she assessed him with cautious curiosity, hoping he wouldn't notice her.

His ears were the size and shape of tulip tree leaves and age lines like waterless rivers snaked through his leathery skin. He didn't look human. But then, what was he?

The man reached a stubby arm to scratch behind the wolf's ears. The animal rumbled its agreement and pushed its head further into the man's hand, licking his fingers with its long black tongue.

"Lots to do today, Kahu." He turned suddenly to face to Talullah. His eyes were void of surprise as they flicked from her face to the knife in her hand. She flinched.

The man laughed so hard he wheezed, a sound like wind whistling through cracks in a cave. When he'd composed himself, he said, "Have a seat. It's rude to leave before tea." He pointed at one of the kitchen chairs.

Talullah didn't move.

"I don't have all day. I got things of my own to tend to, and I don't appreciate when my time is wasted. Especially by Wreckers." From his tone he might have said "flesh-eating slugs."

Talullah observed, never lowering the borrowed knife, as he moved into the kitchen and filled a kettle with water from a stone basin.

He glanced back at her and snorted. "If you want to get on with your suicide mission of going to Terrapese to find your family, you might want to sit. The sooner we start the sooner we can both be doin' what we need to."

A jolt sizzled through her veins. "Who are you? Do you work for the Terrapesian Regime?" She narrowed her eyes, hoping she looked fiercer than she felt. If he was a Terrapesian soldier, the knife in her hand wouldn't save her. But he didn't look like any soldier—any person, for that matter—she'd ever seen.

Another snort and a wheezy laugh. "I wouldn't work for those lyin', cheatin', traitors if they offered me a ten-story tree-house and a lifetime supply of elderflower honey." He spat in a second, empty basin. "Wrecker filth. No offense. But I do know what you're up to and you're goin' about it all wrong." He hung the kettle on a hook above the fire and patted the wolf on the head. "You can put that down. If I wanted to hurt you, you'd be dead already. Lucky for you I don't like killin'. Here, I found this outside the tree. Might work better than that." He drew her hunting knife from a sheath on his leg and offered her the hilt. "I cleaned and sharpened it for you. If you're plannin' on stabbin' me that should make for a quick, clean job." A hint of a smirk crossed his lips.

Talullah placed the borrowed knife on the table in front of her—out of his reach—and accepted her hunting blade. She tested its sharpness on her thumb, drawing a thin line of blood on the tip. It was sharper than she'd ever managed to get it.

He poured tea into a chipped mug from an orange teapot painted with blue flowers and set it next to a plate of steaming food on the table. Her stomach growled.

"If you're not working for the Regime, why bring me here? Why not just leave me?"

"Couldn't. Who knows what kind of damage you could have done. Couldn't risk it. Really, put that away, will you?"

He could have slit her throat with her own blade while she slept if he'd meant to harm her. She needed information about her family, and if—*if*—he had it, she'd play by his rules. For now, at least.

She sheathed her weapon in her thigh holster and breathed in the smell of venison jerky, eggs, and slightly burnt toast. Her mouth watered, but she hesitated.

"It's not poisoned."

Talullah lifted her eyebrows. "How do I know that for sure?"

He huffed and crossed the room. He took a swig of her tea and a bite of each item on her plate. "Satisfied?"

She took a cautious sniff of the tea and lifted the cup to her lips. "Who are you?"

"The name's Gillie. And to answer your other question, I'm a wood faerie."

Talullah inhaled mid-sip and choked, spraying tea all over the table. "You're a what?" she said between coughs.

"Wood faerie." He gestured from his head down to his feet as if it were obvious. "What else?"

"Faeries are myth." Gillie tossed her a worn tartan cloth and she dried the table.

He shook his head, pity in his eyes. "Wreckers just think we are. They have the hardest time seein' what's right in front of them. Only notice what they want to."

"And what exactly is a Wrecker?" Talullah's head spun. Giant trees, rainbow threads, and now wood faeries.

Gillie grunted, assessing her as if trying to decide something. "Wreckers are"—his face scrunched up as if he'd eaten something sour— "humans."

"Why do you call—"

"Because they destroy things!" He pounded the table with his fist, making Talullah jump. "Do you always ask this many questions? Never mind. We don't have time. Sit." A few leaves and twigs fell from his hair to the aged oak floor, shaken loose by his outburst. He grunted at the mess, swept it into a crude dust pan with a broom, and flung it out an open window.

Talullah wanted to ask what humans had ever done to him personally, but she bit her tongue. No need to make things more difficult. He might know something important about her family. She needed to stay on his good side.

"Why were you sneakin' around Igdrasil?" It was an accusation, like she'd committed a crime.

She shook her head, taking a bite of toast. "I have no idea what you're talking about. What's an Ig-dran-sool?"

"Ig. Drah. Sil. Igdrasil. That giant tree you somehow managed to get yourself into. The one with the sparkly insides. What were you doin' sneakin' around there?"

She set her jaw. "Not *sneaking*. I was running from your...*that*"—she pointed at the wolf, which sat looking up at Gillie and licking its chops. "I thought it was going to rip me to shreds. So, it seems, whatever happened last night was your fault. If you hadn't sent your *pet* after me, I would never have ended up in...whatever you said."

Gillie's face hardened. "I didn't send Kahu after you. She does what she pleases. And she wasn't goin' to kill you. She sensed some...things." He patted Kahu's head and poured a cup of meaty kibble into a wooden bowl. "And I believe you owe us thanks for savin' your life."

An incredulous laugh burst from her mouth. "You call chasing me into a tree and kidnapping me saving my life?"

"That was an unfortunate by-product. The savin' part happened when we stopped you from drinkin' from the river Lethe. Unless you prefer to live without your memories?" His eyes glowed in challenge.

This gave Talullah pause. "What do you mean?"

"Wreckers. Unbelievable," he muttered, dragging his long-fingered hand across his face in disgust. "If you drink from Lethe, the orange river, you forget things," he said, as if explaining the weather to a child. Kahu's head bobbed, following the motion of his arm as he gestured.

"That doesn't make any se—"

"We don't have time to debate the probability of what I say. Let's just assume it's true, since accordin' to your logic I'm not supposed to exist and obviously I do. There's a reason Wreckers don't travel through Nainehta Forest. It's full of dangerous things they don't understand and don't care to learn about. The forest's magic isn't somethin' they can control, so it terrifies them." Kahu bumped the back of Gillie's knee with her fluffy head and he set the bowl in front of her. "Sorry, girl."

"But what does Nainehta Forest have to do with my family? You said my way is wrong. How do you know where I'm going at all?"

"There's all sorts of stuff you don't understand. I'm not the right one to tell you."

"And who is?"

Gillie stared at her. Blinked. Frowned.

She stood and squeezed her hands into fists. "Who do you think you are? You bring me here against my will and talk some cryptic nonsense. You said you know something about my family, so tell me."

He pinched his earlobe and focused on a spot behind her head. She followed his gaze to a large quilt hanging on the wall. A tree in the center of the quilt took up most of the space, and four smaller trees decorated the corners. Dulled with age, the colors blended together in muted versions of the originals.

"This is all a lot more complicated than kidnappin'—which *I* didn't do, by the way—and as much as I'd prefer not to consort with Wreckers, it seems neither of us has much of a choice. You would have died in that tree had Kahu and I not pulled you out. You want to save your family, you got to trust me. Understand?"

She touched the eye charm through her tunic and took a deep breath. Even if she decided not to take his advice, wasn't it better to have options?

"One second I was trying my damnedest to scale that tree to avoid—" She glanced at the wolf, who munched her breakfast and licked her lips.

"Kahu."

"Right. I was trying to get away from Kahu. The next thing I knew I was inside the tree." Talullah's fingers tingled at the memory of how the threads danced and how she felt compelled to touch them.

"No one can just get inside the tree without magic. It's impossible. What's that you're holding?"

She hesitated but pulled the necklace from under her tunic and showed it to Gillie. He crept closer. The aroma of freshly dug earth wafted toward her.

"Where did you get this?" he whispered, his face lit by disbelief.

"My mother."

He waited for her to elaborate.

She didn't.

"But that means..." Gillie paced, muttering to himself. "...interesting possibility..."

Finally, he stopped in front of Talullah. "Ever heard of the Tree of Destiny?"

She shook her head.

"That's Igradsil's nickname. Legend says the authors of destiny formed Igdrasil at the beginnin' of time and from it flows everythin' that has happened, is happenin', or will ever happen. There's a network of smaller ones throughout the Four Worlds, but Igdrasil is the original. The most powerful. Those with the Gifts of Sight use the trees to travel between the worlds. And the ones with Dunamai's Eye? Well, they do more than travel."

"Did you say Dunamai's Eye?"

"You've heard of it, then?"

"Briefly. I overhead Terrapesian soldiers talking about it. They're looking for it."

"Of course they are. Renevelda's been searchin' for years." Gillie massaged his caterpillar-like eyebrows. "How to explain this in Wrecker's terms? The sparkly, stringy things you saw inside Igdrasil are threads of time. Each one represents an event that has happened, will happen, is happening currently, or might happen in the future."

Talullah nodded, brows furrowed. She sat.

"The Suditzas—the original authors of destiny—gifted some creatures, includin' Wreckers, with the Gifts of Sight. You've heard of clairvoyants and the like?"

Again, Talullah nodded, remembering the blonde woman she'd seen gazing into a crystal ball and reading tarot cards at the last Hidden Market. She'd assumed it was all just a performance.

"That's one of the Sights. Some Seers —called Sezna Seers—have all four. They see the past, present, future, and possible. And Dunamai's Eye, like the one you're wearin', helps them See more clearly. And change things."

"What does this have to do with my family? Even if what you say is true, what's the point?" She stood suddenly, knocking her chair over.

"Renevelda wants to alter time, you understand? That kind of magic—*seith*—is powerful. It isn't a simple potion you whip up on a Tuesday with whatever's in your cupboard. It requires tools, specifically Dunamai's Eye. And I'm bettin' there's a reason she took your sisters, too. You want to save the people you love, you'll use everything the universe gives you. And right now, the trinket around your neck is the best chance you've got. But you've got to find the missin' stones first. Without them, the magic won't be strong enough."

A sour burn crept up Talullah's throat. Could he be telling the truth?

Gillie's expression softened. "I hope I'm wrong. Unfortunately, I don't think I am. This story has been circulatin' the forest for weeks. Renevelda's goal and her tactics are widely known. You heard it with your own ears from her henchmen. News travels fast in Nainehta, and if you pay attention, you can find out almost anything. Ghosts are terrible gossips."

Talullah's voice came out strained when she spoke. "You're telling me a lunatic witch kidnapped my sisters, and you expect me *not* to get to them as fast as possible? I don't know why I'm still here. I have to go to them."

She shouldered her pack and crossed to the door.

"Only strong magic can beat her, Talullah. If you go to Terrapese now you're doomin' your sisters, and yourself, to certain death."

Talullah whirled with fury in her eyes. "What would you have me do instead?"

"If you want a fightin' chance, you'll keep the Eye far away from Renevelda. Without it, she can't enact the spell and your sisters are safe. Once you've found the stones, you'll be able to win." Gillie glanced at the tree quilt again, whispering something like a prayer under his breath. "If you'll wait a minute, I've got a few things that might help."

Chapter 9

Gillie disappeared down the hall and Talullah turned toward the door, fully intending to leave. Her hands swiped the surface of the door. Still no knob. Hell and a half.

The open window in the kitchen caught her eye. It just might be big enough for her to squeeze through.

She crossed the room, her mind reeling. Her family was being held hostage by a sorceress in Terrapese and the only way to save them, according to this wood faerie, was to find the missing gemstones from her necklace.

That could take years. Decades even. She wouldn't have a clue where to start looking if she did believe that was the best plan. Which she didn't.

She cranked the lever on the wall and the window pane pushed outward. It groaned loudly and Kahu howled.

"Shhh, be quiet," Talullah whispered to the wolf.

Kahu cocked her to the side and padded over to the window.

"No, stay over there." Kahu sat at Talullah's feet. Talullah turned the crank faster, her mind keeping pace with her motions.

If what Renevelda wanted more than anything in the world was the charm hanging from Talullah's neck, why hadn't the soldiers kept looking for her? Why had they been content to return to Terrapese without it?

She hoisted her pack through the open window. It was heavier than she'd remembered, and it landed with a *thunk* on the forest floor.

Gillie's warning be damned. She had to save her sisters.

Perched on the ledge, she swung one leg through the opening. Kahu latched onto her other boot with her teeth.

"Kahu, let go." The wolf's grip, though not painful, was too strong.

"Good girl," gruffed Gillie as he re-entered the room.

Kahu swished her tail and gave one hard tug. Talullah toppled backward onto the hard floor.

The window shut with a lazy wave of Gillie's hand. "You can go as soon as I give you these."

He unfurled a weathered piece of parchment on the table. Kahu, her job done, chased her tail. She caught it and flopped down on the rug in front of the fireplace, looking pleased with herself.

"By the Founders, get on with it then." Talullah joined him at the table. "What's that?"

"Map."

"Obviously." How stupid did he think she was? "A map of where, exactly?"

"Not sure."

"Helpful. Where did you get it?"

"It was a gift."

Talullah bit her tongue. The fewer questions she asked, the sooner she could leave.

Silence descended for a moment. Finally, Gillie shook his head, sadness in his eyes, and handed the map to Talullah. "Take it."

"If you don't even know what it's of, how am *I* supposed to know?"

Gillie either didn't hear her or chose not to answer. Instead he busied himself sweeping invisible dirt off the floor while she studied the map closer.

It was worn all over, as if it had been handled often over many years. An uneven edge suggested it had been torn in half, the rest of it lost. But the charcoal lines remained un-smudged. They might have been applied that very morning. Looking at the drawn curves and lines made her heart hurt.

Dhalian. Her best friend had been obsessed with maps ever since they were five. They'd found one in the library that showed the continent before Terrapese and Viltresor split into two nations. Dhalian's hazel eyes had sparkled as he took the map to a corner and curled up to study it. Hours passed before he remembered they were supposed to be creating their own language. When he finally returned the map to its shelf and they cracked open *Ancient Languages* for inspiration, Talullah knew he'd found his trade. Normally it took children right up until their fourteenth birthday to decide what apprenticeship to pursue the following year. Talullah had been happy that Dhalian found his calling so early. She just hadn't realized what it meant for their friendship.

How long had it been since he'd written?

Months.

The realization knocked the breath out of her. This was the longest they'd gone without contact since he left the previous summer. Did he love his work so much he couldn't find time to scribble a few lines on parchment?

She folded the map as if it were made of fine silk. A pang of missing rose in her chest, but she pushed it down.

"Gillie," she said, redirecting her thoughts before the 'what ifs' could creep in. "I'm going now."

"There's one more thing you should have." Gold foil symbols embellished the outside of the black garment box he slid toward her. The symbols seemed familiar, but she could quite place them.

Gillie drew a deep breath. "I need you to listen carefully. Don't interrupt, just let me finish." He arched one bushy eyebrow. "Can you handle that?"

Talullah shot him a look.

"This cloak is a *Nemosyn*." He removed the lid and held up a black cloak decorated with golden swirls. "An object that, with the help of magic, holds memories. It memorizes how a person feels and what they see and experience."

"Like a souvenir?" Talullah asked, unable to swallow the words before they leapt from her mouth. "Sorry."

"Exactly," said Gillie. "Most folks use them to remember vacations and things. Except if you know how to work them, they're more than glorified photos. Here, touch the cloak. The sleeve will do. *Gently*. Don't choke it."

Talullah let the end of the sleeve rest in her palm and curled her fingers around it. It slid across her skin like a mix of satin and velvet. She was about to ask what it was made of, but she tucked the question away. She *had* promised not to interrupt. Moths fluttered in her stomach.

Magic.

"This cloak not only holds memories from its previous owner, but also adapts to its wearer's needs." With his stubby index finger, Gillie traced an invisible symbol in the air. The cloak vibrated gently in Talullah's hand. "It can shield you from the most blistering of heat or bone-cracking cold and repel water so you're always dry. If it's external, this cloak can help."

The cloak fell limp once again and Talullah stared at it, brows furrowed. Years ago she would have danced in circles and sung with joy at discovering something with this kind of power. Traders at the

Hidden Market would drool over it, knowing what kind of price it would fetch in Viltresor's outskirts. A small piece of her heart still reached out toward the idea that magic could be good, that it could help or even save. That part of her said not to dismiss the gift, but to trust in its power. She might have listened to it too, if it hadn't spoken in her mother's voice.

"I can't do this." She released her grip on the sleeve and it slid like water from her palm. The voice inside pleaded she reconsider.

Through the fire blazing bright...

"Not now!" She hadn't meant to shout, but Gillie stared at her wide-eyed and grimacing. "I wasn't talking to you. Sorry. I just...I can't take the cloak. Once, a long time ago, maybe. But not now. I don't..." How to explain her distrust of magic? The creature standing before her was obviously steeped in it. She didn't want to offend him, but this was something she couldn't compromise.

Saving her family without magic would prove she'd been right all along. Magic couldn't and shouldn't be trusted.

"Thank you, but no thank you. I'll be out of your way." Leaving her pack on the floor, she took her breakfast dishes to the kitchen. Manners were important to Gillie, and after all, he had rescued her from the tree. The least she could do was clean up after herself.

When she returned, Gillie appraised her, smirking. Then he looked her dead in the eye. Signing, he brought his hands together so the tips of his fingers touched, then pointed his left hand at Talullah and touched his own chest with his right. He moved his right hand, palm down, from the left side of his chest to his right. Finally, he nodded and said "Turas sabalt."

Talullah gaped. She had spent countless hours studying old languages, but nothing compared to experiencing one firsthand by a native speaker.

"It's an ancient wood faerie language. Basically unused now." He stared at the tree quilt again, his eyes misty.

"What does it mean?"

"The signed part means, 'Good to have met you' and the words mean 'safe journey.'"

"Thank you for sharing it with me. Why isn't it used anymore? You must speak with others of your kind."

A flash of pain lit up Gillie's eyes, but a second later it was gone. "Long journey. You'd better go. Head back to where the rivers converge. That's where we met the first time and should orient you. Follow Lethe until it disappears, and you'll be well on your way to finding one of the stones. At least finding its last known location. Do not drink from Lethe for any reason."

She nodded. Never mind she wasn't planning on searching for the stones.

At the door, Kahu nudged Talullah's hand until she scratched behind the wolf's ears.

"Thank you," Talullah said, and after a moment's pause she signed to him what he'd shown her. *Good to have met you.* He didn't respond, but as Talullah stepped into the forest and he disappeared behind the closing door, she thought she saw him smile.

TALULLAH REFERENCED the crude map Gillie had drawn on the back of the worn parchment one. She couldn't guess how long it would take her to reach the place where the rivers converged. Last time she'd made the journey she'd been unconscious. Gillie had only said she'd reach it before dark if she was smart. Whether that was a dig at her navigational skills or sound advice, she wasn't sure. Regardless, she didn't have time to waste. She'd get back to the rivers and head North, toward Terrapese.

Face flush from the afternoon heat, Talullah stopped to rest. It felt like she'd only left Gillie's house an hour ago, but already the sun hung high in the sky. She sipped water from her canteen, which had somehow remained cold despite the heat outside. According to Gillie's map, she should reach Lethe soon. Which was good. Stumbling around the dark abyss once the sun went down didn't seem like a good idea.

A sawed-off stump made for a good place to rest. Gillie must have stocked her provisions, because when she opened her pack, various foods spilled out. She ripped off a hunk of bread and dunked it in a jar of elderflower honey. Floral sweetness flooded her taste buds. It was the most delicious thing Talullah had ever eaten.

Birds chirped a lively melody in the trees, and an unexpected breeze cooled her skin, bringing with it the scent of fresh dew. Which was strange. Any dew that had been present that morning had long since evaporated, leaving the tall lavender grass dry and wispy. Maybe she'd imagined it.

Not long after she'd packed up and continued toward the rivers, she spotted fresh hoof prints in the soft ground. A loud *thump* drew her attention to a group of trees in the near distance.

"Could that be our guest of honor?" The familiar brogue rang through the forest.

Talullah slid behind a tree, heart pumping.

Rantoul emerged and headed for the group of trees, his cloak billowing as his horse picked up speed.

Caprico and Fallon followed.

Talullah released her breath. Adrenaline buzzed through her blood. She wasn't too late.

When she was sure they were out of earshot, she moved from behind the tree and silently thanked whatever had drawn the soldiers' attention.

"Don't fight us," Fallon said. "We don't want to have to hurt you."

"Like hell we don't. I've got him, Cap!" Rantoul boomed. "Hold still, earthworm. The sooner we get back to the castle the sooner I get to have my date with Verita."

"Look, messenger boy, I don't know why you ran away, and I don't care. Hell, I don't even care how you did it. All that matters is that we get you back to Renevelda. Apparently, she didn't authorize your release. Imagine that. Wrap him up, Rantoul."

Talullah's breathing quickened. Could this be the person they'd been searching for before? The realization hit her like lightning. Margot hadn't escaped, and they didn't know Talullah was there. But why, then, had they taken the path through Nainehta Forest? And who *had* they captured?

The convoy cantered back through the trees and Talullah dashed into hiding. For a moment it looked like they were going to head south—straight toward her—but Caprico turned the group north. All three soldiers kicked their horses into a gallop. A lumpy figure bounced on the back of Rantoul's horse, but Talullah couldn't see any defining features.

As she watched them disappear, though, a familiar voice caught her ears.

"By the Founders, could you loosen these ropes just a touch? I have sensitive wrists."

Talullah's whole body tingled with recognition. It couldn't be. But there was no mistaking it. She would have known his voice and wry humor anywhere.

Shock glued her boots to the ground as her mind processed. Terrapesians had not only kidnapped her family and ransacked her home, they'd also captured her best friend.

Chapter 10

Breathe in, breathe out. Talullah had to repeat it over and over to make her lungs work. The realization that Dhalian was on his way to Terrapese turned her blood cold. First her sisters and her father, and now the only other person who mattered to her. A sharp twinge shot down her clenched jaw. She'd acted too late to save Margot; she wouldn't let the same thing happen to Dhal.

The horses had slowed to a walk, so at least she didn't have to run. She didn't dare follow too closely. Instead, she used trees and bushes for cover and crept with delicate steps, staying just close enough to eavesdrop.

"Guess it's good that damn bird tagged along," Rantoul said. "Though I hate to admit it. Still, at this rate we should be back earlier than expected."

"I wouldn't get too far ahead of yourself, Rantoul. Night's already on its way." Captain Caprico gestured to the sun, which was significantly lower in the sky, despite the fact they'd departed less than an hour ago. "We'll have to make camp soon. Don't worry, I'm sure Verita will understand."

"I told you this forest is creepy. The stories I've heard would give even you nightmares, Rantoul." Fallon's voice shook, and for a second Talullah almost pitied him before she remembered he was part of the Terrapesian guard.

"Who'd you hear these stories from, kid? Been fraternizing with traders?" Rantoul's tone was teasing yet accusatory.

"Just these girls I met in town. They said the trees have powers and the nights are so dark they swallow all light." He fidgeted and kept his eyes trained on his horse. "They told me about people who lost their minds drinking from the river and others who were burned alive by invisible fire."

"Let's stop here." Caprico dismounted abruptly and wagged a finger at Fallon. "Come here. Look at this tree for me." Fallon did as he was told. "Really get your nose close."

"What am I looking for, Captain?"

"How does the tree feel?"

Fallon placed his palm on the trunk. "Uh? Like bark?"

"Does it seem to have any...powers?"

There was a moment of silence and then Caprico and Rantoul burst out laughing. "Tether the horses, kid. We're making camp."

Fallon's shoulders slumped while he worked. Talullah watched him loop the rope around the nearest tree and knot it multiple times.

He bound Dhalian to the same tree with different rope. "Watch your hands, soldier. I'm not that kind of girl." Even in capture Dhalian maintained an airy positivity. It was almost annoying.

Talullah, on the other hand, held her breath. The men dragged fallen logs close together. Caprico pulled a circular rock from his bag and placed it on the ground in the center of the logs. "A gift from the She-Devil," he said. The rock sparked and instantly caught fire.

Talullah stifled a gasp. Had Renevelda given the soldiers magic? And if so, what other weapons might they have?

Rantoul removed provisions from his bag and the three soldiers sat on the logs and gorged themselves. Fallon held a long stick of dried meat over the fire and it crackled. The smell of smoked beef and roasted potatoes made Talullah's mouth water.

It didn't matter. She would eat when she'd freed Dhalian.

But how to do it? The men planned to camp for the night and there was no chance she'd best three of them with just her hunting knife. Not to mention they'd probably kill her the second they realized she had Dunamai's Eye.

Subconsciously she touched the amulet through her tunic. She stole a glance at the sky.

Stealth may not have been her strong suit, but in less than an hour that wouldn't matter. The forest was about to lend her a hand in the form of a total blackout. All she had to do was wait.

Surely only one of the soldiers would stand guard once night fell. Her money was on the youngest recruit, Fallon. She was confident she could slip past him, untie Dhalian, and steal a horse.

Talullah moved as close as she dared during the last few minutes of light. The soldiers were busy setting up their tents and making enough of a racket to cover the low *shush* of her boots in the leaves. A golden strip of fabric hid Dhalian's eyes. Talullah willed him to know she was there, but he gave no indication he felt her presence. She swallowed the river-stone wedged in her throat.

Her plan played on repeat in her mind. Once it got completely dark, she'd walk the thirty or so paces in a straight line to Dhalian. She'd saw through the rope binding him to the tree, and he could fend off Fallon while she untethered a horse. They'd be gone in no time. Of course, if the men woke up before she'd freed Dhalian, it would be her versus them and whatever magic tricks the sorceress had provided. And what if Fallon was a better fighter than she suspected? She shook away her doubts.

By no means was it foolproof, but it was the only plan she had.

The charred smell of the soldier's fire almost convinced her they'd built it for real instead of using magic. Talullah had always loved the smell of wood smoke. It reminded her of winter nights spent huddled around the fireplace in her cottage, reading aloud to her sisters.

She blinked the tears away. She would save them, protect them. Her sisters and her father. But first she had to save Dhalian.

Shuffling and groaning echoed through the otherwise silent forest as the soldiers finished readying their camp. Talullah blinked in their direction, but their forms had already disappeared into the night. She held her hand in front of her face. If her palm hadn't been touching her nose, she wouldn't even know it was there. Darkness had fallen.

"Put out the fire and use the lantern," Caprico said.

Hell and a half. Of course they'd have lanterns. Why hadn't she realized that? What if they were magic, too?

The green fire light extinguished, and the clang of metal reached her ears.

"Where are the matches? I can't even see my boots. Was it this dark last night?" Rantoul bellowed.

"We went to sleep before dark last night," Fallon said. "What's wrong?"

Objects clanged for a few seconds. "Damned thing won't even catch. Must be out of fuel."

"It's hot," Caprico said. "I can feel it. But I can't see it."

"I told you," Fallon's small voice cut in. "The forest swallows light."

"Bet that magic woman knew this would happen. She-witch devil," Rantoul grumbled.

Talullah shivered as a breeze swept through the area. Despite having experienced it before, the blindness unnerved her. But she steeled herself and thought only of her plan.

Knife unsheathed and held at the ready, she placed one foot directly in front of the other, hoping she was moving in a straight line toward Dhalian. The soldiers yelled at each other, cursing, so she chanced moving quicker. They didn't seem to notice.

Sooner than she'd expected, she reached the tree.

"Dhalian," she whispered. "It's me."

He flinched as she removed his gag. "Tules? By the Founders, what are you doing here? How did you find me?"

"Lucky coincidence. But we don't have time." She groped for the rope holding him to the tree and placed her knife edge against it, sawing back and forth.

Not one thread frayed. Sweat beaded on her forehead as she pressed harder.

"Are you trying to slice it? It won't work. It's laced with magic. It can't be broken, only untied."

A shot of panic ran through her. She should have known.

"Tules, you can do this. I trust you."

She sheathed her knife and gulped down her fear. The rope slid like silk in her palm, different than the jute she was used to. A series of knots secured it, instead of just one. Seven in all. Apparently, they'd wanted to be extra sure Dhalian wouldn't escape. Her fingers set to work, clumsy at first. It had been a long time since she'd practiced on her loom, but soon her muscle memory took over.

Within minutes, she'd undone five of the seven knots. As she started on the sixth, Dhalian drew a sharp breath and she felt his body go rigid.

"What is it?" she whispered.

"They've stopped talking." It was true. In fact, Talullah couldn't remember the last thing the soldiers had said.

"Who's there?" Caprico's voice sliced through the silence. The distinct grating of metal-on-metal, of a sword being drawn. And then two more just like it as the others followed their leader. "Fallon, check the boy."

"Captain, I can't see a half-step in front of me."

"Just do it."

"And if you hear or feel anything moving, start swinging," said Rantoul.

"Just make sure it's not one of us," Caprico added, a bit of worry tinging his tone.

Footsteps shuffled across the ground. Talullah forced her fingers to work faster. She had no way of knowing how close Fallon was. His movements grew louder, though it was hard to hear them above the hammering inside her chest.

Cold fear dripped down Talullah's spine. She needed to hurry, but her shaking hands fumbled. If the soldiers caught her, who would save her family? *No one, Talullah. You have to do this.*

She gritted her teeth. The rope slipped like sand from her hands as the last knot released. She pulled Dhalian to standing and groped for the horses' tethers, whispering soothingly to keep from spooking them.

Thank the Founders, she thought, when she latched onto a familiar jute rope. She drew her knife and set to sawing it. Before she'd finished, the horse moved. The others whinnied in terror. Talullah continued her soothing talk and attempted to steady the one she was trying to free.

"The horses!" Rantoul bellowed. "Fallon, what in the blazes is going on over there?"

"I d-don't know, sir. I can't s-see." A second later, "Oh, I see something now."

"Well, what is it?" Caprico shouted.

"Eyes."

Talullah's first thought was of Kahu and her tension lifted. Maybe the wolf had followed. Maybe she was there to help. But a glance dashed her hopes. Kahu's eyes were gray. The round, cat-like pair staring directly at her glowed as yellow as the midday sun. It was impossible to tell how big the animal was.

"Dhal, make sure that animal doesn't get too close. It's spooking the horses," Talullah whispered.

"Never mind the horses. It's spooking *me.*"

"Just watch it, Dhal. I'm almost done."

A dull light broke through the darkness, casting a faint purple glow across the forest. Silhouettes of trees illuminated in its path. Though the light source was still far enough away she couldn't identify it, sudden sight after total blindness caused her muscles to tense. Another magic fire, maybe? She pulled Dhalian behind the tree and out of the light's range. If she could see, so could the soldiers. Which meant she and Dhal needed to go *now*.

And then Fallon uttered two clarifying words that zapped her insides. "Captain? *Ghosts*."

Chapter 11

Dozens of semitransparent figures appeared in the approaching glow. Talullah recoiled and shielded her eyes.

Humans of all ages and animals of varied species. Either they didn't notice they had company, or they didn't care. They floated across the forest without making a sound. Fallon, on the other hand, whimpered from somewhere to Talullah's left and Rantoul muttered something so vulgar Talullah would have been embarrassed to think it, let alone say out loud.

Dhalian nudged Talullah in the side and whispered, "Do you think now might be a good time to, you know, get out of here?"

"Absolutely." She reached for the reins of the horse she'd cut loose but found only air. She swore.

"I don't think we have time for the horse, Tules. Plus, we'll be quieter on foot." Dhalian gripped her elbow and the warmth of his hand traveled up Talullah's arm. Her pulse thrummed in her wrist.

"But the horse will be faster." She felt for the other horses' tethers.

Just as she'd hooked her hand around the rope, the sensation of being watched prickled her skin. All the air left her lungs when she glanced up.

Every one of the ghosts stared directly at her.

"Dhal," she whispered, panic rising in her like a river during a thunderstorm. "What do we do?"

Before Dhalian could answer, one of the ghosts spoke in a low rumble. "Find the keys." The words echoed inside Talullah's skull, though she couldn't make sense of them. The ghost's body flickered as if lit by purple candlelight blowing in the wind.

"The keys," he repeated. And to Talullah's horror he lifted a hand and pointed at her.

"There's someone else over there," said Rantoul.

"Don't swing your sword, Rantoul. Or we'll all be ghosts." Caprico bit off each word, his anxiety evident. Whether he was more concerned about being stabbed by his own solider or by the presence of the ghosts was unclear.

"Dunamai will reward the Keeper of the Keys," the ghost called, still pointing at her while the rest of the shimmering apparitions chattered in hushed voices.

"D-Did he say D-Dunamai? Isn't that the ancient witch Renevelda mentioned? The one whose necklace we were supposed to find in River Hill?" Fallon's voice trembled with every word.

"Tules. We have to get out of here."

They eased backward in tandem. She couldn't turn away from the ghostly figures no matter how hard she tried. There was something almost pleading in the man's face as he locked eyes with her. He cocked his head in contemplation and lowered his hand.

"Dunamai is with you, child, no matter where you are. Embrace your Gift, or may we all perish."

A series of lightning bolts illuminated the forest, a sound like a whip cracking with each one. Her heart raced as the forms of the soldiers appeared in the flashes. Through squinted eyes, Talullah saw the ghosts flicker once more and vanish.

"Is that the Eye?" Rantoul yelled.

"Tules, your neck!"

She'd thought anxiety had caused the heat creeping up her chest, but touching it revealed her necklace was to blame. It glowed the ghosts' shade of lilac.

During each flash the soldiers moved closer.

"Capture them, get the necklace, and let's get out of this haunted hellhole." Caprico's gold-capped teeth glinted in the brief light. "And the she-devil will want answers. Which means keep them alive. We'll get nothing if we deliver corpses."

They were close enough for Talullah to see the insignia on their cloaks once again.

She covered the charm with one hand and drew her knife with the other. "Dhal?"

"Yeah?" His eyes narrowed on the approaching men.

"Run."

The necklace brightened their path, its faint light somehow repelling the soul-crushing darkness their lanterns couldn't.

Behind them, a thunderous explosion of hooves pounded the ground, echoing the thunder in the sky. Talullah gasped. There was no way she and Dhalian could outrun them.

Talullah reached for Dhalian's hand to change their direction, grabbing his wrist instead. Raised flesh pushed against her fingers through his tunic sleeve. He swore and jerked his arm back.

The tight bindings, she remembered too late. "I'm sorry!"

"No problem," he hissed through clenched teeth. "I'm right beside you. Any idea where we're supposed to be going?"

"No. And we'll never lose them as long as this stupid necklace glows."

"Remember she wants them alive!" Caprico's voice carried through the night.

The ground vibrated as the horses drew nearer. Talullah could almost feel the beasts' hot breath on her neck. She headed for where the trees seemed thickest. The necklace had been flickering and fading, and she hoped they could hide long enough for it to extinguish.

Talullah traced the eye's frame and willed its light to die, to coat the forest in thick darkness once more. Other threats may have lurked in the shadows, but at that moment she didn't care. As her fingers grazed the smooth silver, her ears blocked out the crunching leaves and hollering soldiers.

A voice crept into her mind, soft yet urgent. *Touch the tree.*

She couldn't identify the speaker.

The tree!

Talullah slapped her palm onto the trunk of the closest tree. A zap of energy ran from her fingertips to her heart.

The lightning ceased. And the light from the eye charm faded.

They were in pitch dark once more.

Dhalian hooked his arm through hers and whispered into her ear, his warm breath sending a shiver up her spine. "When we're done with this running for our lives bit, you're going to have to tell me how you did that."

In response she tugged him away from the tree, listening for their pursuers. The men hadn't been far behind.

Voices bounced off the trees, though Talullah couldn't make out what they said. "We need a place to hide until morning," Talullah whispered.

"That might be difficult since we can't see anything."

"We don't always see with our eyes." She didn't know where the words came from. They bubbled up from somewhere in her memory, spilling over like an unattended pot. Words her mother had said long ago. About trees and roots and strength.

A feeling of certainty swelled in her stomach.

"This way." She pulled Dhalian so hard he almost fell, but she caught him.

"How do you—"

"Just a feeling," she said, not knowing how to explain this sudden surge of intuition because she didn't understand it herself. For some reason she just knew it was the right way. The way to safety.

Talullah moved with sure, brisk steps, not taking care to cover the sounds her boots made in the dry leaves.

Branches clawed at them, scratching marks into their arms and faces. But they moved on, undeterred, the sounds of their pursuers still ringing in their ears.

Anticipation and adrenaline coursed like a river in Talullah's veins. Though she couldn't see her actual surroundings with her eyes, her mind created an image of what she felt. She used it to guide her. She would lead them out of danger and then she'd rescue her family.

They rounded a corner and Talullah sucked in a breath. Dhalian did the same beside her.

An enormous tree stood directly in the middle of the path. Light from above bathed it in a glow, revealing an ornate door carved into its trunk. Raised symbols that looked spun from multicolored sugar wound around its frame.

"There they are, by that tree!" Rantoul called.

"We can hide in here," Talullah said.

"There's no handle. How do we get in?" Dhalian asked, panic increasing his pitch.

She touched the door and recoiled. "It's pulsing. Like a heartbeat."

Dhalian placed his own hand next to Talullah's on the door and his upper body stiffened.

The eye necklace warmed again, but it did not brighten.

Horses whinnied in the near distance. They needed to hurry.

Again, seized by a feeling in her gut, she hooked her arm through Dhalian's. "Close your eyes."

Talullah closed her own and with her free hand traced the eye charm. *We need to get in here. How do we get inside?*

A floodgate opened in her head, spilling thoughts of her sisters and father and all the other families who had been separated during the raid only days ago. Her mother's face. The brightness of her eyes before the sickness had dimmed them. The smell of lavender and honey and fresh morning dew so strong she almost convinced herself she hadn't imagined it.

The door radiated heat. Dhalian's arm trembled in hers. When she opened her eyes, she realized why.

The shining curls that framed the door rearranged themselves into scrawling words across its middle.

"*If you seek,*" Talullah whispered.

"Looks like we got here just in time." Caprico and his soldiers surrounded them and dismounted. Fallon tied the horses to the closest tree.

Dhalian squeezed Talullah's hand. They turned their backs on the door to face the soldiers, knives raised in defense.

Fire burned in Talullah's stomach and she forced it into her eyes, making them blaze with her anger. These men had destroyed her home. They'd kidnapped her family. And who knew what else?

Despite her physical size, she felt more than capable of fighting three grown men, and the desire to do just that fueled her.

"Does she have it?" Rantoul asked, huffing. "Because if it's not her and we've spent all night out here—"

"Quiet," said Caprico, stroking his jaw. The light from the tree cast his face in shadow. He didn't raise his voice, but his tone commanded silence. "The resemblance is uncanny," he said, barely audible.

"We're not going to hurt you, doll," Rantoul said, running his thumb down the blade of his sword.

Fallon stayed quiet, his large eyes widening even further at noticing the door.

"Not unless you make us, right Captain?" Rantoul winked at her.

She arranged her face into a sneer and spat. Her knife hand quivered. With rage, she decided, not fear. She wouldn't give them the satisfaction of making her afraid.

The Captain smiled, a good-natured, mean-you-no-harm kind of expression. "You're valuable, Miss Bridgestone. I think you've figured that much out by now. As is your friend. This chase has been fun, but it's over now. Bind them."

Rantoul reached out to grab her. She slashed at his arm, drawing a trickle of blood. He looked at the wound, shocked she actually attacked him. And then he laughed. A deep belly laugh that didn't suit him.

Talullah backed up further so her knapsack pushed against the door. Dhalian faced Fallon, who despite having his sword raised, looked as intimidating as a small child. In fact, he looked like he might be sick.

"We don't have time for any more games, Talullah. Don't make this difficult, like your sister," Rantoul said.

At the mention of Margot, the thread holding Talullah's emotions together snapped. She lunged toward him. "Don't you dare speak of her! What did you do to her—to them—you monsters? She's only ten. And Penny. And Father." Her body blazed. Her voice quaked with each word. "They did nothing to you. Any of you." She pointed to each of them with her knife, jabbing it in the air. Her braid had loosened and pieces of hair, slick with sweat, stuck to her face.

None of the soldiers moved.

"They don't deserve this, and you know it." She spat on Caprico's boots. "Carp scum." The insult slipped off her tongue, but she didn't try to backtrack. Instead she gritted her teeth. She'd never used that word before, but if anyone fit the description, it was this Captain. A bottom-feeder in the polluted waters of Castle Terrapese.

"You're right." His response caught her off-guard.

She pushed against the tree further, using it to support her tired body. "What?"

"You're right." He dared look her in the eye.

"Then why—"

A symphony of screams echoed from behind the door. Talullah and Dhalian both jumped away from it. Her hair stood on end, but she didn't break Caprico's stare. Dhalian shuddered next to her and he tightened the grip on his weapon.

A soft click emanated from the door.

Dhalian used his free hand to graze the surface of the tree. His mouth curled into a smile. "Handle."

She nodded.

"Don't do anything rash, Talullah," Caprico said. The other men tossed glances from her to the door to Caprico as if trying to decide of whom they were most afraid.

"Don't go through that door."

She pushed down the handle and the door swung inward, revealing a drop of unknown depth into more darkness.

The sun had begun to rise, the first pink rays creeping up the horizon.

Talullah and Dhalian turned back-to-back and stepped sideways onto the first step.

"Don't make us do it, Talullah." Caprico sighed. "Alright, Rantoul."

Rantoul lunged toward Talullah at the same time Fallon disarmed Dhalian and kicked him to the ground. Fallon grimaced as he pinned Dhalian with a foot on his chest and a sword pointed at his throat.

Rantoul grabbed her wrist, twisting her arm around her back and pulling upward until she dropped the knife. Despite herself, she cried out, her eyes watering. He brought his sword to her neck, pressing the blade just enough for her to feel the pressure. Sweat dropped from her forehead and stung her eyes. She couldn't let them win. She wouldn't.

Dhalian's gaze flicked to hers. She blinked twice to say, *I'm okay.*

Caprico went to fetch the horses, satisfied that his men had everything under control.

As soon as he was gone, Talullah channeled all her strength into her free elbow and drove it into Rantoul's diaphragm. He wheezed and coughed, loosening his grip enough for her to slip free. She grabbed her knife and slashed his leg.

Fallon, distracted by the scene, had removed his foot from Dhalian's chest. Dhalian kicked Fallon's legs out from under him, sending him stumbling sideways.

They ran for the door. Halfway through, Rantoul grabbed a fistful of Talullah's braid and yanked her backward. She let out a guttural yell and sliced through her hair, freeing her braid and the soldier's hand from her head. A stinging sensation sliced across her face.

Jump, said the voice in her head. *Trust and jump, now!*

Without a backward glance, she grabbed Dhalian's hand and flung them both through the open door into the black abyss.

Chapter 12

They plummeted.

At least that's how it felt at first. Flowery air whipped Talullah's hair into her face. But seconds later her backside landed on something solid and she and Dhalian slid through a cramped tunnel. An unseen force propelled them up and over hills and around curves. The movement tickled her stomach.

A tapestry of glittering colored threads covered the interior of the tunnel. They moved too fast for Talullah to make out what the pictures were. Dhalian gripped her hand so tightly she lost all feeling in her fingers.

They landed with a hard *thunk*.

Talullah whipped her head around to see if any of the soldiers had followed. She breathed a sigh of relief. They'd gotten away. They were alive.

The square room they'd fallen into couldn't have measured more than five feet on any side. It was, however, dimly lit by curls of colored threads dangling from the ceiling. Talullah ran her hand along the wall in search of the tunnel opening through which they'd arrived. It had disappeared.

Dhalian groaned beside her. "That's going to leave a mark. Or ten. Are you okay?" He released her hand and immediately pulled his sleeves down over his wrists. Sharp needles stabbed at her fingers as the feeling returned.

"Yeah. I think so." She ran her hands over her arms and legs. "Some scratches but nothing major."

She turned to him. "You?"

He drew a sharp breath and faltered. "Oh, yeah, me? I'm great." A second hesitation and then, "Tules, your face."

Talullah touched her cheek. A bloody slash ran from just below her cheekbone to the bottom of her earlobe. Now that her adrenaline had faded, the wound stung. She winced. Rantoul must have caught her with his sword. "It's not too deep," she said, trying more to convince herself than Dhalian. "I have some healing salve in my bag. More importantly, we're alive."

"Did I just imagine sliding through a hole in the wall?" Dhalian raked the walls with his eyes, perplexed.

Talullah shook her head. "It's gone. And I think it's safe to assume the soldiers aren't coming through it any time soon."

"Right, yes. But, then, how are we going to get out?" Dhalian picked a spider off his tunic, grimacing.

"Good point." Talullah bit the inside of her cheek. For the first time since landing, she took a real look around the room. Her eyes lit up.

Books.

Shelves upon shelves of them. The whole room—or, closet, more like—was bookshelves. She approached one and peered at the spines. Symbols from every edge of the world decorated the covers, spelling titles she could have read years ago. But she was out of practice.

The largest book sat in the middle of the shelf at eye level. Something about it seemed...off. It didn't match the rest. Talullah grazed the spine with her index finger, poised to pick it up.

A scream pierced the air and Dhalian dropped a book behind her. Talullah pressed her hands over her ears to try to drown out the sound. She stumbled into another shelf, knocking it and all its books to the ground. Clouds of lavender dust puffed from the shelves and coated them. The harder Talullah pressed her hands to her ears, the louder the voices echoed inside her mind.

Dhalian's lips moved, but she couldn't hear what he said. The books vibrated on the ground, as if seizing in pain. Dhalian dropped to his knees and slammed them all shut.

Dead silence washed over them, leaving a ringing in Talullah's ears.

Panting and grinning sheepishly, he said, "My bad."

"Hey, look."

The odd book still stood upright on the shelf in front of her. An iron curlicue handle stuck out from its spine. Through a gap above the book, Talullah spied parts of another room.

Dhalian raised his eyebrows.

Talullah grasped the handle and pulled it downward from twelve o'clock position to six o'clock. A slight vibration shook the room and the outline of a door appeared around the bookcase.

"Let's get out of here." She pushed against it. Nothing happened. Narrowing her eyes, she tried again, more forcefully. Still nothing.

Dhalian slid next to her. "On three, we push. One, two, three." They heaved their shoulders into the door, sending them tumbling out into a brightly lit room and landed sprawled on the floor.

"Well, that worked," said Dhalian, sitting up and shaking the dust from his hair.

Talullah rubbed her raw elbows, which she'd scraped on the dark stone floor.

"Sorry," said a girl's voice. "I've been meaning to fix that for ages. It sticks something awful."

Talullah and Dhalian both jumped. The girl, who looked only a year or so older than Talullah, assessed them with curiosity through cloudy brown eyes. Her dark hair fell in waves across her shoulders. As she helped Talullah stand, Talullah couldn't shake the feeling she'd seen the girl before. "I'm Hazel."

"Hi. I'm Talullah. This is Dhalian."

Dhalian gave a little wave. Talullah brushed the dust from her clothes and hair. "Sorry about the door..." She flushed, realizing it hung cockeyed on its hinges.

"Never mind that," Hazel said. "How'd you get in there anyway? I thought I locked that room." She furrowed her brows as if trying to remember.

"We came through the for—"

Talullah elbowed Dhalian in the side. He coughed and shot her a look.

"We thought we heard screaming coming from inside, so we went to make sure everything was okay." A partial truth, sort of. They *had* heard screaming.

The girl gave Talullah a half-smile, nodding. "The Unforgiven. We keep them in there so they don't disturb the patrons, but sometimes they get out of hand anyway. Poor souls."

"The Unforgiven?" Dhalian asked.

"The books in that closet. They're the stories of people haunted by their past. The rest of these"—she gestured around her— "are fairly happy. Everyone's got their demons, of course, but the ones in that room just can't get past theirs."

Dhalian raised an eyebrow.

"The books hold their souls. But their bodies live here." The girl took a swig of a cloudy orange beverage, her teeth clinking lightly against the glass bottle. She gestured to the drink. "This juice is the best. I'm completely addicted."

"Sorry, their *souls*, did you say?" Dhalian eyed the books as if they might attack him. "So this is what, the afterlife or something? Are we dead?"

Hazel laughed. "An afterlife of sorts. And no, you're not dead." As if reading the question poised on Talullah's tongue, she added, "And neither am I."

Talullah stole a glance around. Her heart leapt as the familiar scent of parchment wafted into her nostrils. "A library."

Hazel laughed again. "Of course. Finest history section in all of Praeteriti, to be more specific." She pointed to a carved stone panel hanging from the wall in front of them.

"Praeteriti," Dhalian read. "The past *is* the present *is* the future."

Before Talullah could ask exactly what the panel's saying meant, Hazel ushered them into the hall and down a steep spiral staircase. "I've never seen you two before. Well, obviously you're new seeing as you didn't even know where you were." She tilted her head in thought. "It's been a while since we've had anyone new. Especially full bodies. That's because all the passages in and out are sealed." She snapped her gaze to Talullah's. "How did you say you got in?"

"Uh..." Talullah racked her brain for an explanation and came up empty.

"Oh, well. Maybe someone fixed the passages. Finally. They've been working on them for ages. At least, as long as I can remember. I'll ask around."

Passages. That's how she and Dhal would get out of there and back to Margot.

"Where did you say the passages lead?" Talullah asked in what she hoped was a nonchalant tone.

"Oh, everywhere." Hazel flipped her hair over her shoulder. "But I wouldn't get your hopes up that they're fixed. Every few weeks there's a rumor one's been repaired, but it's never true. Hey, are you hungry? I know a great place."

They crossed a marble-floored lobby and followed Hazel out the oaken double doors and onto a bustling street. "After breakfast you can clean up at my place."

Talullah flushed at the mention of her appearance. She hadn't seen herself in days, but the layer of grime covering her skin was evidence enough she could use a shower. And they needed sustenance if they were going to figure out what in the name of the Founders was going on, where they were, and how to get out. "Breakfast would be marvelous."

Outside the library, the dull gray sky looked as if it might open up at any moment and rain. Two men in togas and sandals passed by, and Dhalian just managed to sidestep a woman in a silk corseted gown to avoid being skewered by her lace parasol. Talullah's legs moved to keep up with Dhalian and Hazel, but the rest of her was completely absorbed in her surroundings, her brain trying to reconcile a man in a red military coat talking with a bald woman draped in a striped poncho.

"So, Hazel, are *these* people dead?" She cringed at her bluntness, but she was too tired to be tactful.

"Technically, sure. They're dead to the rest of the world. But they're also alive. The books that hold their souls keep their consciousness aware, and the magic of Praeteriti preserves their bodies. Whatever form they were in when they first arrived here is the form they take whenever they're within range of the magic. So, if you two were to leave and come back, you'd return looking like your current selves." Her eyes clouded a bit more as she finished off her drink and tucked the bottle into her leather satchel. "It's like the plaque said. The past is the present and the future. Each person in Praeteriti experiences it as if they were still alive in their own time and place. When they interact with another person, they don't notice their differences. And there's no language barrier."

"But why don't I see everyone dressed in tunics and boots?"

Hazel pulled open the glass door of a diner and gestured them through. "Because, Dhalian, you're still very much alive."

Talullah's mind reeled as they slid into a corner booth, the well-worn material creaking beneath their weight. "So how did you get here, then? How long have you been here? How is any of this possible?" The questions flowed from her mouth in an anxious burst.

There were too many to keep caged inside her mind any longer. Not to mention the questions she had for Dhalian, like how he'd gotten himself into Nainehta Forest and why the Terrapesian guards were after him. But those would have to wait until they were alone. They'd only just met Hazel and Talullah wasn't ready to trust her with all their secrets.

"Tules, let the girl breathe for a minute." Dhalian patted her on the arm, one brow raised and a crooked half-smile on his face. He always looked like that when she got carried away.

Her face warmed, but Hazel just flipped her curtain of glossy black hair over her shoulder, seeming unbothered by the barrage. "I don't really remember how I got here or anything about who I was before. One day I just woke up in the library, about the same place I found the two of you, covered in purple dust. I wandered around and stumbled upon the Records of the Living, but not knowing my own name I didn't make much progress there."

"You don't remember anything?" Talullah whispered, breathless.

Hazel shook her head. "I chose the name Hazel for myself. And after talking with some of the residents, I learned the passages they use to travel between worlds had been sealed somehow. I looked for a way out, but after a few weeks I realized it was useless. We've all been trapped here ever since, which is why it's curious that the two of you showed up."

At that moment a waitress approached the table, her tray laden with dishes of delicious smelling food. Talullah's stomach growled. When had she last eaten? Suddenly she felt exhausted, every inch of her weighed down by the events of the past few days.

"Wow. Great service!" Dhalian said, unfolding his napkin on his lap.

The woman blinked at him, finished setting the food on the table, and walked away without a word.

"I come here a lot. They know my order." Hazel pulled back her sleeves, and Talullah glimpsed a tiny arrow-shaped tattoo on her left wrist.

"Do you remember that tattoo?" Talullah asked, her chest tight.

Hazel glanced at it. "Nope. Why?"

"I used to know someone who had one like that." Her mother, though she didn't want to say it out loud.

"Arrows are popular, it seems. I've met a few others here who have them. Go ahead and dig in," she said, picking up her fork. "The cinnamon pancakes are the best. Trust me."

The warm food and tea replenished Talullah, but she still didn't have enough energy to ask Hazel everything she wanted to know. If Hazel was right and the passages were open again, it wouldn't matter. By that time tomorrow, she and Dhalian would be back in Nainehta Forest rescuing Margot.

At the end of the meal, Hazel removed a leather pouch from her dress pocket and poured its contents onto the table. A handful of white, silver, and black spheres rolled between the plates.

"Money," Hazel said, nodding at them "Even in the afterlife." She laughed lightly, grabbing a few white marbles and handing them to the waitress who had appeared silently at the table. "It's a simple system, though. Fifty of the white Luz equal one Meitat, the silver. And twenty Meitat to one Nokto, the black. You'll get the hang of it after a bit." She placed the rest of the marbles back in the pouch and handed it to Dhalian. "You'll need some for basic expenses, since now you're stuck here, too."

"Unless the passages are working," Talullah said. "Then we'll be gone tomorrow."

HAZEL'S HOUSE TURNED out to be a small stone cottage in the middle of town. Flowered bushes lined the front porch and a mature tree shaded the yard.

"I like to garden," Hazel said, as she unlocked the front door. "At least, this version of me does. I'm not sure about the other me, but I think she probably does, too. Planted that hazelnut tree when I first figured out I'd be here for a while. It felt right to call myself Hazel after that. Bathroom and a spare bedroom are down the hall. Help yourselves."

Even a hot, soapy shower couldn't wash away Talullah's jumbled feelings about Praeteriti. On one hand, it was the kind of adventure she'd dreamed about as a kid, and she almost felt guilty for being curious about the place, for wanting to learn its secrets. And the library. A whole library full of history books, of people's stories.

If she was honest with herself, the Records of the Living held even more of a draw for her than the history section. A tingle ran down her spine at the thought of whose book she might find there, and a second later her stomach dropped with the realization that the record she most wanted to find may no longer exist.

Choking back tears, she forced her mind to the tunnel she and Dhalian had come through. The one that had disappeared. Even if one of the passages was fixed, would it take them to Nainehta Forest?

Thoughts of Hazel nagged at her. Why couldn't the girl remember who she was? Or was she just pretending not to? Talullah appreciated the hospitality, but she couldn't help thinking Hazel had secrets. The way her eyes clouded over reminded Talullah of magic she'd seen in the Hidden Market. Generally harmless, but she knew sinister varieties existed as well. The idea that Hazel could be working for Renevelda almost made her laugh, but she couldn't disprove it. She and Dhal would just have to be careful what information they revealed.

She combed her fingers through her hair, pulling bits of gold and silver leaves from its tangles. When the steam cleared, she gasped at the face staring back at her in the mirror. She touched the gash on her face. It was worse than she'd imagined. Deeper. It would scar for sure. She cleaned it carefully and slathered a palm-full of healing salve onto it.

Her hair was just as much of a shock. The longest of the uneven ends reached just past her chin, a good twelve inches shorter than before she'd cut it. Each time she ran her hands through she was surprised to find the braid missing. She'd kept her hair long for so many years that it had become her defining feature. Now that it was gone, she felt a little less like herself. But what was done was done. Only thing left to do was even it out.

When she'd fixed her hair as best she could, she located the dresser in the spare room, where Hazel told her she'd find extra clothes. She pulled on the top drawer's star-shaped handles, but it was locked. The second drawer, however, held clean tunics and pants. Once dressed, she padded barefoot into the kitchen. Dhalian's thick curls dripped water onto the carved wooden table, still wet from his own shower, as he bent over his cup of tea. His hair was almost longer than hers now and for some reason this struck her as amusing.

"You look freshened," Hazel said, setting a mug in front of Talullah as she took a place at the table.

The peppermint scent stung her eyes a bit as she sipped—it was strong—but she relished its flavor and familiarity. "I do feel better." She ran a hand over the back of her wet hair, feeling for the absent braid.

"I like it short," Dhalian said, touching the ends with his fingertips.

Talullah raised her brows. "Yeah?"

Dhalian avoided her gaze. "I mean, you looked fine before, but I don't know." He stared into his mug searching for the right words. "I think you look more like *you*, I guess. It's good, Tules."

She hadn't been thinking about her appearance when she hacked off her hair, and though a piece of her missed the main physical trait she'd shared with her mom, it *was* just hair. It would grow back. Plus, she liked how light her head felt without the extra burden.

"So," Hazel said, breaking the awkward silence, "I've been thinking. You guys should just stay here with me for a while. It makes sense, don't you think?" She turned to open a fresh bottle of juice. "And there is someone you should meet, now that you're presentable."

Dhalian swallowed hard. "Alive? Or dead?" He shot Talullah a look and she shrugged.

Hazel laughed. "Alive. But it can wait until tomorrow. After you've rested. Go on and sleep. I won't be offended. It looks like you both could use it."

The spare bedroom wasn't large, but it held two beds, each big enough for one person, the dresser where Talullah had found the clothes. Talullah chose the bed to the left and snuggled under the covers. All she wanted to do was find the passage and get back to her sister, but she knew she needed rest. Her muscles ached and fog rolled around inside her head. In sleep she'd regain her much needed strength. And if she had to fight the soldiers again, she'd need all she could get.

Dhalian shut the door behind him before crawling into his own bed. Now that they were alone, Talullah's questions pressed against her skull, begging to be let out. But where to start?

"Dhal?"

He glanced over, his tired eyes already drooping. "Yeah, Tules?"

"It's just...I don't even..." She took a deep breath and started over. Just pick a question. Any of them. "Why were those soldiers after you?" She'd meant to start by asking about the letters, but her subconscious had chosen for her.

Dhalian propped himself on his elbow and ran his other hand through his hair. "I trespassed on the castle grounds." At her shocked expression he continued, "Accidentally. I...well, I was charting for Norr, and I kind of got off track. Saw a super interesting formation that wasn't too far from where I was working, so I thought I'd check it out. Turns out it was further than I'd expected. Ended up in an unmarked area that turned out to be Terrapesian territory. They...well, they didn't like that I'd managed to get past their defenses so easily."

"Defenses?"

"They were supposed to have some kind of barrier or something, but apparently the guy in charge never handled it. Since I knew where their weak point was they wanted to hold me there until they'd fixed the issue. In case I was a spy from Viltresor."

Talullah laughed out loud and slapped a hand over her mouth. Dhalian? A spy? It was the most absurd thing she'd heard all day. And that was saying something.

"You laugh, but I can be pretty good at secret-keeping. They were right to lock me up. I could have compromised their whole strategy." His toothy grin sent a shot of warmth into Talullah's cheeks.

Talking to Dhal was like being wrapped in a warm quilt on a cold day. After the intensity of the past few days, she needed the comfort of normalcy, even if only for a short while.

"Regardless, how'd you escape? And into Nainehta Forest, no less."

"Superior skill. And I could ask you the same thing. How did you end up in that place?"

Sharper than steel, emotion pierced her insides. She'd forgotten Dhalian didn't know about the raid. About her family. She'd screamed at the soldiers when they'd mentioned her sister, but she hadn't had the chance to explain why. She swallowed the lump in her throat, but it got stuck in her chest.

Before a word could pass her lips, tears soaked her pillow. Dhalian threw off his blankets and in an instant hugged her to his chest. She sobbed, her whole self quaking against his warm body. The familiarity made her cry even harder. The last time they'd done this she'd been thirteen years old. His arms had been less toned, and he'd been shorter than her, but his grip had been just as sure.

Through hiccupping breaths, Talullah told him everything. She talked until her voice rasped. He didn't interrupt or ask questions or tell her it wasn't her fault. He just squeezed her tight and let her cry until she felt she would dissolve into nothingness.

In that moment, after nearly three months waiting and wishing for his letter, she realized she didn't need him to say anything at all.

Chapter 13

"That's the clothing shop. And the apothecary. And there's the grocer. And there's—well, you've already seen the library."

Talullah's brain couldn't keep up. They'd been following Hazel through the town for only ten minutes and she'd already forgotten where everything was. It felt like a labyrinth, the way the cobbled roads twisted and turned without warning. Smells of freshly baked bread and smoked meats and flowery teas wafted out periodically from shop doors. And the noise was almost unbearable. The streets flowed with people, all bustling to their destinations and speaking much louder than Talullah thought was necessary. Her head pounded. The whole experience was making her dizzy.

"And that's where the Mazuchawi course appeared last time!" Hazel stopped abruptly, causing Dhalian to smash into her back.

"Sorry." He smiled sheepishly. "You were saying?"

"The what course?" Talullah squinted in the direction Hazel was pointing. An open field off the road.

"Mazuchawi course. It's a game. But the course only appears every so often. There must be a pattern, but no one's been able to figure it out yet." Her eyes lit up. "Oh, I hope it comes back soon so we can play together!"

"What's it like?" Dhalian asked.

"The course is a maze, and you complete challenges to work your way through. And if you don't finish your game, you pick up where you left off the next time the course appears. Whichever group gets to the maze first gets to continue their game, and only one group can play at a time."

"Sounds like quite the marathon," he said.

Hazel nodded. "And if someone from your group is missing, you can't play. Lots of people have had to forfeit the course because their friend was traveling when the Mazuchawi arrived. Some games have been going on for years. I have three in progress myself. Turn here."

They veered right, climbed a small hill, and stopped.

"Who exactly is the woman you're taking us to see?" Dhalian wiped his brow. It wasn't exactly hot, but it wasn't cool either. The sky was painted flat gray again, and though there was a light breeze, the air smelled stale and musty.

"The Diviner. I met her soon after I arrived. Sweet woman, but a bit...eccentric. Anyway, she asked me to bring any newcomers to her so she could give them a proper greeting."

"A diviner? You mean like a soothsayer?" Talullah's heart stuttered. She didn't like the idea of meeting with a woman of magic. But, if this woman truly was able to tell the future, maybe she could tell Talullah what would happen with her family. Maybe she could help Talullah succeed.

Her hand touched the eye charm through her tunic. She had decided it would be best not to tell Hazel about it. Not yet anyway. They'd only known each other for a day. Talullah had to be certain she could trust whomever she told about the necklace and the sorceress's desire for it. It was still possible that Hazel was working for Renevelda.

"Yep, but she doesn't practice often. Mostly just gardens. I think that might be why she took a liking to me so quickly. She keeps to herself mostly. Doesn't get many visitors. Of course, that could be because it's a bit of a journey to get to her house. That green roof is it."

Talullah glanced up. Her body tingled with awe. Just down the hill sprawled a field of fifteen-foot-tall, golden sunflowers. A deep pang of emptiness wrung her insides.

Sunflowers.

Images of the festival flooded her mind. Penny's crown of flowers perched atop her stuffed rabbit's head. The way her sister's face had radiated joy when she'd put on the dress Talullah made for her. Margot's insistence at having a lemonade. Her face screwed up in defiance as the soldiers carried her away.

Warm sadness pulsed through her veins. Had she not cried herself to sleep only hours before, she would have broken down in an instant. But she'd emptied her reserves. Instead, determination rooted itself in her heart. No matter what, she'd convince the soothsayer to help her.

Once they reached the edge of the field, Talullah noticed a shift. It was brighter than amidst the shops and the air smelled fresh and clean, like after a spring rain. The flower petals' luminescence made Talullah squint. Their light made up for the lack of sun.

"Almost there," said Hazel. Seconds later they cleared the stalks and stepped into a clearing at the edge of a wildflower garden.

"How often do you come here?" Dhalian asked, panting slightly.

"A couple times a week."

"That's dedication."

Hazel shrugged and smiled. "The walk is relaxing. And I like the company."

Talullah gaped at the garden. Butterflies swooped to and fro, landing briefly on roses or daffodils before taking off again. Birdhouses of all shapes and sizes seemed to grow out of the flowers. The longer Talullah looked, the more birdhouses she saw. One looked like a tiny watermelon, another resembled a cloud. A book, a basket, a tiny bell-tower. Talullah breathed in the flowers' sweet perfume. For the first time since leaving home, she felt comfortable.

She felt welcome.

Behind the flowers sat a stone building about the size of her own cottage with a thatched conical roof.

"Hazel, how do we get through?" Any path that existed had been overtaken by the waist-high wildflowers. They couldn't get through without trampling them.

"Not a problem." Hazel reached a hand toward a metal cube-shaped birdhouse and pulled the small knotted branch attached to its side. The front flap popped opened. A canary hopped out and surveyed the three of them. It cocked its head to one side, uttered a melodic chirp, and fluttered away.

"She knows we're here," Hazel said. "Just a second."

Out of the corner of her eye Talullah spotted a quivering of color. She turned and her jaw fell open as the wild flowers swayed away from her, as if blown by the wind. But there was no breeze. She watched, unblinking, as the section of flowers rolled back on themselves and disappeared, leaving a space big enough to walk through. The clover covering the ground dissolved in front of her eyes and revealed a cobblestone path where it had been. Talullah rubbed her eyes and blinked to make sure they weren't playing tricks on her. Definitely real. She readjusted her knapsack on her shoulder.

"Come on, then." Hazel led them around the spiral path to the front door.

"Don't be alarmed if it's messy. She's always getting distracted halfway through tasks and leaving things around. I usually put everything away before I leave so she can find them, but I haven't visited in a few days."

They stepped onto the porch. A round, polished maple door sat just off-center, flanked on either side by two circular windows. Hazel lifted her hand to grab the sunflower-shaped knocker hanging in the center of the door. But before she could grab it, there was a click and the door swung open.

A small, thin woman stood in the doorway. A messy gray bird's nest of a bun wobbled on top of her head. Her sharp eyes peered out from behind magenta cat-eye glasses.

Talullah's throat tightened and her mouth went dry. It had been years since they'd seen each other, but she would have recognized this woman anywhere.

"Hello, dear. I thought I'd be seeing you soon." The woman's voice was just as she remembered. Soft and sweet. And those eyes. Though the rest of her had changed with age, those golden eyes still shone bright and clear.

The words felt foreign on Talullah's tongue, like a language she'd once spoken fluently but now stumbled over, out of practice. "Hello, Aunt Mirella."

Chapter 14

Mirella's eyes filled with tears, her lip curling into a quivering half-smile. Before Talullah could say anything else, her great-aunt wrapped her into tight hug.

Talullah returned the hug, surprised at the wetness rolling down her own cheeks. Though she hadn't seen her aunt in years, unconditional love warmed their embrace. She wanted to tell Mirella how much she'd missed her, how glad she was to see her, to be with family again. But overwhelm paralyzed her vocal cords. If she opened her mouth now, she'd only sob.

"I knew you'd come. Follow me." Mirella released her hold, turned, and disappeared inside the cottage, Hazel on her heels.

Talullah and Dhalian followed Mirella's messy gray bun through two long winding halls but hung back enough not to be overheard.

"Are you okay?" Dhalian touched her forearm, his brows furrowed in concern.

Talullah nodded and drew a deep breath. She concentrated on stilling her lip. "How did she get here, Dhal? What if she's—"

"She's alive, Tules. Hazel said so, remember? You haven't lost her. You haven't lost anyone. They're all okay."

Dhalian was mostly right. She *had* lost someone, though, a long time ago. But she couldn't focus on the past.

Talullah's head swam with possibilities. Why, then, was Mirella in Praeteriti, and how long had she been there? She shook them away. No use driving herself crazy. Mirella would tell her.

When they entered the kitchen, Mirella stood on a chair and pulled mugs out of a cupboard, and Hazel set a kettle on the stove to boil.

Talullah's attention wandered, catching on various objects. A glass teapot caught her eye. Though a thick layer of dust coated the outside, hints of cerulean peeked through. If Mabel Miller could have seen it, she would have had a heart attack. She'd asked for blue glass at every Hidden Market since Talullah could remember. No one had any, the merchants always said. It was too rare and too expensive.

Yet here it was.

She glanced at the far wall where a slab of lattice leaned. It was covered in thorny vines of some sort, and Talullah moved closer to examine them. The tendrils glistened like a misty morning rainbow but the leaves looked sharp as Talullah's pocketknife blade.

"Look but do not touch," Mirella said. Talullah jumped. "Luna Vine is useful in healing wounds, but only the juice in the stems. The leaves will slice you to the bone. And the thorns? Well, the thorns could knock a grown man unconscious for days. Got to use thick leather gloves if you're trying to harvest it." She met Talullah's eyes, her expression searching. "Fully mature vines each have twelve thorns and twelve leaves. You could set your sundial by these things. Each part takes an hour to grow. Easy to transplant, too, since they don't have roots."

"Aunt Mirella?"

Talullah wished she'd thought further ahead. She didn't know what she meant to say, but she needed to say something. "It wasn't my choice. I hope you know that."

Her aunt nodded. "I know, dear." She squeezed Talullah's shoulder on her way back to the stove.

"Mirella, I—"

"There will be time for questions, dear. I'm sure you have many." She poured the water over leaves and strained them. "Hazel, dear, could you do me a favor and tidy up a few of the rooms? I'm afraid I've let my wandering mind get the best of me these past few days."

"Of course. I'll do that and then I've got to run. I'm sorry. I promised I'd cover a shift at the diner tonight."

"Talullah, and Dhalian, I presume? Let's take tea in the library."

They passed an assortment of rooms on the way. Humming and clanging noises filtered through the cracks in closed doors, and wafts of colored smoke drifted beneath one into the hall. Talullah's skin prickled.

Magic.

She hurried by, unnerved by the tingling sensation in her collarbone.

Sturdy mahogany shelves lined all four walls, each one stuffed with books of all sizes. The familiar scent of paper and ink reminded her of home.

"Dear, I know you must have a thousand and ten questions, and the Founders know I'd love to answer them all. But there are some important things we have to discuss first. Sit."

Mirella disappeared into the rows of books and Talullah and Dhalian settled into leather armchairs, placing their mugs of tea on the round table. Steam rose from the mugs and disappeared into the ceiling. So many strange things had happened to her in such a short time, she soaked up every familiar piece of her situation.

But the calm in her mind ended sooner than she'd have liked. Another memory rose to the surface. A slip of parchment with three small words. She could almost feel it crinkle in her hand, could see the unfamiliar scrawl.

Go see Mirella.

Had the note's author known Mirella was in Praeteriti? Had they meant her to come to this place?

Mirella plunked a large volume on the table in front of them. *Legend of the Suditzas* sparkled in thick gold script across the cover. "What I'm going to say might come as a bit of a shock, but we can't avoid it any longer."

"Suditzas," Talullah said. "Gillie mentioned something about them. "They're the original authors of destiny."

Mirella nodded, her glasses magnifying her eyes to twice their size. She adjusted the frames on her nose. "They are. And their tale is inextricably linked with your own. Have you had any strange dreams lately?"

"Occasionally, yes, but doesn't everyone?"

"Of course, dear. But yours are different. You experience them through veils of color?"

Talullah's mouth went suddenly dry. Her recent visions flashed behind her eyes. The ruby forest and the wall of fire. The purple room with the boy and the bird. How did Mirella know about her dreams? Talullah had told only her mother years ago. "Not always. But sometimes."

"These dreams are not just your imagination. They're events throughout time, some of which have already happened, and some have yet to be. Others may never come to pass. The Sights manifest themselves in different ways depending on the Seer. Sezna Seers often have visions like yours. You're like your great-great grandmother in your Gift."

Again with the *Gift of Sight*. When Gillie had first mentioned it, Talullah dismissed it without a second thought. But the seriousness in Mirella's expression gave her pause. Could it be true? She shifted in her chair. Dhalian gave her an encouraging smile.

Mirella flipped through the book and pointed to a page about a quarter way through. An inked timeline stretched across the parchment. "This was when Aurinia held the eye charm you wear now."

Aurinia. Talullah had never met her mother's grandmother, but she'd heard the name a few times throughout her childhood.

"She was one of the most celebrated Sezna Seers of all time. The Eye worked for her as it had never worked for anyone before. She commanded it with unmatched grace and firmness. People came from all over seeking her counsel.

"Aurinia knew warring kings would fight to enslave her in their quest for power and force her use her Gift to destroy others. Instead, she broke apart the amulet and hid the four stones that complete its power. She weakened herself, but she succeeded in keeping the Eye out of ill-intending hands. She hid the frame as well and disappeared. No one's seen or heard from her since. We know this much from the diary she left with the Eye."

Talullah touched her necklace through her tunic, feeling each of the holes where gems should have been. Concentration lines formed in her forehead.

Mirella flipped to a page with a diagram. There, in black and white, was a picture of Talullah's necklace. It matched curve for curve, line for line. Talullah traced the image on the page.

"You have inherited Dunamai's Eye and Aurinia's Gift. But it goes beyond just Seeing. Sezna Seers have the power to affect time, to change its course. The colors of your visions match those of the missing stones."

"Gillie mentioned this," she said, more to herself than anyone else. "He said something about needing to find them in order to beat Renevelda."

Mirella dipped a long finger in an inkwell, muttered a few words, and touched the corner of the page. From her fingerprint flowed a line of ink. It traced the eye, just as Talullah had done, and when the liquid pooled in the pupil, the image glowed. Each of the circles representing the stones pulsed a different color: sapphire, ruby, amethyst, and emerald.

Talullah gaped. Dhalian squeezed her hand, his gaze glued to the book.

"Each of the Suditzas imbued a stone with her particular Gift. Amethyst from Urtha to represent the past. Sapphire from Katamai to represent the present. Ruby from Cesera to represent the inevitable future. And Emerald from Dunamai herself to represent potential futures. They placed the stones in the frame of Dunamai's Eye, uniting their powers into one Gift. They created one hundred copies of the Eye and disseminated them among various species to ensure balance. Few remain. Those who still command Dunamai's Eye must protect it. Changing events creates ripples throughout all phases of time. It must be done with great care."

Questions raced through Talullah's mind, but none stayed still long enough for her to catch it on her tongue. For the first time in a long time, she was speechless.

Dhalian, however, said, "How can the future or present affect the past? The past is over. It can't be changed by something that happens now or later."

"Time is cyclical and exists in parallels. If you travel to the past, the present and the future still exist where you left them. Nothing stops moving."

Talullah pinched the bridged of her nose. "What does this all really mean?"

Tension pulled at the corners of Mirella's mouth. When she spoke, her voice belied the calm expression painted on her face. "Again, the nations are on the verge of war. Renevelda was a Seer's apprentice as a girl. Now, she's one of the most powerful sorceresses our world has known. Many people fear if she controls the Eye, she'll use it to start—and end—the war."

"But why kidnap my family, if she means to destroy the whole country anyway?"

Mirella sighed. "I can only See the present, so I don't know exactly what she means to do. Whatever spell she intends to enact, it will destroy the current timeline. Many lives will be lost."

Talullah's insides knotted, like a skein of yarn wound tight.

"Finding the missing stones will strengthen your power of Sight and enable you to rewrite time to avoid Renevelda's threat. I can teach you to control your Gift."

Talullah's hands clenched her now-cold mug. "Isn't there another way?"

Mirella shook her head. "Renevelda wields powerful magic. Anyone who opposes her must employ multiple strengths. Magic is the only way to win."

"What about the other Sezna Seers? You said there are more." Surely any of them would be better equipped than she. She cast a hopeful glance at her aunt.

Compassion warmed Mirella's face. "No one's heard from them in years. They went into hiding during Aurinia's reign. For all we know, their amulets have been destroyed. Some may have even chosen not to use their Gift, consequences be damned."

"They can do that? What happens if a Sezna Seer refuses to use her power?"

Mirella wrung her hands in her lap. "It is a decision that one must not make lightly. Headaches are the first warning of what comes if the Gift is unused and power unfulfilled."

Talullah swallowed hard. She'd been having headaches recently. "What comes next?"

"The eyesight grows foggy. A cloudy layer of film develops over the eyes. Total blindness. Slowly the rest of the senses fail." Mirella's voice cracked like splitting wood.

Talullah forced her mouth to close. She imagined a life slowly sucked dry of its senses until only a shell remained, unable to experience the world's great glories. A world absent of the smell of salty sea spray or the sweet flavor of elderflower honey.

"Most do not choose this path, though some would say it's easier than living with the responsibility of their Gifts. What has become of them does not matter at the moment. The only way out of Praeteriti is with the amethyst stone."

"Hazel said the portals might be fixed," Dhalian interjected.

"She was mistaken. The portals—including the one you came through—are sealed. I checked. The stone is the key, and it's here somewhere. If Renevelda finds it first, Founders know we'll be stuck here for eternity."

Convenient that the only way to get out of their prison was also a step toward completing Dunamai's Eye. Talullah pursed her lips. Almost too convenient.

"If it's here, why has no one found it yet?"

Mirella closed the book and adjusted her glasses. "Many have searched for the stone, but none had Dunamai's Eye." She fidgeted with the book cover.

"Mirella, what aren't you telling me?"

"I didn't know if I should show you. But I think it's important. Come."

They followed Mirella to a small wall mirror, which hung between bookshelves. Mirella closed her eyes and touched its golden frame.

A puff of midnight blue smoke replaced her reflection. It shimmered, suspended for a moment, and then faded, replaced by a scene in a stone room. Talullah's heart leaped when she saw Penny and Margot huddled together on a gray stone floor.

Tears welled in her eyes. Talullah scanned Penny's arms and legs, looking for wounds or bruises. Other than the thick layer of dirt coating her normally blond hair, she seemed unharmed.

Purple splotches lined Margot's neck and a black and blue bruise ran the length of her right hand. But she smiled at Penny, a warm look that rarely passed her lips.

"The guard—the large, boisterous one—grabbed her by the neck. She punched him in the eye —drew blood, even—before the Captain could pry her away from him. The Captain sees to their needs himself. Brings them blankets and food and books. I don't think Renevelda's privy to all of that, but the rest of the guards follow the Captain. His kindness will buy us some time, but he can't keep it from Renevelda forever."

Talullah wiped her face on her sleeve. She wanted to call out to her sisters. Hug them close, breathe in their scent of rosewater soap, and never let go. Convince them it was going to be okay. That she wouldn't abandon them.

The scene dissolved in a puff of fog and the mirror returned to its normal state, Talullah's blotchy face centered in the reflection.

A steady rhythm beat in her chest, like a war drum calling her to battle. "Have you Seen them in the future, Mirella?"

"The future is not my burden to bear. But I don't need to See it to believe. My heart tells me it will be so. Your sisters are strong. Like you. Trust them to carry on and trust yourself to do what you must to save them. First you must learn to control the visions."

"What about my father?"

Her aunt's face fell. "I don't know. I haven't been able to See him yet. We will bring them home. All of them. But we have work to do."

Seeing her sisters strengthened Talullah's resolve for what she needed to do.

Find that Founders forsaken stone and get the hell out of Praeteriti.

Learn to use her Gift and save her sisters from whatever evils Renevelda had planned.

Locate her father.

The thought of using magic made her stomach turn. But whatever she needed to do to save them, she'd do.

If she succeeded, her family would be whole again. That was all the motivation she needed.

Chapter 15

Though she knew she lay fully awake in her bed at Hazel's, Talullah couldn't stop trying to wake herself up. This had to be a nightmare.

How could she of all people be a Sezna Seer?

Sure, she obsessed over this kind of magic as a small child. People who delivered messages through tarot or communicated with the dead. Who could change their physical form into something other than what they were. Conjure and manipulate objects—or people. Hours spent in the library ignited her imagination.

To travel to Viltresor before the war, when the gifted ones were free to practice in the open without fear, would have been a dream come true. But King William outlawed magic in Viltresor when he took the throne, threatening death for any caught practicing. Many people had fled to the outskirts, setting up small tribes and living in the shadows. Some had come to River Hill. But to see the city in its prime, with healers on every corner next to trinket shops and fortune tellers? She'd wished for it on every passing star.

As a child, she believed anything was possible, and the fact that she'd seen evidence of magic in her own mother only confirmed her beliefs. Her mother had come from Viltresor, after all, the originator of the craft. Each Viltresse grew up learning a specific style of magic. Talullah's mother had specialized in potion making.

Often, Talullah had watched her mother work, perched on a chair near the kitchen counter. She always hurried through weaving practice so she could help stir and mix. Most of all she loved her mother's recipe book. It was the largest book Talullah had ever seen, even bigger than *Ancient Languages*, which topped three thousand pages.

She frowned now, remembering the last time she opened that book. Hell, the last time she'd even looked at it. It was two weeks after her mother left and Talullah lay awake in the middle of the night. An idea came to her. She flung off her blanket and, careful not to wake Margot or Penny, crept into the kitchen. The lantern they kept lit at night cast a soft glow over the room. She smiled. Just enough light to read by.

Her palm glided over the smooth, worn leather cover of the recipe book and her body buzzed with excitement. She flipped past potions for forgetting and for healing, past Third's Revenge and El-lo's Triumph and countless other recipes, until she found the page she sought—The Locator Potion.

Brows furrowed, she mixed the ingredients with precision. She even counted the exact number of dried Lavandula buds, though she'd seen her mother estimate those kinds of things. If her plan was going to work, she couldn't leave room for error. The potion had to be precise, perfect. The floral scent worked its way into her nose, familiar and comforting. The potion would work. It had to.

When the solution shimmered silver, halfway between translucent and opaque, Talullah clapped silently to herself. It looked exactly like the picture in the book. Her heart swelled. She'd done it. She was going to find her mother and bring her home. With a steady, assured hand, young Talullah squeezed two drops of the Locator Potion onto her mother's hunting knife. The book said to use an object important to the person because the potion would trace memories. It needed a strong starting point—an object full of memories. Her mother went almost nowhere without that knife. That's why Talullah knew—or thought at the time—that she couldn't have gone for good.

Talullah held her breath until she thought her lungs would burst. She watched, unblinking, as the lavender smoke danced like a charmed snake around the knife's blade. Her hand gripped the hilt tighter.

Ten seconds later the smoked disappeared, leaving no path for her to follow.

Her stomach dropped. She must not have made the potion properly.

She reread the directions five times. Her measurements had been exact.

A silent sob escaped her mouth and hot tears raced down her cheeks. Maybe her mother didn't want to be found.

After that night, she chose to ignore magic's existence altogether, instead thinking of it as the kind of story she could fall into when she was especially tired of her real life. It was disconnected from her. Apart. She bought healing tonics from the apothecary in town instead of making them herself, though she easily could have done so. Her mother's recipe book gathered inches of dust. Disbelief had blanketed her heart like snowfall covering footprints, burying all hope of finding her way back.

Talullah blinked the memory into the back of her mind. After that night she'd sworn to never again deal with magic in any form. She massaged her clenched jaw. It seemed now she had no choice.

The only way to save the people she loved most was to trust in forces that had already betrayed her twice. Salty tears carved warm streams in the chill of her cheekbones. Despite doing everything right with the Locator Potion, she had still failed to find her mother. And the protection spell over River Hill had been broken. How could she believe this time would be different?

No matter how hard she tried, she couldn't push away the question that haunted her most: had her mother known any of this?

What were the chances her mother had known what the necklace truly was when she'd given it to Talullah on her birthday eight years prior? Had her mother simply found it at the Hidden Market, its seller unaware of the power it held and the impact it would have on its owner? Surely anyone who knew what it was wouldn't have let it go so easily. And if her mother had known, why would she have given such a dangerous and powerful object to her young child?

The longer she thought about everything, the tighter her muscles clenched. Hopelessness numbed her so she no longer felt the warmth of the blankets cocooning her body. If she'd thought rescuing her family from Terrapese would be dangerous and possibly deadly, her new task was even worse.

And near impossible.

TALULLAH BROUGHT THE flowered teacup to her lips. Before she could take a sip, a smell like charred wood and onions filled her nostrils. Saliva pooled beneath her tongue and her stomach lurched. She pulled the cup away from her face, gagging. "I thought you said this was tea."

Mirella shrugged. "It's much more pleasant to think of it as tea. It's an herbal solution, and while it smells to the high heavens, it will help with the pain. So, bottoms up."

Pinching her nose between her thumb and forefinger, Talullah raised the cup to her mouth again.

"Don't think, just do," Mirella said.

Talullah tipped the offensive liquid into the back of her throat and swallowed. She gagged once more, coughed, and wrinkled her nose.

"Please tell me I don't have to drink this every day."

"Only for a little while. I have capsules as well. Don't worry, they're odorless and taste like cherries." Something in the sparkle of Mirella's eyes told Talullah that had to be an exaggeration.

"Then why do I have to drink this stuff now? Can't I just take the pills?"

"The tea will help your body get used to the herbs. The capsules are more concentrated and will shock your system without proper preparation. Now, ready to proceed?"

Talullah swished and swallowed three mouthfuls of water before the taste of the tea had faded enough for her to pretend she didn't taste it anymore.

An owl hooted from its perch outside Mirella's library window. The sun still slumbered beneath the horizon, but Mirella had insisted they start Talullah's Sight lessons as early as possible. Talullah had stolen a glance at Dhalian's sleeping frame as she left Hazel's house but immediately dismissed her jealousy. If sacrificing sleep would get them out of Praeteriti faster, she'd wake before dawn every day.

"Concentrate. Relax your shoulders. Take a deep breath. Focus on what you want to See."

For two hours she reached out with her mind, willing the vision to come. She was supposed to be Seeing herself entering Mirella's garden, from Mirella's point of view. Vivid, recent memories would be easiest to recall on command, since they were at the forefront of her Sight. Or so she'd been told.

"It's bound to be difficult at the beginning. Your mind isn't used to bearing this kind of strain. Time and practice are all you need."

"I don't have time, Mirella." Talullah buried her face in her hands. "Can I see my sisters? Please?"

"You must focus, Talullah. Watching will not help you save them. Trust me. I've had plenty of practice." Mirella cleared her throat. "We must move toward a solution."

"I just want to know they're okay."

"It's unlikely much has changed in the ten minutes since I last checked on them. Now, focus please. I will give you regular updates if you promise to practice."

Mirella was right, of course. Watching her sisters huddle together in a prison would not free them. Her heart ached all the same. When she could see them, she knew they were safe. Her mind couldn't conjure horrific images of what the soldiers—or Renevelda—could be doing to them. But spying on them was selfish. It only appeased her own guilt and anxiety.

She tried again to call forth the memory that was not her own.

The day faded into a blur of failed attempts to command her Sight with short meal breaks sprinkled in.

"The visions have always come so easily before, but they seem to be actively fighting to stay out of my mind." Talullah swigged from a glass of cold water. "Why is that? Why do they come when I don't expect them?"

"Could be your mind trying to tell you something. Or it could be triggered by external forces. Tell me about a vision you had without trying." Mirella gestured for Talullah to sit in an armchair.

"It was the morning of the raid in River Hill." Talullah sank into the chair, her muscles finally relaxing. She closed her eyes, remembering. "I was about to leave for the library when Father asked me to bring him his cane. When I touched its handle, the vision filtered into my mind. Everything was red. The forest trees sparkled like rubies. A girl—I couldn't see her face—walked into a wall of fire. And then it was over." Talullah shivered and opened her eyes. "What could it mean?"

"Red is the color of the inevitable. What you saw has not yet happened, but it will." Behind her magnified eyes, Mirella's wheels turned. "As for who and when, I can't say. If you had the red stone, the vision would be clearer, more detailed. That cane is intriguing, though. Is there anything distinguishing about it?"

Talullah's mouth wound into a slight smile as she remembered her father's fondness for the object. "It has a carved fish on top."

Mirella cocked her head in consideration. "Well, that was an ordinary morning for you. Perhaps the visions come when your mind is most at ease. But we must do the best we can with what we've got." She gestured for Talullah to stand. "Just once more and we will be done for the day."

Mirella's consistent encouragement grated on Talullah's nerves, but she obliged. She closed her eyes and rolled her shoulders a few times. She let go of her thoughts, not trying to make them do anything. Thin fog settled over the folds in her consciousness. It was like the moment right before waking up.

Color flickered in the corners of her eyes. A shape began to form. She furrowed her brows, willing it to manifest into something recognizable. Shards of other figures rotated into the scene. They positioned themselves, though she couldn't discern what they were supposed to be.

Hope trickled into her doubt-stained veins. She had called forth something. Whether or not it was what she meant to conjure didn't matter. Every second she held on, the picture grew clearer. A moment more and she would be able to identify the scene and its characters.

"Hi." Dhalian's voice broke her concentration and the vision dissolved.

She opened her eyes and pierced his gaze with hers. "Thank you, Dhal, for interrupting the best chance I've had all day. I was so close."

He stopped, his face falling. "Oh. Sorry. I didn't realize..."

Immediate regret bubbled in her stomach. "No, I'm sorry. I'm just tired. I've been at this for hours." Black spots filled her vision and she swayed on her feet. Her stomach churned. "Mirella, can you make the room stop spinning?" She pressed her palms over her eyes.

Mirella guided her to a chair. Talullah sat, fighting the urge to vomit.

"The dizziness will subside. Just give it a minute. It will get easier as you improve your control."

Two blurry Mirellas swayed in front of her. "Can we afford to wait that long? What if I can't find the stone before Renevelda? What if it's already too late?"

"You will find it. You've already made good progress. And you're one step ahead of Renevelda—you're already in Praeteriti. We have some allies outside here that can buy us time. A few weeks, probably. That should be enough."

"Weeks?" Talullah stood, swayed, then sat back down, her face in her hands. "My sisters cannot stay in that castle for weeks. I need to get out of here now."

"They are fine for the time being, Talullah. Trust me. Get some rest and we will resume lessons tomorrow morning." Mirella squeezed Talullah on the shoulder as she exited the library, leaving Talullah and Dhalian alone.

"Don't rest too long, Tules." A Cheshire grin spread across his face, mischief illuminating the golden flecks in his eyes. "The Mazuchawi just appeared. And Hazel got there first."

Chapter 16

The Mazuchawi. The game that appeared from nowhere.

It had manifested in a field near Fisher's Diner. But Talullah couldn't focus on the game. She barely registered her own feet, heavy with fatigue, carrying her toward it. Instead, her mind repeated the memory of her sisters in their cell.

"I'm going back," Talullah said to Dhalian. "I can't spend precious time playing a game when I should be finding the way out of here."

"A little bit of fun might actually help your Sight skills. You've got to reset every once and a while. Even Mirella said so."

Though Talullah had tried to nap in Mirella's sunroom after her lesson, her mind hadn't quieted enough for sleep. She'd lain awake, blinking at the ceiling. Her limbs had twitched with anticipation. Twice, her aunt caught her trying to sneak out to check the portals, just in case, and sent her back to bed.

Now, tired as it was, her body drew toward the maze like a mosquito to light, even as her mind wandered. She'd made Dhalian and Hazel check the portals on their way to the maze, her one condition for agreeing to play. Locked, every one of them. She sighed. Maybe Dhalian was right. Thinking about something else for a short time might inspire new ideas.

They stopped on a braided rug directly in front of an archway made of twisted tree trunks.

"Isn't it magnificent?" Hazel's voice took on a dreamy quality. "It's been months since it appeared last. I saw the lightning strike and I dropped everything and ran as fast as I could." She rested her hand on the brick wall that ran along the game's perimeter.

A bronze plaque hung to the right of the archway, and when Hazel touched it, purple sparks darted across its face. In flourishing script, the light engraved Dhalian and Talullah's names into the plaque alongside Hazel's.

"There. Now only we can play." Hazel gestured through the archway. "Shall we?"

"Tules? You in?"

Uneasiness settled in her chest. She could only see the outer wall, but the maze's magic was palpable, almost magnetic. It tugged at the hairs on her arms and made them stand on end. A sudden urge to turn and run washed over her.

She forced her feet to stay planted while she searched for a logical explanation.

Maybe spending so long with magic that day made her more sensitive to its power. Neither Dhalian nor Hazel seemed to feel anything other than excitement and awe. Hazel had played the game before and was fine. There was nothing to be afraid of. Surely Talullah's tired mind was overreacting.

A bolt of lightning drew her attention to the sky. Next to her, Dhalian jumped.

"That's just the maze showing it's claimed. Nothing to worry about," Hazel said.

But Talullah's skin hummed as if the bolt had struck her. It curled in the sky, gold and bright, like hot metal manipulated by a smith. The J-shaped bolt hovered for a second. She blinked, and it was gone.

"Is that normal, too?" she asked.

Engrossed in conversation with each other, neither Hazel nor Dhalian heard her.

The symbol in the sky looked like a part of Dunamai's Eye. Had she been the only one to see it? It could have been her mind playing tricks on her, but what if it wasn't? What if it was a clue? A tingle in her bones urged her to find out one way or another.

Talullah hooked her arm through Dhalian's. "I'm in. But I'm making no promises about my ability to actually play this game." She wobbled. "Or walk without falling."

Dhalian's face brightened. "Neither of which are issues. I expect to be extremely good at it. And just hold onto me. I promise I won't let you fall."

"Ready?" Hazel asked.

Dhalian squeezed Talullah's arm. She forced a smile.

Hazel stepped through the archway, the others trailing close behind.

Talullah gasped. Candles in sconces illuminated the small room. Ten-foot tall hedges surrounded them. Tiny white lights twinkled from within the plants. A blanket of stars stretched overhead, forming the summer constellations. Jasmine vines wove in and out of the hedge walls, and its fragrance settled over them in an intoxicating, floral cloud. Talullah swayed on her feet, but Dhalian steadied her.

"Incredible, isn't it? And this is only the beginning of the maze. Just wait until we get to the middle." Hazel's face lit up, full of wonder.

"What's in the middle?" Dhalian asked.

"I don't know. But if this is the beginning, can you imagine what the rest is like? It's a different game every time. I can't wait to see the first section."

Vines slithered down from the tree trunks, closing them inside the Mazuchawi. Talullah's heart pumped harder.

"Don't worry. That's so no one else can sneak in while we're playing. It will recede when we're ready to leave." Hazel's voice buzzed with excitement.

"What does the winner get?" Talullah asked, her senses on high alert for anything related to Dunamai's Eye or the lightning bolt.

"Bragging rights, first of all. Other than that, I'm not sure." Hazel shrugged. "This is one puzzle that's never been solved."

"Then why play?" Talullah moved closer to the dozens of stone pedestals, each topped with a colored glass orb the size of a pomegranate.

"For a while we thought the Mazuchawi might be a new passage out of Praeteriti. It appeared for the first time after all the others sealed. Most of us have given up that theory. Now it's something to pass the time. Being stuck in a place for too long can do crazy things to a person's mind. Even if they're already dead. And this is a fun challenge."

This gave Talullah pause. It still *could* be a way out. Just because no one had found their way through didn't mean it wasn't a passage into the world. If the stone from Dunamai's Eye was hidden in the maze, it would be the opportunity she'd been looking for. A way back to her family.

But it could also be a sinister trick. Renevelda—or any number of other dark magicians—could have sent the Mazuchawi. Talullah dialed up her awareness and adjusted her knife in her boot holster. Maybe it was just a game, but she would be prepared just in case.

Hazel gestured to the orbs. "First, select a token. Each has the power to remove one obstacle from the game."

Dhalian bent down so the orbs were at eye-level. "How do we know what they do?"

"Touch it and you'll get a glimpse of its power. Be careful, though. If you smash it, you lose it. We break the token inside the game to spend it."

They scattered throughout the rows of pedestals to choose their tokens.

Hazel found hers first, an emerald one she thought could cloak them from enemies. Dhalian chose his quickly after. Out of the corner of her eye, Talullah saw him stop in front of a midnight blue orb with white streaks like lightning.

"I think this one conjures water, or something. So cool." He picked it up, fumbled, and almost dropped it. "Whoa, everything's fine. Nobody panic." Flashing a sheepish grin, he added, "It's a lot heavier than I expected."

Talullah wandered, stopping occasionally to observe the orbs. She reached a hand out to a few of them to see if she'd feel an energy shift or something, but nothing happened. To be honest she had no idea what she was looking for.

And then she noticed a token much different than all the rest. Where they were dark, this one was light. Its surface shifted like fluffy white clouds passing through a metallic gold sky. She removed it from its pedestal and assessed it. The smooth glass chilled her palm.

A sudden jolt of energy sparked in her brain. The fog of fatigue receded, and she could think clearly for the first time since she'd begun practicing her Sight with Mirella that morning. "I think I found mine."

"What's it do?" Dhalian asked, joining her.

"Not completely sure, but I feel better than I have in days. Maybe it heals." Healing magic Talullah could deal with. She could just pretend it was salve or tonic, something ordinary. If the maze did run on darkness, it might come in handy.

"Let's get started," said Hazel.

The rules of the game were simple enough. Each section of the maze had a specific goal they had to achieve before they could move on. Obstacles of varying kinds would try to hinder their progress.

Hazel placed her palm on the weathered door opposite the entrance gate. It split down the middle and the two halves pulled apart. They stepped into the first section.

Doors of all shapes and sizes lined the outer walls. Talullah spun in a circle, considering each of them. Metal, wood, stained glass. Some with knobs, others with handles. Others' surfaces smooth and undisturbed.

Large stacks of boxes and furniture occupied most of the floor space.

With the toe of his boot, Dhalian lifted the edge of a tartan blanket. A small creature darted from under it and disappeared somewhere in the mess, leaving a puff of smoke in its wake.

Even in its extreme chaos, the room reminded Talullah of the antique shop. Musty, yet comforting. A pang of missing pulsed in her heart.

"Remember, we only have one hour at a time in the maze," said Hazel.

"How do we know how long we've been in here?" asked Dhalian, scanning the area as if expecting to find a clock.

Hazel gestured to a vine snaking across the top of the brick wall. "Our timekeeper. When the first thorn is fully formed, our time is up. The maze will give us warning, and we'll meet at the entrance. Unless we solve this room before then."

"So, we just have to pick a door?" Talullah asked. She squeezed past a writing desk and approached the cornflower blue door nearest her. "What's all this stuff for then?"

"Bet they're locked," Dhalian said, tugging the brass handle on a walnut door. "Yep."

"Be careful," Hazel said. "We don't know what's behind these doors. Could be anything."

"Can't be too dangerous though. I mean, no one's ever *died* playing Mazuchawi." Dhalian chuckled. "Right?"

Hazel furrowed her brows, and when she spoke her voice rose to barely a whisper. "Well, most of the people who play are already dead, you see. But someone almost died last time living people played…"

Talullah almost dropped her token but recovered. "What do you mean the last time living people played?"

At the same time Dhalian asked, "Who almost died? And how?"

They looked at each other, then both snapped their attention back to Hazel.

"Didn't you say you've played before?" The cogs in Talullah's brain creaked as if they'd been turned on for the first time in months.

Hazel shook her head. "I wasn't there. I heard about it from one of the ghosts."

"Who was it, then? There aren't that many living people here," Talullah said.

"The ghosts wouldn't say."

Talullah gave her a skeptical look.

"I couldn't have been there, because, well, this is the first time I've actually played." She fidgeted with her sleeve, and Talullah caught a glimpse of her arrow tattoo.

Dhalian folded his arms. "I thought you said you had multiple games going at once."

"Not actual games," she said, not meeting either of their gazes. "Ones in my mind. I dream about the Mazuchawi. There, I've played almost every night since I got here." Her hair fell into her face making her look like a small child. Even her lip quivered. "I'm sorry. I didn't mean to lie. I just thought if you thought I'd done it already it would be easier to convince you to play with me. Mirella refuses, and I don't really have anyone else…"

Talullah shook her head. "But if someone almost died, why do you still want to play so badly?"

"I thought maybe if I played and won the dreams would stop." Hazel's voice cracked. Tears glistened in her eyes. They were the clearest Talullah had seen them. "I feel like I'm going crazy. This place is making me crazy. And every night when I go to bed I dream of this maze. It has to mean something, doesn't it?"

Hazel's words resonated deep within Talullah's bones. She knew what it was like to have dreams that didn't make sense, that had to be more than they seemed. The last few days had proven her right. Maybe Hazel was right, too.

Placing a hand on Hazel's shoulder, Talullah said, "It's okay. We'll be careful."

Hazel nodded and wiped her eyes.

Time passed as they rifled through drawers and cupboards, carefully opening boxes. The maze's magic throbbed in Talullah's blood. *Se-crets. Se-crets,* it chanted, daring her to discover its purpose. She couldn't ignore it. Especially not if it could lead her out of Praeteriti.

Dhalian slammed a drawer shut. "Nothing in there. Except half a dozen rats." He gagged and moved on.

Knife raised, Talullah eased open a drawer in an ornate bureau. At first glance it looked empty. But as she made to shut it, a colored thread near the back caught her eye. With care she pinched it between her thumb and forefinger and tugged. The false bottom lifted with it, revealing a dusty tin.

"I think I found something." A handful of palm-sized flying creatures rose from the drawer, their wings beating so fast smoke curled off them.

Hazel pulled Talullah back.

Dhalian appeared to Talullah's left. "What are those things?"

"*Kleindraaks,*" Hazel said. "The dragons that devour the sins of new ghosts so they can be at peace."

"What are they doing here?" Dhalian asked.

"Guarding something," Talullah said. "What happens if they don't do their job?"

"The new spirits remain Unforgiven. And the dragons get restless."

Twenty Kleindraaks brandished flaming forked tails, hovering in midair around the bureau. Dense smoke descended in a suffocating cloud as they beat their wings in tandem.

"Dragons?" asked Dhalian. He looked like a six-year-old on Christmas morning. "Are you serious? This might be the best day of my life."

"How do we get rid of them? That box must be important." Talullah gestured with her knife.

"Get rid of them? Tules. *Dragons*. I don't think you're appreciating this childhood moment come true."

She ignored him. Supposedly-mythical beasts or not, if the Kleindraaks had something she needed, she wouldn't dwell on their majesty.

"We can't kill them. Without them, all souls remain Unforgiven. If we can find some water, we can just scare them off. They don't usually attack the living, but they are protective by nature. Avoid their fire. It's poisonous."

"Perfect," said Talullah.

Slowly, they backed away from the swarm of dragons. The creatures fanned out into a semi-circle.

"There are some bottles in those boxes." Dhalian gestured behind him.

The Kleindraaks moved toward them as one, screeching. Talullah pressed her hands over her ears to dampen the piercing sound. She knelt beside one of the boxes and set her token on the ground. Dhalian and Hazel each dug through their respective boxes.

Almond extract. Lavandula solution. Lemon juice. At least fifty bottles of half-used potion ingredients. But no water.

Two Kleindraaks spat flames at her box. It instantly caught fire. Talullah rolled behind a chest of drawers, barely avoiding their next assault. "No luck here. Hazel?"

"Nothing," Hazel called from her left.

"All empty here," said Dhalian.

Sweat beaded on the back of Talullah's neck. Another spray of fire ignited the chest she hid behind. Frantic, she crawled to another box. "There's nothing here."

Dhalian ducked behind a large painting. "Where are they all coming from?"

At least fifty Kleindraaks circled them. Flames consumed half the room, the crackle of burning wood almost deafening. Smoke suffocated them. Talullah coughed.

"Hazel? Dhal?"

"I'm okay," they called in unison.

Talullah followed their voices, dodging screeching dragons and falling embers. "What happens if we leave without finding the key?"

"Maybe that's why I've never seen the same room twice in my dreams," Hazel rasped. "I think if we don't reach a milestone before we leave, we start a new room the next time."

But they'd figured it out. A vibration in Talullah's soul told her the key was in that drawer. They just hadn't managed to grab it. Starting over would waste too much time. Precious time her sisters didn't have. If this was the first step to getting out of Praeteriti, she had to take it now.

Lightning struck overhead.

"That's the warning," said Hazel. "We have to get back to the entrance before the third strike."

"What if we don't get out before it disappears?" Dhalian asked.

"I don't know. But I don't want to be the first to find out." Hazel tugged Talullah's tunic sleeve. "Come on."

A drop of rain plopped on Talullah's cheek. The Kleindraaks ceased their attack and took cover beneath a writing desk at the edge of the room.

Now's your chance, said a familiar voice in Talullah's mind. The same voice that told her to touch the tree when she and Dhal needed to lose the soldiers in Nainehta Forest. It was right once before.

She broke free of Hazel's grasp and sprinted to the open drawer.

"Tules, come back!"

Smoke curled off the Kleindraaks' wings as they watched her. She leapt between two piles of burning boxes, gagging on the thick air.

Another bolt struck across the sky. *Two.*

Quick as a cobra, she pulled the tin from the drawer, ignoring the searing sensation in her hands. Movement in the corner of her eye caught her attention.

"Let's go!" yelled Dhal. He pushed her toward the entrance, hacking.

She stumbled but kept her balance.

Next to her, Dhalian yelled out in pain. "My shoulder. It's like fire in my veins." His breathing grew shallow, his voice softer. "Not again. I can't handle this again."

Hoping Dhalian's instincts were right, Talullah grabbed his token and smashed it on the ground. Water fell from above in cold sheets, drenching them and scattering the dragons. She snatched a fistful of his tunic and shoved him toward Hazel and the entrance just in time.

The third bolt. A shape this time.

A jolt of realization shot from her heart to her head.

White light washed over the maze. Though she squeezed her own shut, the image of Dunamai's Eye blazed on the inside of her lids. Its metallic twin numbed her collarbone with a wintry chill.

When she pried her eyes open again, the Mazuchawi was gone.

Chapter 17

"Dhal!" Talullah crawled to her friend's splayed body. Scorch marks blackened the shoulder of his tunic.

"I got…" he whispered.

"Burned? I know. But you're going to be fine." She placed her hands gingerly on his arm.

A smirk brightened his face. "By a *dragon*. How cool am I?" He laughed, which dissolved into a cough.

Hazel tore Dhalian's shirt and inspected his wound. "It's not too deep," she said. "I can heal him, if we act quickly. We've got about thirty minutes before the poison gets to his heart."

"What happens then?" Talullah held her breath.

"It's not going to. Let's get him to my house."

They scooped him up and raced down the street, ignoring the staring ghosts as they passed. Bursting through Hazel's front door, they lay Dhalian, shivering, on the sofa. Hazel disappeared into the kitchen. A layer of ash and sweat dulled Dhalian's normally warm amber skin. Tears pricked Talullah's eyes. She stroked his dark, curly hair. If anything happened to him…

"I found the antidote recipe and I have almost everything to make it," Hazel said, returning. "I can start, but I need you to go to the apothecary and get three aloe leaves. The ghost who runs it lives above the shop. Go now." Hazel's calm control snapped Talullah into action.

She dashed out the door and made a right, sprinting three blocks before realizing she'd gone the wrong way. Damnit, where was it? Near the grocer. She reversed her route and pushed her legs as fast as they'd go. *Hang on, Dhal. I'm coming.*

As she rounded the corner, a streetlamp illuminated the apothecary storefront. Breathless, she flew onto the stoop and threw her fist against the door. With one hand she pounded while the other jiggled the door knob. "Hello! Please, I need aloe leaves! My friend—"

The pink paisley door opened, and she stumbled inside.

"Aloe leaves, please, it's an emergency," she said. No response. A small lantern in the window cast enough light for her to see, with a quick glance, she was alone. "Hello?" she called, louder. "Mr. Apothecary ghost?" Nothing.

That settled it. Dhal couldn't wait for her to find the proprietor. She'd have to help herself.

Ingredient jars sat in alphabetized rows on shelves throughout the small shop. She located the A's to her left. Her eyes tripped on the space between allspice and Amalaki berry powder.

The aloe should be there.

Each jar she knocked over with clumsy hands ticked another second off the clock. Off Dhal's life.

Alfalfa root. Anise seed.

Where was the damn aloe?

What if she couldn't find it? What if the apothecary had run out?

And then she spotted it. Tipped on its side behind the bilberry fruit.

Thank the Founders.

She pocketed the full jar. No time to count.

Ignoring her guilt, she shut the door behind her and darted back to Hazel's. She'd come back and pay tomorrow.

"HURRY, HURRY," HAZEL urged.

Talullah thrust the jar at her, wheezing. "Save. Him." She checked the cuckoo clock on the wall. Three minutes left.

Hazel pulled three leaves from the jar, dropping the lid on the ground. "Give me your knife."

Dizzy from lack of air, Talullah blinked at her.

"You knife!" Hazel repeated, reaching out for it, her face tense.

Dhalian drew a shallow breath. His hands trembled atop his chest.

Talullah scrambled to free her knife from its holster. Hazel took it and sliced the leaves open. Green gel oozed from their flesh. Hazel squeezed it into the goblet on the coffee table and stirred the solution with her fingers.

Talullah guided the goblet to Dhalian's mouth. "Come on, Dhal. You can't leave me now. Not after everything."

"Tules?" he said in a weak voice. His lids flicked opened and she glimpsed the golden flecks in his irises.

She squeezed his left hand. "I'm here, Dhal. Drink this."

She nodded as she tipped it toward him.

His body seized before the cup touched his lips, his eyes rolling back in his head.

"Hazel!" Talullah yelled.

Hazel held Dhalian's shaking head in place. "Just get a few drops on his tongue."

Talullah plunged her fingers in the cup and moved them toward his face. Solution splashed onto his chest, pooling over his heart, as her hands shook. Two shiny droplets fell into Dhalian's open mouth. *Founders, please let this work. Please. I can't lose him, too.*

Time stopped as she watched his movements slow, then still.

"It's okay," Hazel said, panting. "He's going to be okay."

Only when Dhalian's chest had risen and fallen five times and color returned to his cheeks did Talullah dare to believe her.

"WHAT'S IN IT?" DHAL asked, his voice filling the bedroom. Once the potion had begun to work, Talullah and Hazel carried him to the guest room so he could sleep.

"Hmm?" Talullah leaned toward him in her chair.

"The tin. What's in it?" he rasped. His voice hadn't yet returned to its usual baritone.

"I don't know. I didn't open it."

Dhalian eased himself upright on the bed and clicked on the bedside lamp. "Are you kidding me? I got burned saving you, and you didn't even look inside?" He smiled. "Inconsiderate."

He joked, but even two hours after she and Hazel had managed to force-feed him the potion, the guilt still pierced her insides. Dhal's injury had been *her* fault. Had she not been reckless, he never would have been burned.

He wouldn't have almost died.

But she didn't want him to see her worry. He'd just spin it to absolve her, and she didn't deserve that. "You're unbelievable, you know that?" She gave his good arm a playful shove. "I'll get it."

"How is he?" Hazel asked, when Talullah returned to the kitchen and grabbed the tin.

"He's more concerned about the contents of this than his own health. So, I'd say he's on his way back to normal."

Hazel followed Talullah and they both sat on the edge of Dhalian's bed. Its wooden frame creaked beneath their weight. Outside, crickets chirped in the early morning darkness. With her tunic sleeve, Talullah wiped the dust from the lid, revealing faded words in the middle and a small arrow in the corner.

"Let's see what's inside tin number one," said Dhal. He removed the top.

Keys. Dozens of iron keys.

Find the keys. Dunamai will reward the Keeper of the Keys. The ghost's words returned to Talullah, the ominous tone ringing in her ears. Could he have meant these keys? If so, she was right. The maze did connect to Dunamai's Eye.

"There's something else." She dumped the contents onto the bed. The keys clanged into a pile, and a scrap of parchment fell on top. "It says, 'A star bow takes you backward; What's revealed will lead you forward.'"

"Well, that's cryptic," said Hazel.

"A bow is part of a boat. Maybe there's a ship or something?" Talullah mused.

"There's a drawing on the back." Dhal took the parchment and studied it. Brows furrowed, he ran a hand through his hair. A nervous habit Talullah recognized from ten years of friendship.

"What's wrong?" she asked.

He blinked and looked up at her. "Hmm? Nothing." He handed it back to her.

"Doesn't mean anything to me either. But we did it. We made it to the first milestone. I've never done that alone. Not even in my dreams. Thank you." Hazel stood. "I know it could have been smoother..."

"It turned out okay. Dhal's going to be fine," Talullah jumped in.

"Never better," said Dhalian.

Hazel nodded. "Rest will help your shoulder heal. Actually, we should all get some sleep." She directed this at Talullah as she stood.

"But what about the keys?" Talullah asked. "And the note and the drawing?"

"We'll think clearer with rested minds and bodies." The door clicked softly as she shut it behind her.

Talullah moved to her own bed, her mind still churning.

"Goodnight, Tules." Dhalian turned off his light.

"Hey, Dhal?"

"Yeah?"

"The last lightning bolt. Did it look like Dunamai's Eye to you?" He sighed, and his bed creaked as he shifted positions.

"Tules, you practiced your Sight all day and didn't really rest before jumping headfirst into a magical game. You could barely even stand up straight, for the Founders' sake."

She bit back a retort about him practically dragging her into the maze and pulled the fleece blanket to her chin.

"I know it's my fault you went at all. I know you didn't even want to go—"

"I wanted to go..." she whispered.

"—but I made you, and I appreciate you doing that for me. All I'm saying is you were exhausted. Your mind, especially so. Maybe you saw Dunamai's Eye, maybe your mind played a trick on you. Hell, maybe it was the game itself that made you see it."

"I didn't think about it being a mirage..." But she should have. Hadn't Nainehta Forest taught her to be cautious with magic? She toyed with the necklace, chewing the inside of her cheek.

"We won't know whether or not it was really there until we go back." He paused for a moment and then continued, unsure. "You do want to go back, don't you?"

Now that she'd seen the symbol, she couldn't stop thinking about it. But Dhal could have died during their first round. Could the rest of the maze be just as dangerous? "Considering what happened tonight—"

"Because I do. The Mazuchawi could still be a way out of this place. And I for one think it's worth the risk."

"MIRELLA, I KNOW WHAT I saw."

"You shouldn't have been playing that game in the first place. It's dangerous." Mirella bustled around her kitchen without looking at

Talullah. Her face had been scrunched up in distaste ever since Talullah had arrived for her Sight lessons fifteen minutes prior and told her about seeing the symbol in the Mazuchawi.

"Dhal is fine." Talullah tried to inject confidence into her tone, but the thought of his singed flesh still rattled her.

Mirella uttered a "hmpf" and narrowed her eyes at Talullah.

Talullah flinched at the danger in her aunt's expression, then steeled herself. "I'm not asking how dangerous it is. I want to know why the symbol of Dunamai's Eye was inside the maze. If it has something to do with finding the stones I need to know. It could be the key to getting out of here."

Mirella stared through her pink cat-eye frames, unblinking, and Talullah could tell an internal battle waged in her head. A full minute passed in silence. Talullah held her breath, hoping if she waited long enough, she'd get some answers.

"No," she said finally, scooping up the pot of tea and a patterned mug. "The key is learning to control your Sight. Not roaming around the Mazuchawi. I ask you, Talullah, to please stay out of there." She swept from the kitchen and down the hall without waiting for a response.

"I can't promise that." If her aunt wouldn't tell her about the connection between Dunamai's Eye and the Mazuchawi, she would figure it out for herself.

Mirella kept her practicing all day. Talullah had a sneaking suspicion her aunt thought if she kept Talullah busy and tired her out, she wouldn't have the energy or the desire to go back inside the Mazuchawi that night.

Whether to spite Mirella or to learn her skills, Talullah focused as hard as she could on her Sight lesson. She managed to swallow the tea without gagging, an improvement over her first attempt. It took less time for her to block out the outside world and focus her energy inward. Within ten minutes she had conjured the image of herself walking up to Mirella's front door.

Lines wavered in her peripheral vision, but the scene was mostly formed. Instead of colored blobs she recognized specific shapes. Shrubs, flowers, people. An ember of pride glowed in her chest as she dropped focus and let the image slip away.

"I did it," she said, almost in disbelief. The ember caught fire as realization set in. A genuine smile stretched the width of her face until her cheeks hurt. "By the Founders, I actually did it!"

"How did it look?" Mirella handed her a cool, damp cloth to place on the back of her neck.

"Fairly clear. I could tell who everyone was and where we were." The bookshelves behind Mirella swayed, Talullah's dizziness not severe but still present. "How long did you say before I stop feeling the side-effects?"

"Depends. Your body has to get used to the sensation. The more you practice, the less intense they'll be." Mirella removed the cloth and placed it in a bucket of water. "Are you ready to try again?"

Talullah sighed. "I've practiced this one for the past two hours. Is there something else we can try?" She shifted in her chair.

"Getting confident, are we? Okay. Close your eyes. I'm going to describe a setting. I want you to See the event that took place there."

Talullah did as she was told, a spark of excitement blossoming in her stomach. She blocked out everything except the sound of Mirella's low, smooth voice.

"You're in Nainehta Forest. It's getting dark. You look up at the trees. The gold and silver leaves tarnish to black."

She pictured the image as clearly as she could, placing herself in the memory, despite not knowing whose it was. Mirella's voice had faded away, though it was possible she still spoke details into Talullah's subconscious, building the world around her. An owl hooted nearby. Judging by the warm breeze, it had to be late summer. Her insides hummed with inexplicable nervous energy. She was alone. There was nothing to fear, yet her chest tightened as if her body sensed something her mind hadn't yet noticed.

A hawk screeched overhead. She whipped her head around to locate it. Her heart-rate skyrocketed. She couldn't let the animal find her, though she didn't know why. She tried to run, but her feet rebelled, staying planted to the ground.

Spots flashed in her vision. She blinked to try to refocus, to push herself back into the event Mirella wanted her to See. But color bled across the scene like ink spilled on parchment. Its purple hue changed to blue. She rubbed her eyes with her palms.

Then she noticed the small girl standing a few feet to her right. Where had she come from?

Talullah tried to call to her but nothing came out.

The girl raised a finger in front of her unsmiling lips. "It's almost time. Don't forget what you've learned." The vision wavered, and the blue veil melted away, revealing the true colors of the scene.

"What do I need to remember?"

The girl smiled at her, gap-toothed. "The song, of course." And then she sang. "Through the fire blazing bright, trust yourself, harness your might. Inner struggle blinds your eyes, let it go and win the prize." She turned and skipped away, still humming, her bright red ponytail swishing behind her.

Talullah didn't need to hear the rest of the words. Her own memory finished it for her as she watched the girl disappear into the distance.

Use your heart, keep your mind, and what you seek, you shall find.

Chapter 18

Talullah remained in the vision, alone once more.

Who was the girl? And how did she, who couldn't have been older than Penny, know that song? Talullah had only ever heard her mother sing it. She'd said it was a special rhyme just for Talullah, her bookworm with a love of words.

Sweat slid down her nose like raindrops on a window pane. Her skin burned, though absent flame.

The scene dissolved in front of her, each tree melting like wax on a lit candle. Pain pounded behind her eyes and at the base of her skull. Saliva pooled beneath her tongue a second before her stomach heaved. It was an inadequate warning. She closed her eyes and let her stomach convulse, though nothing came out.

Her head spun. It had all been a vision. But had it been what Mirella wanted her to See?

She waited for the knot in her stomach to unravel before daring to let her watering eyes flicker open. Two blurry forms hovered in front of her. Their muted voices sounded as if she listened from underwater. She pushed on her ears. "Sorry for this," the male voice said.

A wave of cold water smacked her in the face. The contrast of its coolness on her hot skin sent a shiver up her spine.

"Talullah, can you hear me?" Mirella asked.

She sputtered. "Loud and clear."

"Oh, thank the Founders!"

Mirella's library came into focus one piece at a time, the bookshelves first, then the mirror to her left. A twinge worked its way up her hip. How long had she sat in that wooden chair?

Dhalian offered her a fluffy towel. She glared at him, but took it, wiping her face and neck.

"It wasn't my idea."

"That smirk says you *definitely* tried to stop it." She scrunched her hair dry. It still surprised her how short it was.

He shrugged. "Of course not. Mirella said it was the fastest way to get you back." With his un-bandaged arm, he pulled a chair next to hers and sat down. "Plus, this was the closest I've been in months to repaying you for the time you snuck up on me and shoved me in the lake. To have squandered an opportunity like this would have been shameful." His toothy grin warmed her, counteracting the chilly water.

"Talullah, what happened?" Mirella scooted her own chair directly opposite Talullah's. The setting sun pinked her aunt's messy gray bun.

"Did you mean to change the vision in the middle? Who was that girl, and did you give her the song?" She searched Mirella's face for recognition.

"What girl? What song?" Mirella's lips pursed. "Tell me everything."

Steadying her hands, she recounted the events. Surely there was a logical explanation. One that didn't involve her mother.

Mirella focused on a spot behind Talullah. "Sometimes spiritual messengers interrupt visions. In this case, the blue indicates it's about something happening in the present."

"What did she mean, 'It's almost time'? Time for what?" Dhalian asked.

"I don't know for sure, but my hunch is that Renevelda knows you're in Praeteriti."

"The soldiers must have returned to Terrapese and told her what happened." A shadow fell over Dhalian's eyes.

"Even if they didn't, Renevelda has other ways of gathering information. That hawk of hers, for one, is a force to be reckoned with. The sorceress may have known even sooner, but she's chosen now to reveal it." Deep creases etched themselves between Mirella's eyebrows. "If that is the case, we must be quicker in our work. If you are going to locate the stone before Renevelda, you must master your Sight. We must double our efforts. We cannot afford distractions if we are going to succeed."

If Mirella was correct, Renevelda's threat had just grown exponentially. That she could understand. Still, she couldn't help hearing a different warning in her aunt's words. Was Mirella telling the truth, or just trying to keep Talullah out of the Mazuchawi? Maybe the messenger hadn't meant Renevelda at all.

Either way, the magic in the maze tugged at a piece of her soul. She'd practice her Sight to appease her aunt. But she, Dhal, and Hazel would also solve the Mazuchawi. She didn't care what Mirella said. The next chance they got, they'd go back in.

RELIEF WASHED OVER Talullah as soon as she crossed the threshold of the library's large oaken doors after dinner that night. The scent of parchment wrapped itself around her in a comforting cloud. The Mazuchawi had not yet appeared. It still could, but she wouldn't waste time waiting.

"Did you forget about me?" Dhalian huffed as he ran to her side.

Actually, she had. Her face flushed. "Sorry..."

"I figured it would happen. You've got that glint in your eyes."

"What glint?"

"The one that says you mean business."

"Research *is* business. I'll focus on old keys and see if there's anything here about the Mazuchawi."

"And I'll work on deciphering this riddle. See if there's anything about ancient ships with star-shaped bows." His pocket rustled as he withdrew a piece of parchment. "Oops, wrong one. I have it. Promise."

"What's on that other one?"

Dhalian ran his hand through his hair. "Oh, you know me. Always have parchment. You know, Hazel didn't answer her door, but we can fill her in on our findings tomorrow. Unless the maze appears."

"Agreed. I'll be in the history section if you need me." They parted ways.

Talullah wove through the stacks. Rows upon rows of thick volumes rested on dusty wooden shelves. The books called to her, each one begging to be read. She dragged a finger along the spines. Every few feet she stopped to read the titles more closely and add to her growing pile.

Arms laden, Talullah made her way to the violet chairs near the edge of the section. Wingbacks had always been her favorite.

She plopped the books onto a large round table and settled in. Silence blanketed the room save the soft *thwick* of pages turning. Each passing hour scored another line in Talullah's forehead. She scribbled notes about metal and keys onto parchment until sleep pulled at her eyelids.

Midnight chimed on the grandfather clock in the corner of the room. Still, Dhalian hadn't found her. Where was he?

Passing through rows of leather-bound tomes, Talullah massaged her temples. A break might help her refocus. Or maybe Dhalian had made better progress than she had. "Dhal," she said, though not too loud. Libraries demanded a certain level of respect. Even if she hadn't seen anyone besides Dhalian all night.

She repeated his name as she glanced down the endless aisles. All of history lived inside those pages. What she needed to know had to be nestled somewhere inside the millions of books.

Millions. Once, not too long ago, the sheer idea of that many books would have elated her. Now, it soured in her stomach. Even if they searched for years, they still might not find the answers they sought. And her sisters didn't have years to wait. Not even close.

"Dhal, there you are." He sat cross-legged on the floor with dozens of scraps of parchment laid out in front of him.

"Oh, hi." He glanced up at her then back down to the parchment. As she approached, he quickly scooped the pieces into a pile and shoved them into a small pouch. "How's it going?"

"What are those?"

"Hmm? Oh, nothing." He pocketed the pouch as he stood, the slight crinkle magnified in the quiet, and ran a hand through his curls. "Just taking a break from the books. Any luck?"

Talullah sighed and shook her head. "You?"

He held up a notebook. "Some stuff about ships, though nothing about a star on a bow. Also made some notes about bows and arrows. Thought maybe the 'star bow' in the first part of the clue had something to do with archery."

"Like maybe there's a target we have to shoot?" Talullah bit her lip in thought. "I can't remember seeing anything like that in the maze, but then again, we were kind of preoccupied. Can't figure out how that would be connected to the keys, though."

"The keys could also be part of a different room. Or they could be a misdirection."

She hadn't thought of that. Could the riddle be the only important item they'd found in the tin? If so, had the ghost in Nainehta Forest meant some other keys?

"Too many possibilities," she said.

"We just started. We'll figure it out." Dhalian touched her elbow. "Speaking of out, any chance you remember the way back? I didn't pay much attention when I found this spot."

"That's ironic. A lost maker of maps." Talullah hadn't noticed what route she took during her search for Dhalian, either. Navigation never was her strength, unless she had a compass to guide her. Not that that would help them now. She glanced around. Nothing but books. "What section are we in?"

Gold glinted in the corner of her eye, light from overhead reflecting off the titles. She peered at them.

"I keep forgetting how big this place is. I don't know how you ever found me in the first place. I'll go find a sign. Don't move." Dhalian disappeared past the end of the aisle.

Atalissa Cromwell. Adrielle Cromwell.

"The titles are just names," she called, cringing at how loud her voice sounded against silence.

Dhalian returned. "Books of the Living."

An idea burned through her fatigue. "Hazel said there's a book for every living person, right? Why didn't I think to check before?"

"Check for...?" Dhalian raised his brows, an invitation to continue.

"My father's book." Hope brightened her eyes.

"Oh." His face softened. "Tules, what if—?"

"It will be here," she said. "I have to know." After so many elusive questions, this one could be answered. She made her way backward through the 'C' then 'B' surnames, holding her breath.

Brighton. Briffle. Briello.

She couldn't help thinking she'd already know if her father had died. The universe would have shifted. A piece of her own soul would have disconnected and floated away from her body. Same with her mother.

Talullah Bridgestone. Pennilyn Bridgestone. Margot Bridgestone.

Their names wrapped her in a cocoon of comfort. Though she had seen her sisters with her own eyes, this tangible confirmation made it more real, more believable that they lived. Eyes and ears could be fooled. But the woven titles spoke truth into her fingers.

She slid her gaze down the row, heart thundering. Dhalian stood close enough to feel his presence but far enough to give her some privacy.

Daniel Bridgestone.

The name stole her breath. Tears pooled in the corners of her eyes. She snatched the book from the shelf and squeezed it. Droplets plopped onto the cover. Somehow, it smelled like her father.

"He's alive," she whispered, glancing up at Dhalian.

Dhalian closed the gap in two strides and hugged her, resting his chin on top of her head. "Just like you said."

Talullah flipped backward through the pages, stopping at the most recent entry. She sniffed and wiped her nose on her tunic sleeve. "He's ill," she said, her voice quiet and flat. "Someone named Gwendolyn is looking after him."

Watching will not help you save them. Mirella's words filled her mind. Looking up from the page, she paused. She could take her family's books and read them cover to cover, but what good would that do? They suffered; she already knew that much. Details of their pain wouldn't help her save them. Only finding the stone and getting out of Praeteriti would.

When she finally summoned the willpower to place her father's book back on the shelf, her hand ached as if missing a limb.

"Tules? You okay?" Dhalian's soft tone eased her out of her thoughts.

She nodded. "Now I know where to find them."

A pause.

As if reading her mind, Dhalian moved closer to her. "You don't have to do it now." He took her hand.

She hadn't the courage before. But if she didn't look now, she didn't know if she'd ever be able to bring herself to do it.

Bridgestone names—some belonging to relatives she'd never known—filled two whole rows. Only one more name mattered. After so many years, she suddenly needed to see her mother's name. To read her story and find out once and for all why she'd left. And learn how to bring her home.

She drew a sharp inhale. *No.*

It had to be there. She checked again, reading each title with care.

Her breathing grew shallow, her eyes wide.

Maybe someone had moved or mis-shelved it. But who? If Mirella had found it, surely she would have told Talullah. No one else had reason to take it.

Her eyes moved over the spines in a frenzy, like an animal seeking shelter in a storm. The book would validate her theory that her mother had not stayed away of her own free will. Something had made her leave and hadn't let her return.

Doubt rained down her face. She let the tears fall.

For the first time ever, she truly considered the worst.

Squeezing Dhalian's hand, she kept her focus straight ahead. Her whispered words splintered. "It's gone, Dhal. What if she is, too?"

Chapter 19

Each night for the next week, Dhalian held her close while she cried, not saying anything. It was a familiar pattern. One they'd fallen in and out of at various times throughout the years when Talullah particularly missed her mother.

The first time Penny walked.

The time Talullah burned her arm making pancakes.

When Margot had caught a fever so high Talullah thought she might die.

When the Locator spell hadn't worked.

When her body began to change and she was scared and didn't know what to do. She hadn't discussed details with Dhalian about that, but he never required explanation. Every time Talullah needed him, he was there, no questions asked.

She was lucky to have him. Especially now.

He squeezed her hand as they stared at Mirella's front door. If anyone else had noticed her mother's book was missing, it would be her aunt.

The door creaked open. "Would you like to come in, or are you content to stand on the porch all day?" Mirella asked in a gentle tone.

"Hi, Mirella. We'll come in. Thanks." Talullah entered first with Dhalian following. As soon as they crossed into the front room, Talullah turned and the words broke free of her dry tongue. "My mother's book wasn't in the Record of the Living."

Mirella nodded. Likely she'd been waiting for the question ever since Talullah had first arrived in Praeteriti. "I, too, checked the shelves when I got here. For all your books. I hadn't heard from you in so long, but there you were on the shelf. Eldora, too." She ushered them further into the room and onto the sofa. "Don't worry, dear. I'm sure it will turn up."

"How do you know she isn't..." Talullah sat, leaving the rest unsaid.

Dhalian sat beside her, just close enough for her to feel his presence.

Mirella touched Talullah's shoulder with a warm hand. "Just because something isn't where we expect it to be doesn't mean it doesn't exist. Have you never forgotten to return a book to its proper place?"

"Of course I have, but—"

"Then don't you think it's possible the same has happened to your mother's book?"

Talullah stared at the yellow plaid curtains covering the window as she considered this. "I suppose. But I've never seen anyone except Hazel and Dhalian in the library. And neither of them would have moved it."

"Definitely not," said Dhalian, shaking his head.

"Its absence doesn't mean Eldora is *gone*. The magic of time—of truly life-changing events—leaves traces. If your mother had passed on, we'd know. Her spirit would have sent us a sign."

That's what she'd thought in the library. But years spent wondering if her mother was dead had sown deep seeds of doubt. Digging them up would take more than a few words. "How can you be sure?"

Mirella smoothed a few flyaway hairs near her face. "I am sure only of what I see in the mirror glass, Talullah, or what is right in front of me. But without proof of the contrary, why not choose to believe your mother lives?"

Because if that was true, her mother had stayed away on purpose. It wasn't so much her absence that now weighed on Talullah. Time apart had dulled that ache. It was whether her mother had had a choice. Believing she hadn't was easier. Talullah's temporarily softened heart hardened once again. Regardless, focusing on the ifs wouldn't keep her other family members alive.

"Thank you," said Talullah, rising from the sofa and gesturing for Dhalian to do the same. "You've given me a lot to think about."

"Don't lose heart, dear. The book will show itself."

"Trust me. I'm far from giving up." But Talullah had already pushed thoughts of her mother aside. Finding the stone could be her only priority now. And there was one resource she'd neglected.

"REMIND ME WHY WE'VE got to do this," Dhalian said. He handed Talullah her bag and grabbed his own off the bedroom floor. When Mirella had mentioned spirits, it smacked her on the head like an apple falling from a tree. Beings from all eras of history surrounded her. Why hadn't she sought their guidance before? Surely someone knew something about the maze and its secrets.

Ghosts are terrible gossips, Gillie had said. She hoped that was true.

"Two reasons. I'm out of other ideas, and they might actually know something." Long hours in the library hadn't revealed anything helpful, and the maze had been missing since their first adventure. Talullah couldn't guess when it would return, but she couldn't just sit and wait.

Dunamai will reward the Keeper of the Keys. The ghost's words had haunted Talullah's every silent moment. Maybe it was time she paid attention.

"The ghosts do see and hear everything around here." Hazel took a swig of her cloudy orange beverage.

Clinking issued from inside the tin as Talullah tucked it in her bag. "Think about it. Some of them have been here for centuries. If Hazel saw the Mazuchawi first arrive, at least one of them must have. And maybe one of them has played the room we're in." It might be a dead end, but it was a lead to follow. At the very least, asking the question might quiet the voice in her head and make space for other thoughts.

Hazel nodded. "We should start with Mr. Miscian, the apothecary. He's ancient. If anyone knows anything, it's him."

Talullah rolled the marble-like money between her fingers inside her trouser pocket. Intentions aside, she'd forgotten to come back the day after Dhalian's injury. Almost two weeks later, it seemed awkward to broach the subject. Would he still help them if he knew she was a thief?

Hazel rapped on the paisley door and they waited. Shuffling sounds filtered through the crack beneath the door, and a moment later it opened.

Wafts of rosemary and mint and lemon balm swirled through the opening. The scents transported Talullah back to the Hidden Market. The first time she'd visited the apothecary she'd been too distracted to notice, but now she half-expected to see Baako's rich dark skin and conspiratorial smile. Would she ever see her storyteller friend again? Of course she would. She'd make sure of it. Breaking her promise to him would be like lying to herself.

Instead of Baako, a large bespectacled man in a long coat filled the doorway. "Well, if it isn't my favorite patron," he said, stepping aside for them to enter. "How have you been, Hazel?"

"Just fine, Mr. Miscian, thank you. These are my friends, Talullah and Dhalian." She gestured to each of them.

"How do you do?" He extended his hand and they each shook it.

"We're well. Thank you, sir," Talullah said, her face warming.

"What can I do for you today? More ingredients for that beverage of yours?" Mr. Miscian pointed to the bottle in Hazel's hand.

"Oh, no, nothing for me today. I'm all set."

"Did you brew that yourself?" Dhalian asked.

Hazel smiled. "Special recipe." She turned back to the apothecary, who straightened the bottles on display. "Talullah and Dhalian have a few questions. We're hoping you can help."

Mr. Miscian sat on a three-legged stool in front of the counter and invited them to do the same. "I'll do my best."

"Before we start, I owe you this." Talullah's conscience cheered as she offered the apothecary the money. "For the aloe leaves. You weren't here, and it was an emergency—"

"Life or death, sir," piped in Dhalian. "Mine, specifically."

"Or else I wouldn't have taken them..." Splotches painted Talullah's guilt on her neck. Had her selfish need for redemption cost them important information? She waited, hand outstretched.

Mr. Miscian accepted the marbles, understanding lighting his gray eyes. "I thought I must have misplaced that jar. Quite alright, though. Matters of that nature do warrant exceptions to the rules. Thank you for your honesty." The metal till jingled as he deposited her payment. "Now, what can I do for you?"

Talullah sat, her body much lighter now that she'd paid her debt and her head dizzy from the live eucalyptus plant near her. She spoke in a rush, hoping if she filled the space he wouldn't have time to change his mind. "When we were in Nainehta Forest, one of the ghosts said something I couldn't make sense of. He said, 'Dunamai will reward the Keeper of the Keys.' And then we found this."

She removed the tin of keys from her bag, opened it, and placed it on the counter. She lay the lid face up next to the container. "I'm wondering if the ghost could have meant these keys."

The apothecary rubbed his round glasses on his crisp white shirt, then perched them atop his nose. Squinting through the still smudged lenses, he assessed the tin and its contents. "Not these keys, no." He looked up. "You've heard the Legend of the Suditzas, I assume?"

They nodded.

"The gems in Dunamai's Eye are often referred to as keys of destiny or fate. Seers are called the Keepers of the Keys. Coincidence has brought you the metal ones, it seems." He held her gaze, the corners of his mouth upturned, and added, "Or perhaps it was fate." Her necklace lay against her chest, hidden beneath her tunic. But Talullah couldn't help feeling he knew it was there.

She blinked away her discomfort. *Change the subject.* "What about these keys, then, and the container. Do you know anything about them?"

"Where did you say you found this box?" the apothecary asked in a conversational tone, examining the lid.

"We found it in the maze, sir. The Mazuchawi," Dhalian said. He leaned sideways to speak past the row of garlic braids hanging from the ceiling over the counter. "It came with a riddle, which we think will lead us to the next room."

"Ah, the maze. Always the topic of chatter around here." He focused on the engraved design. "This container used to hold moonflower dust. See, you can just make out the words."

"What's moonflower dust used for?" asked Dhalian.

Brows furrowed, Mr. Miscian lifted his eyes. "Among other things, it tempers the effects of Lethe water, the active ingredient in forgetfulness potions."

Lethe. Where had Talullah heard that name before? "The river in Nainehta Forest is called Lethe. Gillie the wood faerie stopped me from drinking from it."

"Good thing. Ingesting Lethe water on its own causes permanent memory erasure. With the right amount of moonflower dust, the brewer can control which memories are lost and for how long. It's tricky to get correct."

Hazel's bottle clinked against her teeth as she took another sip. The apothecary watched her with interest. "You've probably sold a lot of it, right?"

Mr. Miscian shook his head. "No, my dear, I haven't."

Talullah sat up straighter on her stool. "You must remember, then, to whom you sold it? If we know that, we might be able to find the person who put the keys inside."

The apothecary's voice quieted. "I've only sold one tin of moonflower dust in recent times. To Hazel."

Hazel choked on her drink. "What? I don't remember that."

Talullah stole a glance at her. If she bought the moonflower dust, did she also put the keys in the tin?

"Can I see that bottle, dear?" Mr. Miscian asked gently. Hazel passed it to him and he sniffed the top.

"I thought so. This is a diluted solution, but it's Lethe water in there for certain. I never looked too closely before." He sighed and turned to Hazel with pity in his eyes.

"That *drink* has been repressing her memories?" Dhalian asked, incredulous.

The apothecary nodded. "To her credit, she made a commendable batch. Meaning, once it cycles out of her system, her memories will slowly return."

"I'm right here," Hazel said. "I can hear you. And why would I give myself amnesia? Wouldn't it make it easier for me to get home if I knew who I was and could, you know, remember things?" She folded her arms. "It doesn't make sense."

The apothecary stood and moved behind the counter, rifling through a book of papers. "I can't tell you why." He turned the book around so they could read. On the third line of the ledger page he'd written, *Hazel. Tin of moonflower dust. One Meitat, seventeen Luz. Paid in full.*

"For whatever reason, my dear, you chose not to remember."

"HAZEL, LET'S TALK." Talullah knocked on the bedroom door again but received no response. After thirty minutes, she gave up.

"No luck," she told Dhalian as she entered their room.

"She'll come around. She's in shock, I'm sure." He separated the keys on his bed so they lay in a single layer.

"So am I." Talullah crossed the room and plopped down next to him. "She has something to do with the maze, I'm sure of it. But I don't know if that's a good or bad thing." Her insides squirmed. "What if she really is working for Renevelda and she hid her memories so she wouldn't give herself away?"

Dhal gave her a skeptical look. "Really? You think she's the witch's minion?"

She picked up a key. "It's possible. I didn't tell her we thought the stone was in the maze, but if she's on Renevelda's side she might already know. She could be using us to guide her to it, and then once we do, she'll turn on us." She dropped the key. It tinkled against the others.

Dhalian squinted at the parchment with the riddle, Talullah's notes about keys, then back at the key he held in front of his face. "Possible, sure. But what does that mean? If we want to get the stone from the maze, we have to play the game. And we can't play without her or we start over, remember?"

Talullah pinched the bridge of her nose and closed her eyes. "I know, I know. I feel like we're not even close." Margot and Penny's faces, always latent in her mind, drifted to the surface. "I can't make them wait any longer."

Dhalian grabbed one of her hands in his and lifted her chin with the other. "Hey. We're getting there. And Hazel's memories will start returning. Even if she's on the other side, she'll know something useful and we'll weasel it out. In the meantime..." He gestured to the assortment of metal shapes and her notes. "Can you decipher what this says?"

She leaned over her notebook. "Top = bow." She shook her head, flipping her short dark hair against her chin. "Must have been tired when I wrote that. Doesn't make any sense."

Dhal's face lit up. "Yes, it does. What if 'bow' isn't pronounced like 'how,' but like 'know'. 'Star bow' doesn't have to do with boats or arrows at all. It means the top of the key is a star. Is there one like that here?"

Clarity broke through her wall of doubt. She smiled. "Dhal. You might be brilliant."

"What do you mean *might*?"

They scanned the pile.

"Here," Dhalian thrust a key at her. "I've done my part. Now show off those fancy Sight skills of yours. Figure out what it unlocks."

Each of the star's five points poked into her palm as she closed her hand around the key's top. Magic flowed into her fingers. She couldn't control Hazel's intentions or her mother's whereabouts, but she could control her Sight. Finally. Eyes closed, she reached for events attached to the key.

Her arm hair stood on end. A purple image flashed behind her eyes.

Woodgrain. A hand inserted a key into a star-shaped lock. The *click* of the release. Not a creak of a door, but the smooth sound of wood sliding against metal.

Her eyes snapped open. "Dhal. What if the key we're supposed to find doesn't go to a door at all?"

"Are you okay? You look all...crazy. No offense."

She stood, blood pumping hard. The key's magic tingled her skin as she approached the dresser against the wall. "Hazel owned the tin the keys were in, right? She said she lost the key to this drawer. But what if she didn't lose it? What if she hid it in the maze?"

Dhal joined her, his voice animated "People don't just lock drawers for no reason. Let's see what Hazel's been hiding." He gripped one of the drawer-pulls.

She inserted the key and turned it counter-clockwise. A soft *click*. The drawer slid open.

Two weathered pages of parchment sat in the bottom.

"Paper? That's it?" Dhal asked, his face falling.

"Parchment is never just paper, Dhal. You, as a mapmaker, should know that. Remember what the maze clue said? 'A star bow takes you backward. What's revealed will lead you forward.'" Talullah picked them up with care, skimmed the first few lines, and gasped. "Dhal, this story is about Renevelda's past. And something in it will get us closer to the stone."

Chapter 20

Unmarked

Never before had the child of a goddess failed to show the sign of divine power upon reaching the age of maturity. Thirteen-year old Renevelda alone could claim that as her dishonor. Puzzled as to why her tattoo hadn't yet appeared, she hid her shoulders from her mother, Queen Aideen, and her half-sisters, Thena and Eurielle, for as long as possible. She couldn't bear their ridicule. Not over this. Everything else, well, that was another story.

Her tattoo would appear—it had to, didn't it? She was the daughter of the Divine. Surely the mark was just delayed for some reason. But why? Her sisters' marks had appeared right on schedule, the morning of their thirteenth birthdays. Renevelda had reached the age of maturity two weeks prior, yet not even a hint of golden circumference dared peek out. The circle always appeared first, the stars filling in during the following week.

Renevelda bit her lip as she surveyed herself in her oval mirror, trying to think of another excuse to dispel her mother noticing the absence of the mark. Her stomach clenched at the thought of what might happen if it didn't appear soon. No one, in her memory, had ever experienced this. All the children her age proudly flaunted their marks as soon as they appeared, opting for shoulder-less gowns and vests to display their Divinity to the others still waiting their turn.

When they'd asked why she didn't reveal hers, she'd fabricated a lie about her birthday being misreported in the realm ledger. It was two weeks later than everyone thought, she told them with a serene smile. Lucky for Renevelda, her sisters ignored everyone younger. Her mist-thin lie would have evaporated in an instant.

A ball of fire rose in her chest, burning the last piece of hope to ash. Two weeks had passed, and nothing had happened. She paced, wearing a path in the stone floor. How would she explain to the kids today—her fake birthday—that her mark had still not appeared?

More importantly, what would her mother do? Aideen was known throughout the realm as a strict disciplinarian, cold-souled and unforgiving. Apparently, she hadn't always been like that. The way Eurielle and Thena explained it, their mother had been joyous, loving, and warm—until Renevelda's birth.

The thought stung her heart like thousands of wasps. Though the Realm of the Divine didn't have such creatures, she'd watched the humans below caught in their swarms. Their cries were enough to tell her how painful it was.

Aideen had never treated Renevelda like a true daughter. She'd never spent hours brushing her blonde locks the way she did for Eurielle. And Renevelda couldn't imagine her mother ever looking at her with pride the way she did at Thena. The youngest of three, Renevelda never expected to be her mother's favorite. But she'd hoped for something more than loathing. After all, her father hadn't just left her mother. He'd abandoned Renevelda, too.

Tears leaked from the corners of her eyes. She wiped them away, clenching her jaw. Not today. Not on the day of her Divinity Ceremony. Her breath caught in her chest. Would she still be allowed to participate in the ceremony, if her Divinity couldn't be proven for all to see?

Regardless of what happened, she wouldn't cry today. She had to keep her streak of days gone without crying. It was a game she'd started with herself a few years back. Determined to win, she refused to let the tears fall today. She'd managed yesterday, somehow. If she fought them today, her streak would climb to two.

"Rene-smell-da, where are you?"

Renevelda flinched and checked in the mirror that her emotion hadn't reddened her pale skin too much. She couldn't let Eurielle know anything was wrong. The middle sister had the senses of a purebred Crimson dragon. She could smell sadness from a mile away—and would prey upon it with her talon-like words, tearing her victim to shreds without batting an eyelash.

"Eurielle, hello." Renevelda turned to face her sister, steeling herself for whatever verbal assault was on today's menu.

"Hello," was all Eurielle said, though her face betrayed a giddiness Renevelda hadn't seen her sister wear in...well...ever. She sat atop Renevelda's small bed in the middle of the room, pulling apart her perfect jet-black curls with her fingers. Her golden skin was scrubbed clean and anticipation glittered in her large dark eyes. Renevelda couldn't help pine for skin like Eurielle's. Probably because it matched Thena's and Aideen's. Renevelda's pale pallor was yet another brick in the wall separating her from a normal childhood.

"C-can I do s-something for you?" Renevelda asked, cursing her anxious stutter for surfacing. She'd practiced keeping it at bay, but today she was too nervous to concentrate.

"No," Eurielle said, craning her neck toward Renevelda and peering at her exposed shoulder.

Quick as she could, Renevelda pulled her jade silk robe to cover herself. Too late.

"Still no mark?" her sister purred, circling her like a wild cat. Her stilettos clicked the marble floor like claws. "What a shame."

There was no denying it. "Please Eurielle, don't—"

"Thena!"

A puff of glittering smoke appeared near Renevelda's vanity. When it cleared, there her sister Thena stood.

"What is it, Euri? I've only just finished my hair and I have to choose my dress. The ceremony starts in less than an hour." Thena, the eldest, emanated a coolness that could be attributed to being her mother's only companion for the first five years of her life. Aideen's undivided attention had clearly molded Thena into her copy.

"Ren's mark still hasn't appeared." Eurielle bounced on the balls of her feet, unable to contain her glee at her sister's misfortune.

Thena froze. Renevelda watched the realization work itself through her eldest sister's mind, manifesting in a wicked curve of a smile. Thena glided toward Renevelda without a sound, blocking her path to the door.

Renevelda backed into her vanity, Eurielle on her other side. She had nowhere to go. Unless she wanted to jump on the bed and launch herself out the window. Which she considered. Instead, she braced herself for impact. Where Eurielle threw words like daggers, Thena played physical.

"Let me see." Thena's voice dripped with acid.

"I—"

"Do it."

Whimpering, Renevelda pulled aside her robe to reveal her bare shoulder.

Thena drew a sharp breath, then made a tsk sound. Her soft voice sent a shiver down Renevelda's spine when she finally spoke. "Let's see what Mother has to say about this."

"No, please, Thena. I'm not ready—" Renevelda pleaded. Thena's razor sharp nails dug into her arm as she dragged Renevelda down the hall.

"Ready or not, it's time to face the facts. You're not one of us, and you never will be." Thena shoved her through the billowing curtain that led to Aideen's chambers.

Renevelda stumbled, trying not to fall on her face in her mother's presence, but Thena kicked her feet as she and Eurielle passed through the curtain behind her. A sickening crack echoed off the stone walls as Renevelda's chin made contact with the floor. Warm blood trickled from her wound and she pressed her hand to it. She ran her tongue along her teeth and breathed a sigh of relief when she found them all intact. A small cut was nothing. She'd endured much worse.

The second the thought entered her mind it vanished like smoke. Remembering where she was, she struggled to her feet. The air crackled with tension.

Aideen appeared in the time it took Renevelda to blink. Her mother looked her up and down, her thin nose wrinkled and square jaw tight.

"Vellie's got something to tell you," Eurielle cooed, smirking. She lowered herself onto the nearest velvet chaise.

Renevelda bowed her head in respect, watching the bottom of her mother's blood red silk dress inch closer to her. "I—"

"Well, out with it."

"I...well—" Renevelda glanced at the tapestry on the back wall, as if she'd find the right words woven among the History of the Divine.

"I don't have all day."

"If you don't tell her, we will," Thena said, arching her eyebrow.

Renevelda swallowed the bile creeping up her throat. Better to come from her than her sisters. If Eurielle or Thena told Aideen, she'd think Renevelda had been hiding something from her. Which, in fact, she had.

Poking a cobra was less dangerous than keeping secrets from Aideen. At least when a cobra struck, its venom worked quickly, mercifully. Aideen's variety of poison seeped beneath the surface and slowly worked its way into every mental crack.

"My mark...it still hasn't appeared." Renevelda flinched, anticipating a strike that didn't come.

Instead, silence descended over the room. The four women held their collective breath. Seconds stretched into hours as Renevelda waited for her mother to say something...anything. She almost thought Aideen hadn't heard her and prepared herself to repeat the brutal truth.

But then Aideen spoke, composed, her voice sharp and clear as the glass tiara adorning her head. "That is no surprise. Your father was a deceptive traitor of a being, you know."

Thena and Eurielle's soprano cackles ricocheted off the walls and assaulted her ears.

"My father? I don't understand."

"At first I thought my Divinity would prevail. That maybe it wouldn't matter that he was...what he was. But now it's obvious I was mistaken."

"I know he left. But...I've done what you've asked of me. Maybe my mark will still come." Renevelda's hands shook at her sides, mirroring the quaking in her voice.

Aideen stalked toward Renevelda until only inches separated them. "It's not that he left, stupid girl. I'm glad that he's gone." Her inky eyes stared directly into Renevelda's. "It's that he was human. And so is half of you."

Renevelda's lungs depleted as if she'd been punched in the stomach. She wheezed, unable to draw breath.

"Today you must leave. Only the Divine belong in the Realm."

Chapter 21

"She wants to make herself a full goddess. To claim her place in the Realm," said Talullah.

Dhalian's eyes darkened. He fiddled with the end of his sleeve, pulling it over his palm. "When I was captive in the castle, I overheard some of the servants whisper about the third's revenge. I didn't understand, but now I get it. Renevelda is the third sister."

Talullah's muscles seized. *Breathe, Talullah. Breathe.* If she didn't think it, her lungs would stop working, she was sure of it. "Did you say, 'third's revenge'?"

The papers rustled as her hands shook. Dhalian steadied them with his. "Yes?"

How the words squeezed through her compressed throat, she didn't know. "Third's Revenge is a potion. A spell. I came across it in a book once, way before I was mature enough to understand it. One thing stuck with me, though, because I'd never seen such a gruesome description. It requires a sacrifice related to what the brewer wants to change." Her voice dimmed to a whisper. "She has two sisters, Dhal. And, so do I."

"You don't think she's going to…oh, Tules." He pulled her to his chest, the scent of honey and dew enveloping her. "She still doesn't have the stone or the Eye. We can still save them."

Talullah pulled back. "We will." That was the only option.

She wedged the pages into her bag and ran to Mirella's as fast as her feet would take her. Dhalian trailed a few feet behind, wheezing, but Talullah didn't slow down. The crisp freshness of rain-scented air cooled her lungs, clearing them like a broom sweeping cobwebs from a forgotten corner.

Whatever Mirella was doing would have to wait. She'd break down the door to get inside if she had to.

As it happened, she didn't.

A damp squeak issued from her boots as she skidded to a stop on Mirella's front lawn. Her great-aunt stood in the doorway, her hands clasped in front of her and an unreadable expression on her face. Mirella's emerald eyes—just like Penny's, Talullah couldn't help thinking every time she saw them—sparkled behind her pink cat-eye glasses.

"Mirella, I—" She bent at the waist, trying to catch her breath.

"I know, dear. Come in."

"Dhalian—"

"Right here," Dhalian announced between gasps.

They entered the kitchen where three mugs of tea sat waiting on the kitchen table.

"How did you know—?"

"I saw you coming. Follow me." She led them down a hall Talullah hadn't known existed.

"Mirella, I want to see my sisters," Talullah said.

"And you will."

They stopped at the end of the hall in front of a plain brown door Talullah never would have noticed had she stumbled upon the hallway alone.

Mirella pressed a circle on the right side of the doorframe with her first and middle fingers and the door swung inward. Talullah recoiled at the brightness of the room as she entered, her eyes blinking furiously and watering.

"Oh, sorry. Forgot to turn it down. It is a bit jarring the first time, I always forget." Mirella flicked her wrist and the light dimmed enough that Talullah could look around without straining.

Hundreds of mirrors of all sizes and shapes covered the walls, some framed in ornately carved wood, others in simple bronze, and still others without a frame at all. Talullah gaped.

"Over here, please," Mirella called, waving them over to an oval mirror with a black iron frame. "It's almost time."

"What are all these for?" Dhalian caught sight of his reflection in one as he passed and attempted to flatten his curls.

"Not for preening," Mirella said. "These mirrors help me See. I like to say they're my windows to the worlds."

"Worlds, plural?" Dhalian asked, dropping his hands to his sides in an obvious attempt to stop fiddling with his hair.

"Yes, Mr. Philo. Worlds, plural. We are in another one now, aren't we? This isn't the only alternate to the one you know. Ah, here they are." Mirella pointed at the oval mirror.

Cerulean smoke filled the glass and when it dissipated, Talullah's sisters stood in frame.

"Penny? Mar?" Talullah's voice cracked. Penny's hair hung in messy waves past her shoulders. Had Margot grown taller? No. It couldn't have been that long since she saw them last. Not long enough for them to noticeably change. But then, was she misremembering?

Penny and Margot stared at her as if they knew she was there but couldn't see her. "Tuley? Is that you?" they said in unison, their small voices the sweetest harmony Talullah had ever heard.

"I'm here. How are you? Are you hurt?" She turned to her aunt. "Can't they see us?"

"One-way glass, dear. But they can hear you. It's the best I could do, given the circumstances."

"We're okay, Tuley. Auntie Mirella told us you have an important job to do, but then you're coming to get us. Can you come soon?" Penny said.

"As soon as I can. Everything is going to be okay." The second promise tasted bitter, but she masked it with a sweet tone. Her sisters needed to believe it. And, so did she. "What are they doing to you?"

"Nothing much," said Margot, her eyes boring holes into Talullah's, even though she couldn't have known it. Talullah forced herself to hold her sister's gaze. "They ask us questions. Sometimes we get them right and then we get a prize."

"What kind of questions?"

"A lot about Mother," said Penny. Her soft voice faltered. "We always get those wrong."

For obvious reasons. How could they possibly know anything about her?

"And some about you," said Margot.

"Me?" Of course. She should have guessed. Why wouldn't the soldiers exploit Talullah's sisters, looking for weakness? "What do they ask about me?"

"Just things." A smirk dimpled Margot's bruised cheek. "For those we always lie."

Her sweet sisters had done a better job protecting her than she had them. Bruises only hinted at the horrors they'd endured. For her. No, *because* of her.

Margot dropped her voice. "Don't worry about us, Tuley. We have a friend here. He can help us escape, even before you can."

"Who?" Talullah snapped. "You know you're not supposed to go with strangers." Where would he take them? If they left the castle, how would she find them?

"We can't tell you, but it's okay. He's nice. Sometimes he tells us stories, like you used to." Penny rocked back on her heels as she spoke and turned to look over her shoulder.

"We have to go now, Tuley."

In her mind, Rantoul struck Margot's face with a heavy gloved hand. He dragged Penny by her hair across the rough ground. Renevelda whispered curses and her sisters' faces contorted in pain.

"Penny, Mar, listen to me. Do not go anywhere with anyone, do you hear me? I'm coming to get you." Panic fell over her like sheets of freezing rain.

"Sorry, Tuley. We have to go now. We love you," Margot said, and the cerulean smoke seeped into the mirror.

"Hope you have better answers today than you did yesterday. Those bruises look painful. It would be a shame to add more." Rantoul's brogue sent Talullah's mind reeling.

"Don't touch them you bastard!" she yelled, adrenaline coursing through her as if she'd been struck by lightning, heating her blood and vibrating her bones. She banged on either side of the mirror with clenched fists. "Do you hear me? Don't lay your filthy hands on them! Leave them alone!"

But when the smoke cleared, only her own tear-stained face stared back at her.

That carp soldier would keep hurting them. Until Renevelda killed them. No. Talullah's sisters had suffered enough for her mistakes. No more waiting.

"What's the next step, Mirella?"

"Sit down, dear. You're shaking."

"What's next?" she repeated, snapping each word like a twig. "You said controlling my visions is the first. It's time to move on."

"I don't know that you're ready—"

"Were you watching the same cell I was? Because there isn't time to get ready. She's brewing Third's Revenge, Mirella. I need you to teach me. Now."

Chapter 22

"Where are you going?" asked Talullah. She'd hoped Dhalian would be there to support her during her first Alteration lesson.

He glanced at her over his shoulder halfway out Mirella's front door. Shadows obscured the gold in his hazel eyes. "There's something I need to do." He shoved his hand in his coat pocket. It crinkled. "I'll see you later."

"Check with Hazel, okay? About her memories. Anything could help."

Dhalian nodded.

The door slammed shut as Mirella entered the sitting room. "Alteration is much more difficult than Sight." Her aunt gestured for her to sit on the tufted sofa. She undid the drawstring of a patchwork bag and removed a large book. Worn and leathery, a sparkling braided thread ran along its edges. Talullah recognized the style immediately.

"A Book of the Living."

"Yes. To Alter a person's story, you must possess their book. It contains their life experiences, their decisions, their emotions." Mirella handed her the tome. Golden thread spelled *MIRELLA VIDENTE* across the cover.

"Wait. I'm not practicing on *your* past, am I?"

"Don't look so petrified, Talullah. I'm not asking you to change anything of significance. And you need to be able to see the effects, if there are any. I know you're anxious, but we must start small. Consequences of Alteration can be catastrophic, if done incorrectly. If we'd had more time...but here we are."

Talullah traced the thread.

"The key is to feel out the specific event and focus only on that. Don't let the others break your concentration. It will be overwhelming at first, but as all things, it will get easier with time. Open the book to the last page with writing."

The pages glided across her fingers like melted butter. She turned them slowly, taking care not to tear the thin parchment. When she stopped on the last page, her nerves tingled. Was she actually ready for this?

"The threads represent the events that occur on each page, and the knots are the intersection of the events impacted in each of the worlds."

"But some aren't connected at all."

"Good observation. That is because the effect is either yet to be determined or insignificant enough to not impact anything else. These threads are where we begin. You will access the event with your Sight but use your intuitive touch to separate it from the rest. See that loose one, there? Let's use that for our first experiment."

Seeing the past was one thing, but she hadn't mentally prepared for what it would be like to actually change it. Affecting something so small could have a huge impact on the future. And apparently the present, according to Gillie and Mirella. What if she accidentally Altered something she didn't mean to and couldn't reverse the change? Would the people she loved be the same?

Would she?

"Close your eyes and open your heart. You must be receptive to the memories. Good. Relax your shoulders and reach for the thread. No, keep your eyes closed. *Feel* it."

She did as Mirella instructed. A fuzzy sensation permeated her right hand before she even made contact with it, as if the thread held a charge that drew it to her. When she pinched it between her thumb and forefinger the sensation spread through her body and flipped a switch in her brain.

Mirella's voice wove into her subconscious, instructing her what to do next. Drop into the memory. To fully understand what she would change she needed to put herself in Mirella's place.

With only a thought, it was done. She stood inside Mirella's kitchen thinking Mirella's thoughts.

What flavor of tea should I have this morning?

Start small, indeed. But at least no one would die if she got it wrong.

"I chose to drink Chamomile this morning, but I would like you to make my choice Cinnamon instead." Mirella's voice sounded muffled, like water filled Talullah's ears. "Concentrate on this decision with your mind. Twist the thread in your hands and you will See the possibilities. When you've found the one in which I choose Cinnamon, tie a knot in the end of the thread."

Talullah forced her mind and body to steady. She could do this. It was a small event with little to no consequence. Sweat trickled down her palm, the only outward sign of her inner struggle.

Tension developed in the thread as she twisted it, cycling through the potential outcomes in her Sight. Scenes flashed by in seconds. She twitched when the vision's color morphed from purple to green.

Minutes passed. Maybe hours or days or weeks. Talullah's sense of time dissolved completely, lost in her aunt's memory and the possibilities. Fatigue hovered over her like a phantom in the dark. But she pushed on.

Cinnamon. Cinnamon. Where was it?

"Come out of it, Talullah. Let it go. We will try again later," said Mirella.

I can do this. Just a few more minutes. It's here, I know it is.

Possibilities cycled by so fast her head spun. *Focus on one spot. Like dancing.*

She'd never mastered dancing. Especially not the twirls.

"Come back, Talullah." Mirella's voice froze the images.

Three blinks later they'd dissolved and Mirella's sitting room reappeared. Talullah's legs wobbled. Before she could brace herself, her knees buckled and she tumbled, arms flailing, to the floor.

Crash.

Multicolored porcelain shards littered the ground. Amber liquid seeped under her palms. Her head throbbed as she groaned, "Sorry, Mirella."

"Are you alright, dear? Don't worry about the teapot. Very old. It was bound to break sooner or later."

Talullah pushed herself to a seated position on the sofa. Had she managed to fall a few inches backward instead of forward, the plush cushions would have cradled her fall. Just her luck.

She rubbed her scuffed kneecaps. "At least let me clean up the mess."

The room stopped spinning and Talullah's stomach felt oddly calm. She didn't have the slightest urge to vomit. After ensuring she was steady enough, she made her way down the hall. "Broom cupboard is this one?" She pointed at a small closet door.

Mirella nodded.

Inside, she found towels, spare tissue, soap.

Something caught her eye that made her pause. Was she dreaming? She rubbed her eyes. Had messing in Mirella's memory done something to her own?

It leaned against the wall, so innocent.

So out of place.

Impossible.

Yet, there it was, scales gleaming and one red eye daring her to deny its presence.

She reached for it, but her hand stopped short. Hovered over the fish-shaped handle. Her father wasn't in Praeteriti, so why was his cane? And why did Mirella have it?

Bracing herself, Talullah closed her fingers around the top. Puffs of red rolled across her vision. When they cleared, she stood in the same ruby forest. Trees stretched above her, obscuring the sky. Then, fire.

It cascaded from above like a circular waterfall, ash flying like droplets into her hair. Screams echoed off the trees. But where had they come from?

Silent, she watched. From her right, a girl walked toward the flames, her face obscured by her chin-length hair. Symbols swirled on the surface of her cloak as she moved. Its bottom grazed the fallen leaves with a soft *swish*. A hawk screeched. The faint sounds of boots on earth and the whir of flying arrows fought to be heard above the screams.

Not noticing, or ignoring them, the girl tucked her hands into her sleeves and straightened her posture. Then, as Talullah had watched her do twice before, she walked into the fire.

Chapter 23

"What did she say?" Dhalian asked. He nudged the porcelain plate of fries toward her.

Talullah still hadn't gotten used to the fact a place created for dead people had real food. Or that spirits could, apparently, still eat.

She took one, glancing at the "Fisher's" sign glowing in the window. Outside, night had fallen. It had taken her hours to locate Dhalian to tell him what had happened. She still didn't trust Hazel enough to tell her about the visions, and anyway, she'd been ill for the past few days. Recovering memories had side effects, according to Mr. Miscian. Not that Hazel had shared any with Talullah or Dhalian when they'd visited. If she remembered anything, she'd kept it to herself.

"That she'd forgotten it was there. She said she thought it was too creepy, so she never touched it. Apparently, my describing my father's to her a while back didn't jog her memory."

"If she didn't bring it here, then who did?" Dhalian wiped grease from his lips with a lime green napkin.

She shook her head, taking another fry but not eating it. "She won't even say how she got here or when. I can't get anything from her."

"Okay. Let's table the cane for a minute. What about this vision?" He signaled the waitress for more water.

Rubbing her forehead, Talullah said, "I've had it multiple times recently. I don't remember ever having the same one more than once.

And I can never see the girl's face. It's like she's hiding on purpose, but she feels so familiar. Like I know her somehow."

"And you're sure it's going to happen? This girl, whoever she is, walking through a wall of fire?" He munched another fry. At least someone still had an appetite. Talullah dropped her uneaten one back on the plate.

"Yes. It was all in shades of red. Mirella said that's the color of the inevitable. No matter what, it's a fixed event. Unchangeable. I just wish I knew what happened next. Or who she is. Or why I keep Seeing her."

"Seems like she's got everything under control, though, from what you've said." Dhal gestured toward her with a fry.

She had exuded confidence. Head held high, shoulders back. Maybe Dhal was right. "I guess."

Thunder rumbled the diner, shimmying the salt and pepper shakers. A bolt of lightning struck. It hovered in the field outside. Beneath it, the air wavered like when heat made objects dance. And then, there it was. The Mazuchawi.

"It's back!" Talullah jumped from her seat and reached for Dhalian's hand. Instead she caught his wrist, his raised flesh pressing into her fingertips through his sleeve.

He recoiled as if she'd burned him, but he said nothing. As he slid from the booth, he slammed a handful of Luz onto the table. A few rolled off the side and bounced onto the floor. "She'll find them. Let's go."

"Should we get Hazel?" Talullah shouldered her bag.

"She'll see it, I'm sure."

Hazel stood waiting on the mat outside the maze when they arrived, breathless, a few minutes later.

"How are you feeling?" Talullah gave her a wary once-over.

"Better, thanks. I still don't remember much, but at least the headaches have lessened. I couldn't miss this, though. Not for anything."

As they stepped through the arch, the room with the doors manifested around them. The flames had been extinguished by Dhalian's token, but singed furniture and piles of ash lay scattered throughout, evidence of their battle with the Kleindraaks. The dragons themselves, thank the Founders, were nowhere to be found. A smoky scent tinged the air.

"Which door?" asked Dhalian. He walked the perimeter of the room, assessing each one.

"The clue said, 'what's revealed will lead you forward.' So, something in this will tell us." Talullah pulled the pages from her bag and read through Renevelda's story again.

"The doors have symbols on them. Each one has something different," Hazel said. She circled the room with Dhalian. "Crown. Goblet. Cloud." She listed the rest. "Any of these make sense?"

"Could be any of them." Talullah read the story twice more. "But the story is about what Renevelda didn't have. True Divinity. Loving family. A place in the Realm. Which of these most signifies that?"

Hazel joined Talullah in front of an emerald green door. She pulled up her sleeves and Talullah caught a glimpse of the arrow on her wrist.

"Wait, that's it," said Talullah. The image was like the first domino in a line of her thoughts. Each one connected with the last until she pieced it together. "Renevelda's tattoo."

"Sorry, what?" asked Dhalian.

"The key we used to open the drawer had a star on top, like the tattoo of the Divine. That signified Renevelda's past."

"So, we want a door with a star like her tattoo?" asked Hazel.

Talullah shook her head. "The star-topped key led us to this story. Its title is the clue that will lead us forward. *Unmarked.*" She was right. She knew it. Faster she moved around the room, searching the doors. "Renevelda's tattoo never appeared. We want a plain door. This one."

Beneath her palms, the simple walnut door pulsed. Her necklace warmed against her chest. Just like in Nainehta Forest. Yes. This was the one for sure.

Talullah closed her eyes and called on her Sight. If the door had been opened before, she could learn how to do it. Snippets of events circled her like a carousel. There. She latched onto the memory of the door inching open, a stream of light spilling across the floor.

Very good, said a voice in her head, the one she'd heard before. Her intuition, she'd decided. Because that was better than being crazy. *Now tell it to open.*

She imagined the door opening. Coolness spread through her hands and arms. The pulsing ceased. She opened her eyes. The door swung inward on creaky hinges, light dancing across her shoes.

"Way to go, Tules," Dhalian said, his voice full of awe.

"I can't believe we made it through," said Hazel. "Well done, Talullah."

Talullah smiled. For a second her eyes glistened with pride, before dimming with determination. She crossed the threshold and waved the others through.

A large pot encircled by dozens of woven bins occupied half the room. Flames licked at the black stone and thick liquid gurgled inside. Atop a long table at the right of the room, liquids glittered inside glass bottles and jars.

"What are we supposed to do here?" Dhalian asked.

Talullah peered into the bins, identifying their contents without trouble. "Potion ingredients."

"Maybe we have to finish it," Dhalian said, taking a cautious sniff of the steam wafting off the pot.

Hazel shook her head as if clearing her mind. "Yes, could be."

"We'll need a recipe to tell us what we're supposed to add," Talullah said.

"We could just taste it. Smells delicious." Dhalian drew another breath.

"No!" Hazel said. "It could be poison."

"Or Lethe juice," said Talullah under her breath. She snuck a glance at Hazel, who hadn't heard her. "Look for a potion book page. We've got to figure out what this stuff is."

The Luna Vine at the top of the wall grew, adding a leaf to its thorn as time passed. Talullah stared into the bubbling pot. It had been so long since she'd brewed anything, she couldn't recognize it by sight.

"What's lost must be found," a high-pitched voice said.

Talullah drew her knife. A red flash gleamed in the corner of her eye. She spun in a slow circle. "Anyone else see that?"

Was it a trick of the maze? Had it been in her head?

"No need for that," said the voice. "I'm here to help, not to hurt."

"Then show yourself," said Talullah. An invisible enemy would be almost impossible to fight.

A long red ponytail emerged first from behind the cauldron. It bounced as the small child hopped across the room to where Talullah stood.

"Tules, what about this?" Dhalian turned, a scrap of paper in one hand and a beaker of oily blue liquid in the other. At the sight of the girl, he dropped the beaker. Glass shattered and the ground sizzled, absorbing the liquid. "Who are you? How did you get in here?"

A flicker of recognition ignited in Talullah's memory. "I've seen you before."

The girl's mouth spread into a wide smile. One of her front teeth was missing. "I was hoping you'd remember. Sometimes they do, sometimes they don't. It's hard to guess."

"I thought you said no one could get in here while we were playing." Dhalian shot Hazel a look. "Isn't that the point of those creepy vines at the gate?"

"No one's supposed to be able to get in," Hazel said quietly, narrowing her eyes on the girl.

"You interrupted one of my visions." Talullah locked gazes with the girl, who couldn't have been older than Penny, yet whose round yellow eyes held a mysterious wisdom. "And you've been guiding me. It's your voice I've been hearing."

The girl nodded and rubbed her delicate nose, her fluffy hair bobbing like a fox tail. "That's right. Could you lower your weapons? You're making me nervous."

She didn't look nervous, smiling and hopping from one black-booted foot to the other. But Talullah lowered her knife to her side.

"You," Hazel whispered.

Dhalian's hands twitched, occasionally flicking against Talullah's hip. "You both know her? Who is she?"

"I remember," said Hazel. She turned to Talullah with large eyes. "She's a shapeshifter. The Spirit Fox. I met her when I first arrived."

The spirit girl stopped moving. "I see someone's coming back to herself. About time."

"Why are you here, Spirit Fox?" Dhalian drew himself to full height.

"To aid you in your quest, of course." She giggled, the sound as pointed as her teeth. "And my name is Azeria. But I prefer Zeri, for short."

Chapter 24

"We can't trust her," said Hazel, narrowing her eyes at Zeri. "The Spirit Fox is known for her tricks."

Zeri placed a mocking hand over her heart. "Hazel, I'm hurt. After everything we've been through together. After all the help I offered you. I'm only trying to do the same for Talullah."

"What does she mean, Hazel?" Talullah gripped the handle of her knife tighter.

The Spirit Fox circled the room, picking up jars every so often and gazing at them with mild disinterest. "I'm sure she can't recall quite yet. But it will come. We have a history, she and I. But I gave up on her a long time ago. For a while now, I've set my hopes on you, Talullah."

"Hopes for what, exactly?" Dhalian inched closer to Talullah.

"That she would be the one to reopen the portals. It's getting awfully dull being the only one who can travel between time." She tugged on a thin black ribbon encircling her neck. "The ghosts and other creatures are bound by the trees' magic. Lucky for you, however, I'm not. And I can help you find the stone."

"What stone?" asked Hazel.

Talullah still hadn't told her about Dunamai's Eye or the missing gemstone. She'd wanted Hazel to regain her memories first, to see whose side she was on. Apparently that no longer mattered.

"You don't remember that either?" asked Zeri, raising a thin brow. "The stone that opens the portals is hidden in this maze, Hazel. I'm surprised your *friends* haven't shared their plan with you."

Hazel's questioning eyes shot a stream of guilt through Talullah. "I told you my thoughts about this place. Why didn't you say anything?"

"Don't be angry with her," Zeri cut in before Talullah could answer. Not that she'd formulated a good response. "Only time will tell whose secrets are the worst. Yours, Talullah's, or maybe even Dhalian's." She smiled and winked at Dhalian.

He clenched his jaw and took half a step forward.

"Dhal doesn't have secrets. Not from me. You're just trying to stir up trouble." Talullah glanced at Dhal, searching for reassurance. He kept his eyes on Zeri.

"That's not why I'm here, though. I'm here to help you win this game. In exchange for something I want."

"Bargaining with a spirit is dangerous, Talullah," Hazel warned. "I may not remember exactly what deal I made with the Spirit Fox, but I'm sure it had consequences."

"I've been nothing but helpful to you, Talullah. Have I not?" Zeri batted her long dark eyelashes.

Talullah stared into the bubbling pot as if she would find the answer at its bottom. The spirit had to be manipulating her. Driving a wedge between her and her allies. She and Dhal told each other everything. How could Zeri know something about him Talullah didn't? Though she still didn't know if Hazel was an ally. And when Talullah thought back to the times when she'd heard Zeri's voice, she confirmed the spirit had actually helped her.

In the forest, Zeri had guided her to the portal tree so she and Dhalian could escape the soldiers. The spirit must have used her own powers to allow them passage and to keep the soldiers out. Yes, they were stuck in Praeteriti, but she was closer to finding the stone that could help destroy Renevelda and save her sisters. She never could have done that on her own. When the Kleindraaks had retreated in the first room of the maze, Zeri's voice had urged her to grab the tin of keys, ensuring they wouldn't have to start the room over and lose precious time. She'd helped Talullah open the door to the second room of the maze.

And the song. Talullah couldn't ignore that Zeri knew her mother's song.

"She hasn't steered me wrong yet."

"You really believe she's trustworthy?" Dhalian asked.

As far as she could tell, Zeri hadn't lied to her yet. Which was more than she could say for him. She'd had the feeling he was hiding something. Zeri had just confirmed it.

"Believe it or don't. That's of no consequence to me." Zeri's hair swished as she skipped around them, her black boots landing without sound on the stone floor. "I want freedom. For everyone who's trapped." She flashed her pointy teeth in a wicked smile. "And if I'm not mistaken, others count on Talullah for their freedom. Two others."

Desperation and hope washed over Talullah. "What do you know about my sisters?"

"You're trying to save them from the sorceress. And you're running out of time. But I can help you."

A war broke out between Talullah's heart and head. If Zeri really could help her save her sisters, she'd be a fool to deny her. She'd given Talullah no reason to doubt her thus far. And yet, the Spirit Fox's mischievous smirk gave her pause. What if Hazel was right and it was all a trick?

However small the chance Zeri told the truth, Talullah had to take it. With her sisters' lives at stake, she couldn't afford not to.

"Okay," she said.

Dhalian and Hazel tensed beside her.

"Are you sure this is a good idea, Tules?" His warm hand touched the small of her back.

She turned to Zeri, whose face radiated glee. Talullah's stomach turned. She ignored it. Her decision was made. "Help me, Spirit Fox."

Zeri hopped up and down, clapping as if Talullah had said she'd buy the spirit a pony. "Wonderful. I knew you'd come around." She stalked around the cauldron and gestured to it. "You've already figured out what you need to do here. Complete the potion. That much is obvious. But which one is it? The magic prohibits me from telling you exactly, but I can give you hints, like the one I gave when I first arrived."

"What's lost must be found," Dhal recited, frowning. He didn't trust Zeri. But that didn't matter to Talullah.

"That's right. I do believe Talullah has some experience with this particular potion." The spirit met Talullah's gaze, her stormy eyes igniting the memories locked deep within Talullah's heart.

Talullah peered into the cauldron, its fire warming her shins.

"Think, little Seer."

Her mind projected memories onto the surface of the solution. Three years old and perched on a chair next to her mother, she breathed in spicy aromas and watched her mother's skilled hands pull tiny leaves off woody stems and toss them in a bowl.

A bubble in the potion popped and the memory changed. A few years later, when she'd first started learning to read, she thumbed through the butter-soft pages alone, practicing her pronunciation of the ingredients aloud. Words like *camphor* and *mullein* and *jojoba* each a decadent taste of worlds unexplored and adventures to be had.

The image shifted again.

She'd brewed a few potions on her own, under her mother's supervision, by the time she turned seven. Simple ones, but still. Perhaps that's why she hadn't worried as she snuck out of her bedroom that night and brushed the dust off her mother's recipe book. Something inside it would help her find her mother and bring her home.

"No," Talullah said, trying to push the memory back where it belonged. Every cell in her traitorous body screamed *Yes*. For years she'd tried to drown the memory, to sink it like a stone at the bottom of the river. But it rose, undeterred, a leaf that, no matter how hard she pressed it down, floated when she let go.

On the surface of the potion in the Mazuchawi, her failure held her captive. She wanted to look away, but she couldn't. She watched as the child version of herself counted Lavandula buds and stirred until her arms tired. As realization dawned and hope disappeared.

A ripple broke the memory's spell and Talullah returned to herself. Of course. It had to be the one recipe she'd failed to get right. "The Locator Potion."

"Very good." Hunger crept into Zeri's expression, like a predator that knew it would catch its prey. She sniffed the pot. "It seems to need only finishing touches. I think you know what they are."

Of course she did. But that didn't mean it would work. Knowing the ingredients and the steps hadn't mattered last time. They hadn't helped her find her mother.

"If you know what it is, why haven't you finished it yourself?" asked Hazel, approaching Zeri with balled fists. "What's stopping you?"

"If I could have done it, dear girl, I would have long ago. But potion making is near impossible if one is colorblind. Embarrassing inadequacy for someone with my power, but the Suditzas had a skewed view of creating equality." Zeri spoke through clenched teeth. Air whistled through the gap at the front of her mouth. Had her eyes not promised danger, Talullah might have laughed at the sound. "Spirits have specific gifts. Unfortunately, potion making is not one of mine."

Peeking into the bubbling cauldron, Talullah wasn't sure it was hers, either. But she couldn't let past failures hold her back. And if her mother really was dead, as her missing book suggested, then it wasn't Talullah's fault the spell hadn't worked the first time she'd tried.

Now that she knew what the potion was, the missing ingredient called to her.

"Lavandula buds," she said. "Seven of them." She turned toward the cabinets, but Hazel met her halfway, a jar in hand.

Talullah took it and counted the purple buds into her palm, giving the jar back to Hazel. Everyone crowded around the simmering pot. With a deep breath, she dumped them in.

The potion sizzled and sparkled. Dhalian handed Talullah a large spoon and she stirred the liquid ten times. It changed to silver, stopping between translucent and opaque. "It's done." She stepped back.

"But what are we supposed to find?" Dhalian asked.

"I don't think that story just told us which door to go through," Talullah said, removing Renevelda's pages from her bag once more. The smooth parchment sent tiny tremors through her fingertips. "We've got to find Renevelda's book. Mirella said a person's book is necessary for Altering their story. And this is how we find the sorceress's. Dhal, hand me that dropper."

Dhalian retrieved the tool from the counter and handed it to her. Talullah breathed in the floral scent of the potion. Hope swelled in her chest. It wouldn't be like last time.

She filled the dropper and held the pages out in front of her, forcing her voice to remain even. "A smoke stream is supposed to lead us to whatever we seek." Eyes closed, she focused on Renevelda's book. Her necklace pulsed in time with her heart, steady and confident. It would work.

Drip, drip. The liquid fell in perfect silver droplets onto the middle of the page. Ink bled outward, but Talullah focused on the stream of shimmery smoke rising from the story. It danced like a charmed snake before turning bright violet and circling the cauldron three times.

The flames beneath the pot snuffed out. The potion inside gurgled, then a sound like streaming water emanated from it. "It's draining," Hazel said. But it simply disappeared inch by inch. Talullah fought the urge to scoop it in a tube and save it for later. Now wasn't the time. Her mother couldn't be her priority.

When the liquid had all gone, a rectangular object remained. Talullah reached inside the cauldron.

"We found it," she said. Across the cover, golden thread scrawled *RENEVELDA ANAIDEIA*. Somehow, the book was dry. The leather tome weighed heavy in her hands, but her heart felt lighter than it had in weeks. The book didn't only hold the witch's story. It would determine her sisters' fate. And Talullah's own future.

The scent of lavender wafted through the room, calming her buzzing nerves. Now she just had to find the stone, master Alteration, and change the story before Renevelda interfered. Or before the witch killed her sisters. She didn't know at what point in the spell the sacrifice would happen. But she'd stop it in time. This victory proved her magic had improved.

Dhalian ran his finger along the book's spine. "What's it doing here? Do you think someone else figured out Renevelda's plan and stole the book so the witch wouldn't be able to get it?"

"Or maybe someone hid it for the sorceress, to protect it from anyone who might try to steal it," Hazel said. She glanced at Zeri.

A bolt of lightning zapped the sky. Talullah stole a glance at the Luna Vine. Its leaf was almost full. Their time was up.

"Time to go," she said, hugging the book to her chest. She took a step toward the door.

Zeri blocked her path. "I knew you could do it. Now give me the book. Unless you want to find out what happens when the Mazuchawi disappears."

"What? No. Let us leave. I'm not giving this to you." She tried to pass, but her legs froze.

Dhalian rushed to her side. Hazel darted behind a table to the left, out of Talullah's sight.

"Magic," Talullah said. "Dhal, I can't move."

The second warning bolt flashed overhead.

"I said I'd help you find the stone in exchange for my freedom. And that book promises me my freedom." The spirit bared her teeth. Claws pushed through the tips of her fingers. Sparks flew from them as she swiped the air.

A stinging sensation shot through Talullah's thigh. Blood from three long scratches raced down her leg. "I'm not giving it to you." She brandished her knife, securing Renevelda's book with her other arm. Still, her feet stuck to the ground.

"Shame. I was starting to like you."

Glass smashed as Zeri lunged, showering Talullah in sharp emerald slivers. Coolness permeated Talullah's flesh. An arm yanked her downward.

The edge of the book jammed into her diaphragm as she landed on the ground. She wheezed when the wind knocked out of her, but she forced herself to crawl toward the door.

"I spent my token. We're invisible to her for now," whispered Hazel. "But it won't last. Let's go."

Rough fibers scratched her knees, signaling she'd reached the mat. Dhalian's hand pulled her to standing. The third bolt streaked across the sky.

As the maze dissolved, so did Zeri's silhouette. But Talullah had a feeling they'd see her again.

Chapter 25

A full moon cast a silver glow on the field where the Mazuchawi had stood. Talullah sat up slowly and poked Dhalian's cheek.

"Dhal," she whispered. "Wake up."

He stirred, then opened his eyes. "Where is she? Where's Zeri?"

"Disappeared with the maze."

"Talullah, Dhalian, thank the Divine." Hazel crawled over to them, her clothes ripped and her hair wild. "Are you alright?"

Talullah nodded. "Thank you. For getting us out of there."

"You're bleeding." She pointed at Talullah's leg.

Dried blood peeked through tears in Talullah's pants. "I'm fine."

"I have something at home that will help. Come on. We might even be able to prevent scarring." She stood and offered her hands to Talullah and Dhalian.

Talullah hesitated. The revelation that Hazel and Zeri knew each other shook Talullah's confidence in Hazel even more. It was another piece of evidence she might be working for the enemy. Though it made Talullah's skin crawl to think Hazel might have something to do with her sisters' imprisonment, continuing like normal could just save their lives.

Wincing, Talullah took Hazel's hand and stood. She still clutched Renevelda's book in the other.

As they walked, path lit by staggered streetlights, one fact nagged at her, pleading Hazel's innocence. If Hazel was working for the sorceress, why had she helped them escape? Why hadn't she let Zeri take the book?

Maybe those memories hadn't returned yet and she didn't realize whose side she was truly on. Or maybe that was part of the plan all along. Zeri was a decoy meant to distract Talullah while Hazel gained her trust. It would be too easy to sneak into Talullah's room while she slept and steal the book.

"Wait here," Hazel said when they entered her kitchen. "I may have to mix a fresh batch."

When Hazel was out of earshot, Dhalian bumped Talullah's elbow playfully. "Don't look so glum. We found the book. That's a good thing! Pewter for your thoughts?" He propped his head on his hand, leaning his elbow on the table.

Dull pain throbbed at the base of her skull. She stared at the yellowing flowered wallpaper. "I can't stop turning it all over in my head."

"The Spirit Fox?"

Talullah nodded, whispering, "And Hazel. Do you think it's true? Do you think they made some kind of deal?"

Dhalian shrugged. "Hazel remembered meeting Zeri, but that's all. Zeri could have manipulated Hazel's thoughts. Or maybe she flat out lied. After that theft attempt, I'm not sure I believe anything she says."

"So, you think we should trust Hazel?"

"Trust her? Not particularly. Not until her memories return and we find out for sure. But I don't think we should outright accuse her of being the witch's servant. We still have to find the stone inside the maze, which we can't get into without her."

Dhalian was right. They'd found Renevelda's book, but that was only one piece of the puzzle. She couldn't Alter anything important, or get out of Praeteriti to save her sisters, without the stone. Regardless of Hazel's loyalty, they needed her.

Talullah tapped her fingers on the book cover. Zeri had said something else. That Dhalian had a secret. She hated that the spirit made her doubt her best friend, the only person who'd been completely honest with her since the raid. At least she thought he had. But Zeri's cavalier tone echoed between her ears, calling to mind every time Dhalian had dismissed a question or run his hand through his hair. Could he be lying to her, too?

"So...should we open it?" Dhalian gestured toward Renevelda's book. "Wait a second. I'll check on Hazel first. Since we're not sure if...well, you know." He vanished down the hall but returned soon after. "She's still mixing the healing salve. We have a few minutes," he said, sitting back down.

With caution, Talullah gripped the edge of the cover. "What if it screams like the others?"

"Hazel said those books encase souls of the Unforgiven. As far as we know, Renevelda is still alive so I don't think her book would hold her soul. But maybe keep a tight grasp just in case?" He poised his hands near his ears, ready to cover them if necessary.

She took a deep breath and pulled on the cover.

It didn't budge.

Hell and a half. All that trouble and she couldn't even open it?

"It's stuck." She tried again. Nothing. She shook it. Ran her hands over every inch of it. "Useless." Instinctively she traced the eye charm at her neck. It was hotter than usual. And it grew even warmer.

"Tules..."

"I know." The woven threads of the book's cover glowed brighter, sparkling like the silken strands she'd seen inside Igdrasil the magic tree. From the end of the title, four golden threads loosened themselves and slithered like snakes to the top right corner, entwining into the familiar eye shape. "Dunamai's Eye. The necklace must unlock it."

Of course. A spell protected it. And only someone with Dunamai's Eye could break it.

The book relaxed beneath her fingers, as if exhaling years of tension meant to keep the pages bound tight. She tucked a finger under the marked corner and pulled the cover open. The inside pages were smooth with age, and a thin band of colored threads dotted with tiny knots wound around the perimeter of each one.

Talullah flipped through the first few pages with care, skimming some of the words. She stopped a quarter of the way through. An intricate illustration covered the page.

Three female figures draped in long sleeveless gowns stood near each other on a cloud overlooking a city. Each of their exposed shoulders bore a tattoo—three stars enclosed by a circle. A fourth female stood apart from them, her shoulders bare.

Ruffled edges in the book's center suggested removed pages.

"So that's where the story came from," Dhal said.

"This should help your wound." Hazel's voice echoed down the hallway.

Talullah shut the book and shoved it into her knapsack before Hazel could see them reading. She let Hazel apply the salve and bandage her leg.

"Hazel, would you mind if we just went to bed?" Dhalian asked, giving Talullah a just-go-with-it look.

Hazel's mouth smiled, though the spark didn't reach her cloudless eyes. She nodded but sounded hurt when she spoke. "Of course. It's been quite an evening. We'll talk tomorrow."

Once inside the bedroom, Talullah locked the door. She and Dhalian huddled together on her bed, devouring the sorceress's story. Later chapters detailed Renevelda's time after being cast from the Realm of the Divine. She'd sought the magical community in Viltresor and kept her identity a secret. Learning magic became her sole purpose.

"So, no one in Viltresor knew she was half a goddess?" Dhalian asked. "Wouldn't that be hard to hide?"

"She didn't have the mark, so maybe it was easier than we'd think. Or maybe they knew, but people were too scared of her to do anything about it."

Talullah lost herself in the sorceress's rise to power. Dhalian said goodnight sometime around three in the morning, but she, bleary-eyed, continued reading. Changing an event in the book would save her sisters and father. She needed to find it.

"GOOD MORNING, SCHOLAR." Dhalian's baritone broke Talullah's sleep.

She snapped her head up. His warm brown face came into focus as she blinked. "Hi."

"You know, normal people sleep on pillows. Maybe you should try it sometime." He winked and set a glass of water and mug of tea on her bedside table.

A few gulps of cool water tampered the heat creeping up her neck and into her face. She touched a crease in her cheek. "Guess I fell asleep."

"I'd say sleep probably took you by force. But you'd better hurry. You're going to be late for Mirella." Dhal pointed to the bedside clock and took a bite of toast. Crumbs fell onto her quilt.

"Damn. I already have to tell Mirella we found Renevelda's book in the maze, after she explicitly told me not to go in there. I'd rather not be late, too."

She dressed, brushed her hair and teeth, and met Dhalian at the front door. Hazel was nowhere to be found.

"She left for a shift at Fisher's," Dhal said, answering Talullah's unasked question. "Told me to tell you she'd find us after she gets done."

Outside, he turned right while she turned left.

"You're not coming with me?" she asked. He'd promised to back her up when she told Mirella about the book.

He rubbed his jaw. "There's actually something I need to do."

"Something more important than this?"

Conflict clouded his expression. "I'm sorry. I'll catch up with you later."

She watched him go. Had she not already been late, Talullah would have pressed further. But her aunt appreciated tardiness almost as much as she appreciated a bee in her tea. Which was to say, not at all.

The whole way to Mirella's house, Talullah rehearsed different ways to tell Mirella she'd gone into the Mazuchawi. She'd disobeyed her aunt's rules. All she could do was hope Renevelda's book would be enough to earn forgiveness.

The hairs on the back of her neck stood on end and goosebumps rose on her arms. Talullah stole a glance over her shoulder, suddenly overwhelmed with the strange feeling of being watched. Her heart thumped faster as she increased her pace. Her aunt had been checking on her sisters in Terrapese. Maybe she was doing the same to Talullah. Or maybe the guilt of keeping her own secrets had finally caught up with her.

Though ghosts bustled through town, most paid her no attention. Mr. Miscian, however, waved to her from the apothecary's porch and she returned the gesture. A few others smiled at her or nodded. She pressed her palm to the hilt of her hunting knife sheathed at her waist and flicked her gaze through the crowd. Nothing seemed out of the ordinary.

The sensation of being watched followed her all the way to Mirella's doorstep. She tried to ignore it. It was probably all in her head anyway. As a child she'd often felt that way, despite being all alone in her room with the curtains drawn. Her father had explained how sometimes creative imaginations could invent things that weren't there, and on occasion, those things might be scary. Scary things only had power if she thought about them.

Her throat constricted. Her father had always known what to say and do to ease her or her sisters' qualms. Tears threatened to squeeze from her eyes, but she pushed them back and sent a silent plea into the universe that the woman named Gwendolyn had healed him. Wherever he was, she'd find him.

Talullah banged the sunflower knocker against Mirella's front door and waited. Every other time she'd visited, Mirella had greeted her at the door without her having to knock at all. Was something wrong? With a shaky fist she banged the door and called, "Mirella? Where are you?"

No answer. The door was locked. It wouldn't budge when she tried the handle.

She adjusted her knapsack on her back and stepped in front of the closest window. Pressing her forehead against the cool glass, she cupped her hands around her face to better see inside. No movement, but from what she could see nothing seemed out of place. Maybe Mirella had forgotten about her lesson and was caught up doing something else. Based on past experience it wouldn't be out of character. But, today, of all days Talullah needed to speak to her.

She peeked through the other front window and sighed.

A soft noise filtered its way into her ears. Music? There wasn't another building for at least half a mile. So, Mirella was home.

Talullah stepped off the porch and eased her way into the side yard, squeezing past overgrown bushes and ignoring the snags they tore in her tunic. The music grew louder as she crept through the garden, trying her best not to crush any of the flowers.

Maybe she could get in through the sunroom.

Vines tugged at her ankles. Three jerks of her leg made the plants recede. Was it her imagination, or was the garden trying to dissuade her from walking through it?

Finally, she reached the edge of the windowed sunroom. A crisp freshness washed over her. The smell that foreshadowed rain.

A drop of cool water landed with a soft splash on her forehead. Others quickly followed.

"Mirella," Talullah called as she pounded on the glass of the sunroom. "Let me in. It's starting to rain." The music continued playing and there was no indication Mirella had heard her. "Of course she's busy now," Talullah grumbled to herself.

Ducking under a tree for cover, she opened her bag and fished for anything she could use to protect herself from the steady rain. Books, books, more books. Didn't she have anything else in her bag? She opened some of the pockets. Spools of thread, tins of healing salve, a wedge of stale bread.

An unseen force drew her to the smallest interior pocket. Her fingers tingled as she untied the strings. There was no way something large enough to cover her would fit inside it, but she stuck her hand in anyway.

Fabric smooth as silk and luscious as velvet brushed against her fingertips. Her brows knit together.

She pinched the plush material and removed it from the pocket. It was dark as Nainehta Forest after sundown. Hints of embroidered golden swirls peeked out from beneath the folds. When she unfolded it fully, her breath caught in her chest and she almost dropped the cloak.

Gillie had somehow hidden the cloak, the *Nemosyn*, in her bag. Tiny shocks jumped from the fabric into her palms, making them buzz, but not in a painful way. It was the same feeling she'd had when she'd entered the Mazuchawi. *Magic.*

Talullah froze with the cloak held out like a dress she was considering buying at the Hidden Market. What had Gillie said about it? It held memories, but it also could protect its wearer from external forces.

If only she'd realized she had it in the maze. Dhal wouldn't have gotten burned by the Kleindraaks. Actually, that whole room would have been easier to navigate had they been protected. Maybe she shouldn't have dismissed it so quickly.

Clutching the silky cloak to her chest she breathed in its lavender scent, which mixed with the crisp and cool rain. Had it been warmer she might have mistaken it for a summer day in River Hill. On a day like that she would have helped her father organize the inventory and tutored her sisters. When the work was finished, she would have curled up with a book, hearing the promises of faraway lands drip down her window and dreaming of undiscovered adventures. Now, all she heard was, *I miss normal*. All she dreamed of was home.

For half a second, she hesitated. Gillie had used a glittering powder and drawn a symbol in the air when he'd wanted her to use the cloak as a *Nemosyn*. If she didn't do either of those things, it would just keep her dry and warm until she got inside Mirella's. Alteration lessons would be enough magic for her. Especially after her last trip inside the maze.

She closed her bag and slung it over her back before slipping on the cloak, making sure it covered her bag as well. She didn't want her books—especially Renevelda's book—to get damaged. She cinched the belt and pulled the hood over her head. Instant warmth spread through every inch of her body. She stuck her arm into the rain as a test. Droplets plopped onto the thin fabric, but the water didn't soak through. Instead, it evaporated.

Satisfied, she took a step forward. Before she cleared the tree's cover, her vision blurred.

Chapter 26

Her stomach dropped as if she'd missed a step and the pattering of rain, and its fresh scent, faded.

She blinked, and when she opened her eyes, she was somewhere else entirely.

The purple tinted memory flickered into being around her, as real as if she truly stood in the middle of Nainehta Forest. Tall grass swayed in the breeze as the sun made its descent. The smells of pine and earth danced through the air. She sat perched on a smooth tree branch overlooking the forest, waiting for something.

A twig snapped, and she turned to locate the source. A teenage girl, not much older than Talullah herself, crept through the trees. Her waterfall of long dark hair cascaded from under the hood of her cloak as she moved, her hand grasping something at her collarbone. Though her face was hidden, a tingling of recognition buzzed in Talullah's veins.

Talullah watched as the girl scrutinized each tree and finally stopped at one Talullah herself knew—Gillie's house.

In seconds, Talullah's perspective changed. She stood behind the girl, whose hand hovered near the door, ready to knock but hesitating. The swirls on her cloak glistened, despite the fading light.

"Can't help you," said Gillie's gravelly voice from somewhere inside the memory. Even through the muffled filter of her vision, Talullah could tell it was his.

The girl turned without meeting Talullah's gaze, her hair covering her face. "Please, I know you can. Please," the girl begged, desperation thick like sap in her tone.

"You're mistaken. I can do nothin' for you," said Gillie's bodiless voice.

The girl lifted her eyes to Talullah's and brushed the hair behind her ears.

A shock ran up Talullah's spine.

Hazel.

Hazel knew Gillie.

She had worn the magic cloak before Talullah.

Gillie had refused to help Hazel do something.

Was it Hazel's memory she had witnessed, or Gillie's?

The pieces drifted quickly downstream in her mind like a shattered raft, fading from view and threatening to disappear over the edge of a waterfall. She struggled to hold onto every detail. Even if she managed to keep them in her mind, she still needed to know what Gillie refused to help Hazel do. That was the rope that would hold the raft together.

Blinking the world into focus she found herself lying on the wet grass beneath Mirella's tree. Sharp pulses jabbed behind her eyes, and her stomach churned. With caution, she pushed herself into a seated position and leaned against the tree trunk.

I will not throw up. I will not throw up. I will not—

She heaved. Nothing came up, but her mouth watered and she spat over her shoulder. Sweat trickled down her face. A few moments passed during which she concentrated on breathing steadily with her eyes closed. When the queasiness had subsided, she stood. It wasn't the worst reaction she'd had to a vision. In fact, five minutes was a record fast recovery. Maybe she was getting better after all.

Was that the same memory Gillie had tried to show her before she left his house? If so, why would he have wanted her to see him refusing to help Hazel? And why wouldn't he have just told her? Though her stomach felt better, her head throbbed. She didn't have enough information or energy to put it together alone.

Her knocks, again, went unanswered. Fine. Mirella clearly had something more important to do. But Talullah needed answers.

She burst through the glass door of Fisher's Diner still wearing the cloak. The ghosts inside stared at her, but she ignored them. Crossing the checkered floor, she scanned for Hazel's long glossy hair. Three laps around and still no luck. Damn. Where was she?

About to take a fourth lap, she spotted Dhalian in a corner booth. Head bowed, his hands moved scraps of parchment to different positions on the table.

"Have you seen Hazel?" she asked, approaching him.

He jumped, looking up at her. "For Founders' sake, make some noise or something. You'll give a guy a heart attack sneaking up like that."

"Where's Hazel?"

"I'm sure she's around somewhere. Haven't seen her, though. Better question: why are you dressed like Merlin?" He touched her sleeve.

"Actually, that's why I'm here. I think it's Hazel's. I found it in my bag when I got caught in the rain. Gillie the wood faerie gave it to me. Well, he tried to give it to me and I refused, but then he snuck it in my bag anyway. It's an object that holds memories, called a *Nemosyn*. This one also protects against the elements."

Dhalian slowly swept the parchment pieces into a pile and lay his hands on top. "Could we take the speed down a few ticks?"

Talullah huffed. "Sorry. The cloak is a *Nemosyn*. And I just saw the attached memory." She recounted the memory for Dhalian. "So, Hazel and Gillie know each other, or did at some point, and Gillie refused to help Hazel do something."

"Do you think Gillie is working for Renevelda, too, then?" Every few seconds he snuck a glance at the parchment pile as if checking to make sure it was still there.

"That's the funny thing. I don't think he is. The way he reacted when I asked him about it, I may as well have asked him if he murdered wolf puppies."

Dhalian blinked, blank-faced.

"He has a pet wolf," she clarified.

"Right. That makes more sense. Well, then maybe Hazel isn't working for her either."

"That, or Gillie wouldn't help her because he knew she *was*."

Out of breath, Talullah gripped the table. She'd run all the way to the diner and had barely breathed since.

"Do you want to sit? You look like you might spew on my shoes."

She sank into the seat across from him, the booth's vinyl creaking as she moved. "Sorry to dump that all at once."

"It's fine, Tules. I'm here for you. You know that." He smiled, but his eyes didn't shine.

"Do I, though?" She hadn't meant to bring it up. But she couldn't take it back now.

"What?" Dhal's shoulders stiffened.

A sigh escaped her pursed lips. "You disappear for hours at a time. You won't tell me what you're doing. And Zeri said you have a secret." There. She'd said it.

"Zeri said a lot of things that might not be true."

"Was she lying about you?"

He gently tugged on his tunic sleeve. "No," he whispered.

"Does it have something to do with these papers you apparently think I can't see?"

He melted against the booth. "I'm sorry, Tules. I'm not quite finished." He lay the pieces so the lines connected, forming a mostly-complete picture.

Some had been sewn together with thick black thread. Unsmudged charcoal lines formed shapes like paths, winding around the surface, twisting and turning. Where had she seen lines like that before?

As he flattened his final piece, Talullah recalled her vision of a boy in a stone room.

She moved to his side of the booth. "I had a vision when I was in the forest, before I found you. A bird delivered parchment to someone." Looking at him now, she knew it was Dhalian she'd seen. "Someone sent these to you while you were in the castle."

He nodded. "Hours after they caught me, the first one arrived with a note on the back that said, 'Solve the puzzle.' I don't know who sent them, though. Or why."

Puzzle.

"It's a map. I've just figured that part out. To where, though, I'm not sure." The booth creaked as he shifted. "It's still missing a big chunk. I don't know if it's important or not. I was hoping to figure it out before I showed you. Didn't want to give you false hope."

Lines so dark they could have just been applied. Paper like fine silk. A map to an unknown destination. A light flicked on in her brain. Of course. She rummaged through her bag hoping she hadn't lost it. "Where is it? Where is it?"

"Tules?"

"I've seen marks like this before." She unlatched an inside pocket and her fingers grazed the water-smooth paper. "On this." Unfolding it gently, she lay the map Gillie gave her next to the one Dhalian had constructed. The torn side of hers matched perfectly with his unfinished edge. "Gillie also gave this to me before I left his house. He said he didn't know where it led, but that it might help. I figured half a map would be useless, so I never looked too closely."

Considering it now, she realized her mistake.

Square around the outside, the inside of the map divided into different paths. Each path spidered from a section at the top-middle of the page. A flame sat in the section's center. Tree sketches lined the bottom, the only section with an exit. Only two paths opened to the trees. The rest were dead ends. Various other symbols freckled sections of the map, but one caught Talullah's attention. Hidden among the trees, a purple dot marked the end of a J-shaped symbol, the only color in the whole picture.

This is one puzzle that's never been solved. Hazel's comment from their first foray into the maze returned to Talullah. Lost memories be damned, a part of Hazel had recognized the maze for what it was. Dunamai's Eye warmed against her chest as she placed her finger on the dot. "This is a map of the Mazuchawi." The memory in the cloak, the map. It all fit. "Hazel knew the stone was hidden in the maze. And she wanted Gillie to help her find it."

Chapter 27

According to the manager at Fisher's, Hazel hadn't shown up for her shift. No one in town had seen her since the previous night. Except, apparently, Mirella.

"I need to talk to her, Mirella." Talullah's pleading had gotten her nowhere with her aunt, though the worry lines in Mirella's face suggested she knew something she wasn't revealing. She hadn't even scolded Talullah for entering the Mazuchawi. Her sighs hinted she knew even before Talullah told her. Damn mirrors. Of course she knew. But Talullah had things more important than her aunt's spying to worry about. Like whether Hazel was working for Renevelda. And finding the stone.

"I understand your concerns, Talullah. We will address them later. For now, Alteration is our main focus." She held up Renevelda's book. "With the stone—"

"And where were you this morning? And what was that music?" Talullah couldn't help interrupting.

"I'm sorry I was otherwise occupied this morning. I was helping Hazel with something and lost track of time. And sometimes I like listening to music. Last I checked that is not a crime." She raised a brow.

"So, you have seen Hazel."

"Yes. And that is all I will say on the matter at the moment."

"But—"

"Talullah. This interrogation is over."

Talullah shot Dhalian a look to say, *a little help please*? He sank further into the sofa and shook his head.

Talullah grimaced but bit her tongue as Mirella continued.

"As I was saying, with the stone, you will be able to rewrite events within this tome. Until then, we can use it to discover our enemy's weaknesses. Keep it safe." She handed the book to Dhalian. "It's too risky to attempt to Alter the sorceress's story without the stone. We will practice again on mine. Dhalian, you can sit there." She pointed at a peach colored armchair in the corner of her sitting room. "Let's begin, Talullah. Close your eyes. Concentrate. Let my voice wash over you like an autumn mist. Feel it, but See through it. Picture my garden."

The vision came with little effort.

Mirella's garden appeared. Talullah's fingers loosely gripped the purple thread that clung to a page near the back of Mirella's book. Knotted to a green thread, it pulled taut. She hesitated. Mirella had told her to disconnect the threads and change one of the plants in the garden, but she wouldn't allow Talullah to See what events the green thread held. It seemed so insignificant to change what Mirella grew in her garden. And yet, it was knotted with another event. It did have some kind of impact.

"Don't seek the possibilities of the connected event, Talullah," scolded Mirella, somehow knowing what she was thinking.

She wanted to ask why, but speaking would break her hold on the memory and cause her to start over. Fatigue already circled her like a vulture. Beginning again would wreck her, and she needed to conserve her strength. Hazel had told her she was well enough to enter the Mazuchawi that night.

Tendrils of curiosity reached out for the green thread's possibilities, but she froze them.

Concentrate.

Immersing herself in the memory, she allowed Mirella's thoughts to cover her own, leaving enough consciousness to direct the Alteration.

Three small dishes of seeds sat on the ground in front of Mirella, each labeled with a tag.

In the original memory, Mirella chose thyme, but she was supposed to change it to rosemary. Talullah repeated her task three times to solidify it.

Holding onto that thought, she slid her thumb and forefinger down the thread until the knot pressed into the pads of her fingers. She rolled it first to loosen the threads, then used both hands to carefully separate them. It was the first time she'd handled a knot in the threads of Time, but she'd been untangling knots of this kind since before she could remember. Her fingers moved almost of their own volition, quick and precise.

Within seconds the threads hung loose in her grasp, no long attached to each other.

"Good. Now find the scenario in which I choose rosemary." Mirella's voice floated around her in ethereal waves.

Talullah didn't stop to watch each possibility's outcome, despite her intense desire to do so. She plowed through the emerald-tinted scenes listening for that one key word. When she heard it, she grabbed the green thread as quickly as she could. In her haste, she pulled another thread in with it.

The scene froze with her inside of it. For a brief second, she thought she'd somehow broken Mirella's memory.

And then the vision shifted, restarting as if she'd been in it the whole time.

She still stood in Mirella's kitchen, but Mirella wore a dress instead of her robe. Talullah tried to pull herself back to the herb memory, but the threads had tangled, trapping her fingers.

Hazel sat in a chair and spoke to Mirella. "I found it this morning. It's familiar for some reason, like a memory I used to have but can't quite grasp."

"Just put it back where you found it, dear. I'm sure it's nothing."

"Mirella, I've been remembering things." She grabbed Mirella's hand. "I don't know what they mean, but I'm scared."

"It's alright, dear. Are you thirsty?" She uncapped a bottle of cloudy orange liquid and offered it to Hazel.

"Where did you get this? I ran out a few days ago." Hazel accepted the beverage and took a large swig.

"This is the last one. Don't worry about the memories. Everything is going to be okay." Mirella smiled, but her eyes didn't light up. "You'd better go get ready for your shift at Fisher's. I'll visit tonight."

As Hazel left the scene, the vision wavered, but the past version of Mirella didn't seem to notice. "It's happening too soon," she said.

Present Mirella's voice cut through the memory. "Come back, Talullah. It's time to come back."

Talullah harnessed her consciousness enough to work her fingers free of the threads.

"Why?" she said as the sitting room came back into focus. "Why did you make her forget?"

Stars winked in the corners of her vision. The room spun her in circles, like the time she'd ridden the carousel at the Sunflower Festival. She wanted off the ride, but with every inch she moved it spun faster.

Her head throbbed. Five minutes passed before she could look at her aunt and not see double.

"What did you See that got you so flustered?"

"My vision changed. I tangled another thread in with the one you told me to Alter. When I touched it, I couldn't hold onto the rosemary memory. I saw you talking to Hazel. You gave her the Lethe juice."

"Wait, what?" Dhalian said from across the room.

Mirella shifted from one foot to the other. "Yes. I didn't want to. Not at first. But it was for her own good. And yours."

Talullah stood, her fists balled. "You keep saying these things are for my own good. You told me not to go in the maze, but when I did, I found Renevelda's book. Did you know it was in there? Were you trying to keep me from finding it?"

Her aunt seemed to shrink before her eyes. With a shaky hand, Mirella smoothed flyaway hairs into her gray bun. They were as out of control as Talullah felt. "No, I didn't know it was in the maze. I should have guessed. But I didn't."

"Why? I know she was looking for the stone. The memory from the cloak made that much clear. Why would you conceal her memories, knowing that? Knowing they were the key to getting out of here and to rescuing my family."

"Seeing comes with its burdens, dear. We don't always like what's written, but that doesn't mean we ignore it. It doesn't mean we can change it. Even with Dunamai's Eye, some events remain unchangeable. And so, we do what we have to do. I'm sorry for not telling you but doing so wouldn't have changed anything. If it were my choice, I would have told you everything a long time ago. But these are not my secrets to tell, and I have sworn to keep them."

Talullah suppressed the urge to stamp her foot like a petulant child, but she let her words froth with anger. "My—*our*—family is in danger, Mirella. What secret could be more important than saving them?"

Mirella stared at her for a moment, considering yet calm. "Have you not considered that keeping the secret *enables* the saving? I think that's enough for today. I have other things to tend to."

Talullah followed Mirella through the narrow hallway, past closed doors concealing other secrets whose whirs and smoke leaked through the cracks. "Please, Mirella. Help me understand."

"I've tried, Talullah. You don't listen." Mirella turned the silver knob of a dark door. Before opening it, she turned. "I'm doing my best to help you, dear. But I can only do so much if you don't trust me."

The door slammed and locked, leaving Talullah staring at its sleek finish. She knocked, though she knew her aunt wouldn't answer. Turning on her heel and stomping back down the hall, she gestured for Dhalian to follow her out the front entrance. He, at least, was still on her side.

Chapter 28

Talullah stormed across town, her boots heavy against the cobblestones, Dhalian trailing close behind. First, a mystery ally at Castle Terrapese whom Mirella refused to name. Now, modifying Hazel's memories. Secrets. So many secrets.

She whirled without warning, throwing her hands in the air. Dhalian crashed into her and stumbled backward. "Why can't she just tell me? I don't understand."

Three ghosts dressed in saris stopped in front of the grocery store across street, whispering among themselves. Two more in fur coats rounded the corner and stopped at the sight of her and Dhalian.

"No, I'm fine. Yeah, don't worry about me. I'll just pick myself up," he said.

"Sorry." She helped him upright. "Nothing to see here, folks." Talullah waved her hand with impatience and the ghosts went on their way, chattering. "I'm so sick of being lied to."

Dhalian dusted off his clothes. "Understandable. But—"

"But what?" She folded her arms across her chest. "Don't tell me you agree with what she did?"

"Not entirely. But you heard what she said. Maybe something she Saw predicted bad things happening if she told you. Maybe the only way for you to succeed is if you *don't* know."

"Mirella can't see the future, remember? Only the present." Talullah scraped the toe of her boot against the ground. Slowly, connections formed in her mind. "Mirella said it wasn't her secret to keep, meaning she wasn't the one to See it. It had to have been Hazel's vision. Why else would Mirella have suppressed her memories?"

"Hazel made the Lethe juice, though." Dhal adjusted his sleeves.

"Whatever Hazel Saw, she didn't want to remember, so she made the Lethe juice. But she couldn't trust herself to remember to drink it. She needed someone else to do that for her. She needed Mirella. And according to the vision I just had, Hazel's out of Lethe juice."

"Which means she's going to start remembering soon, if she hasn't already."

"I'm willing to bet a hundred Noktos that whatever Hazel's hiding has to do with the Mazuchawi and the stone," said Talullah.

"Then we'd better find her fast." Dhalian raised a lanky arm and pointed. "Because there's the maze."

IT WAS ALMOST AS IF Hazel knew when the maze would appear. When Talullah and Dhalian arrived, out of breath, she already stood in front of the twisted archway. The air hung thick with tension. So much had happened since Talullah had last seen Hazel, she didn't know what to say. What she wanted was to question Hazel about everything she'd seen in her vision and to ask what she'd wanted to forget. But Dhalian spoke first.

"How are you feeling?" he asked, tentative.

Hazel brushed her dark hair from her face. Thin lines at the corners of her eyes and mouth aged her, as if she'd just woken from years of sleep. "I've been better. The headaches are awful, and my vision has been spotty. But I'm doing okay for now. I had to be here. The maze feels like more than just a game now, doesn't it?"

She remembered, then. She must. Before Talullah could speak, Hazel continued.

"Mirella told me what you Saw. I wish I could help, but I just don't remember yet. I have pieces, but I can't quite put them together." Regret stained her dark brown eyes, but their sharpness gave Talullah hope. The clouds from the Lethe juice had receded. She'd remember soon.

Until then, they had to press forward.

"Ready?" Talullah asked.

Vines snaked down to seal the entrance behind them. Through the opposite door, they found the potion room just as they'd left it, except twelve identical doors had appeared along the perimeter.

Dhalian unfolded the map he'd constructed so all three of them could see. "It's—"

"A map of the maze," Hazel finished. Surprise tinged her quiet voice. She traced the path they'd traveled so far. "Where did you get this?"

"Half came from Gillie the wood faerie." Talullah studied Hazel's expression in search of a flicker of recognition. None appeared.

"And someone sent the other half to me in pieces," said Dhalian.

"Lucky," Hazel said, still starting at the parchment. "Well, which way?"

Talullah grabbed the corner of the map. "What's this? She hadn't noticed the faint symbol before, but a tingle in her hands begged her to touch it. Beneath her fingertip, the drawing of Dunamai's Eye glowed brighter. From the symbol flowed a stream of ink-smooth light. It started at the maze entrance and wove through the lines, leaving a trail of glistening purple in its wake. With a flourish, it ended at the purple dot among the trees.

"I guess that answers your question, Tules." Dhalian squinted at the map, then at the doors. "This one." He rapped on the third door from the left.

"Are you sure?" Talullah asked.

"Positive."

"Okay." The simple brass knob turned without a key and she pushed it open.

A forest thick with trees lay ahead of them. Gauze-like mist hovered inches above the ground. Fallen leaves crunched beneath their boots as they moved into the maze's third section. Different from Nainehta, the atmosphere was calm. It reminded Talullah of the woods she explored as a child, full of innocent mystery.

"Now what?" Hazel asked.

"Look." Talullah pointed at the map. A blinking dot marked their location. "We just have to follow the purple path." She gestured for the group to move in the direction the line indicated. But their dot moved the opposite way.

"That doesn't make sense." Dhalian moved them ninety degrees in the other direction and their dot joined the line once more.

"Something must be interfering with the directional charm," Hazel said. "We'll have to navigate on our own, I guess."

"That could take hours to figure out," Talullah said, deflated. "The dot moves somewhere different even if I go in the same direction."

Dhalian glanced around at their surroundings. "And the boundaries on the map don't match with what's here. I mean, we're literally surrounded by just trees."

Talullah rifled through her bag. "I think I still have a compass in here somewhere. That'll be better than wandering aimlessly. Maybe there's a pattern to the directions." She found the golden heart-shaped compass and held it out in her palm. "It points south instead of north, but it's at least a reference point."

"Did you say south?" Dhalian snapped her attention to Talullah. "Let me see that."

Talullah handed the compass to him.

"I've seen this before. In the castle." Words tumbled from his mouth in a hurried stream. "I overheard a man and woman talking while I was being transferred to my cell. He handed it to a woman with bouncy blond hair and said, 'Make sure she gets this.' And then she said, 'Will she know what to do with it?' And then he said, 'Yes. Once the other pieces are delivered.' Where did you get this, Tules?"

"At the Hidden Market the day before the raid." Her speech slowed. "The seller had curly blond hair. I thought it was odd of a fortune-teller to sell something like this. It's outside her normal stock of wares. But it was too interesting to pass up. She made a big deal about the cryptic engravings."

"Sounds like she knew her audience." Dhalian smirked.

"She meant me to have it. And the pieces the man mentioned must have been the map. Whoever they are, they knew even before I did that I'd be looking for the stone. And they knew you'd help me." Both the map and compass had come from Castle Terrapese. Her shoulders tightened. Years of merchants' warnings about Terrapesian soldiers and her own recent experiences with them set off alarms in her head. How did she know Renevelda hadn't orchestrated the plan so Talullah would retrieve the stone for her?

She didn't. But this was the best chance she had at finding it and saving her sisters. Consequences she'd have to deal with later.

"Maybe it points south for a reason," Hazel said.

"Worth a shot." Talullah spun so the compass pointed due south and gestured for the others to follow. Ten minutes later, after turning south every time the arrow shifted and despite the tree line not matching the drawn boundaries on the map, their course still followed the purple line.

"We're getting closer," Dhalian said.

"Very good, little Seer," said a girlish voice.

The sound froze Talullah's blood. A fluffy red ponytail swished out from behind a tree.

Zeri flashed a smile of daggers. "But you're running out of time."

Chapter 29

The Luna Vine crawled across the trunk of the nearest tree. Since they were no longer in a room with walls, it appeared on a different tree every time they moved. Its second thorn had almost fully formed.

Talullah's mouth grew dry. Unless they turned back now, they wouldn't have time to get back to the entrance if the warning bolts sounded.

Zeri stalked toward Talullah, her eyes hungry.

"What do you want?" Dhalian took a place at Talullah's right. His hand clutched his knife.

Hazel stood to Talullah's left. Waves of rage rolled off her like an incoming tide.

"To impart wisdom, of course." Zeri skipped back and forth as she sang. "A simple touch is all you need, for trust and hope and love to bleed. Take the hand and just ask why, you'll find your truth within the lie." A grimace harshened her delicate features. She spat. "Ridiculous rhymes. Curse the Suditzas and their sick sense of humor. Nonetheless," she said, stopping in front of Talullah. "It's time you understand who you can truly trust."

"Not you," Dhalian said. "Obviously."

Zeri raised her brows. "Oh? We don't see eye to eye on that." She yanked Dhalian's sleeve upward, exposing his wrist.

Talullah gasped. A raised pink scar in the shape of an 'R' decorated his flesh.

"That's not a burn," Talullah said, breathless.

"No," Dhalian said quietly, not meeting Talullah's gaze.

"Why don't you tell Talullah how you got it?" Poison dripped from Zeri's words.

"Tules, you have to understand—" He froze.

So did Talullah and Hazel. Zeri's raised hand and satisfied smile told Talullah she'd done it.

"Let's find out," Zeri said. She snapped and Talullah's hand moved to Dhalian's wrist.

When her fingers met scarred flesh, her vision blurred.

They were in a stone cell with one small barred window. Anticipation and nerves strangled the air. A purple film covered everything in sight.

A memory.

She experienced it from the owner's perspective, like when she'd practiced her Sight with Mirella.

Thoughts flicked through Talullah's mind. How had she been so stupid as to accidentally wander onto the castle property? Master Norr wouldn't be pleased about this at all, that was for sure. Norr always said to be aware of one's surroundings. Perfect time to ignore Norr's advice. One year into the apprenticeship and she'd already managed to mess things up. If she got out of there, there was no way Norr would let her go anywhere on her own for a while.

If she got out. The seriousness of her capture finally took root inside her, strangling all thoughts of Norr and his disappointment. What did Terrapesians do with trespassers? Would they cut off her hands, like ancient civilizations did with thieves? Or remove her tongue so she couldn't spill their secrets? She pressed it against the roof of her mouth and grimaced.

Would they let her leave at all, or was she destined to rot in a dank cell with only her regrets for company?

Talullah's mind struggled to separate her own thoughts from Dhalian's memory. She shivered, but whether from her discomfort or his she couldn't be certain.

A heavy metal door clanged open. "Out," a burly guard grunted, pointing first to Talullah then to the hallway through the open door. Hatred blazed in the pit of her stomach. *Rantoul.*

The desire to draw her knife and slice his throat raged inside her. But her limbs wouldn't do what she told them. Stuck in Dhal's memory, she could only do what he'd done at the time, which was to try to stand.

Her hands and feet were bound. She wiggled and swung her arms forward for momentum, but she fell face down on the cold stone floor. "Umm, not to be a bother or anything," Dhal's voice said, "but you wouldn't be able to help a guy out would you?"

A thick hand grabbed the back of her tunic and pulled her to her feet. Her mind urged her to spit in his face, but again the memory stopped her from acting on her own ambitions. "Ah, right, thanks. Bit difficult to maneuver when the hands and feet are tied, you know?"

Remain calm. Think of a way out. Don't let the enemy sense weakness. Maybe if she cooperated, she'd get a lesser punishment.

Rantoul stared at her with a bored expression. Based on what she'd overheard in Nainehta Forest, prisoner duty was the last thing Rantoul wanted to be doing.

"Well," Dhal's voice continued, "I guess *you* probably don't know about maneuvering with bound hands and feet. You're probably more accustomed to doing the binding, I suppose. In your position, that is."

Rantoul pointed through the doorway. "Out. Now."

The metal chains weighed her legs down as she shuffled after Rantoul. Agonizing screams echoed down the hall. The hair on

Talullah's arms stood on end. Punishment? What had they done? Would she suffer the same fate?

Rantoul doubled back. "Why are you so slow?" He looked at the leg shackles as if noticing them for the first time and huffed in annoyance. He produced a small key from somewhere inside his giant cloak then looked at Talullah. "Don't run."

"Run? Me? No, wouldn't dream of it," Dhal's voice said, shaking. Talullah shook her legs, one after the other, as the shackles clattered to the ground.

"Follow. Don't. Run."

Talullah obeyed silently.

Rantoul must have had a bad day that day, Talullah thought in her own mind. Caprico hadn't been able to shut him up that night in the forest. Or maybe he'd just been drunk.

After three long hallways they reached a large painted door. Rantoul pointed at a small wooden chair next to the door and said, "Sit. Wait." He gestured to another guard a few feet away, opened the door, and disappeared behind it, closing it before Talullah could see inside.

She could run. Disappear through one door or another and hide. A diminutive kitchen servant passed by with a curt nod. He couldn't be older than seven or eight. She opened her mouth to address him. Maybe some of the servants would help her escape.

A bitter taste coated her taste buds. Or they'd turn her in. She closed her mouth. Regardless, the castle was huge. She had no idea where any of the exits were, and they'd be guarded, anyway. Unarmed and obviously a prisoner, she didn't stand a chance.

She tried not to think about prison cells or dull blades hacking through her limbs. Still, her leg jiggled in anticipation. Waiting was almost as torturous as the punishments running through her mind.

The door opened and Rantoul reappeared, motioning for Talullah to follow him inside.

Who has a sitting room without anything to sit on? Talullah thought in Dhal's voice as she entered the room. Four jewel-toned tapestries covered most of the stone walls. She was about to ask where she was, but Rantoul was already gone.

She made her way over to one of the windows and peered out. The setting sun's pink light stabbed at her eyes. Rantoul had taken her to one of the towers on the west end of the castle, a few stories up. She wobbled as she gazed downward. Jumping to freedom was not an option.

Talullah smirked to herself, again in control of her own thoughts. Dhal had always been terrified of heights and clumsier than a horse on stilts.

"I believe you know where to find something I want." The silky-smooth voice burned inside Talullah's ears.

A tall woman in a silk gown stepped out of the shadows. Ice blond waves streamed down her back.

Talullah's heart skipped. The woman was beautiful, but something made Talullah avoid the intense gaze pinning her to the spot.

"I see you have good instincts, Wandering Boy," the woman said. "You don't want to look at me directly, but you're not sure why. It's the eyes. There's power in the eyes, you see."

Realization dawned on Talullah. Renevelda. For the Founders' sake, no. Though she'd known Dhal had been in the castle, she hadn't imagined he'd come face to face with the sorceress herself. What could she possibly have wanted with him? What had she done to him? And why hadn't Dhal told her?

Talullah focused on the spot where Renevelda's silver-blue dress met the floor. The sorceress circled her. "Can you guess why I've brought you here?" Talullah stared at the ground. "You have nothing to say? My guard informed me that you've been chatty. I hoped that would make this easy. We shall see, I suppose." She leaned in close.

Her warm breath sizzled against Talullah's skin. "I seek a necklace. An old and special necklace."

"I haven't got a necklace, Ma'am," Dhal's voice said. Talullah forced herself not to make eye contact.

"Obviously. But you know where it is. I believe it's in a town you know well. A hiding place for traitors who fled Terrapese and Viltresor many years ago to avoid the war. They took some important things with them to their new home, one of which belongs to me. An eye-shaped amulet."

Talullah flinched at feeling Dhal's brain work a mile a minute, his thoughts flooding hers. She had seen the necklace in River Hill. But why would this woman want it? It was a family heirloom. She tried to clear her mind of all thoughts of home. Instead she thought about fishing. It had been a long time since she'd been fishing. She tried to remember how to construct a simple fishing pole, like her dad taught her to do when she was a small child.

"Clever boy. I underestimated your intelligence. But I know you know where the necklace is. And though I hoped this would be a simple and easy exchange, I will go about it the difficult way."

Talullah stared at the stone floor, Dhal's half of her mind focusing on fishing. Find a nice sturdy stick for the pole, one with a little bit of give, but not too much. Want to make sure it won't snap under pressure. Tie a piece of twine or long strip of cloth to the end of the pole. Attach a sharp, curved branch to the end to use as a hook. Use short back and forth motions at first, then a longer sweeping motion, fluid and even. Let it fly.

"The hard way, it is." Renevelda turned to face her. Golden rope secured Talullah to an iron chair. She forced herself to keep her eyes downcast. Mumbled words she couldn't understand wove through her mind. A blazing fire rose up inside her. Sweat dripped from her brow into her eyes. She bit her lip hard enough to taste metallic blood.

Talullah wept inside. Sweet Dhalian who'd always been there for her burned alive from the inside out. He'd saved her after her mother's disappearance. But she couldn't do the same for him.

Renevelda changed her incantation and the fire turned to ice inside Talullah's veins. Shivers ran up her spine in unceasing waves. Tiny icicles broke off in her hands when she touched her eyes. "You have willpower," Renevelda said, almost amused. "But even the strongest of wills can be broken."

Talullah raised her eyes just a bit, needing to see what was coming next. Dhal's face reflected back at her in a six-inch long dagger held at Renevelda's waist. "We all have a weakness, Dhalian. The trick is discovering them. Finding weakness happens to be my specialty. A little hint for you. It's always loved ones."

For the briefest of seconds Talullah's smiling face flashed in Dhal's mind. Talullah tried her best to block out his thoughts. Wrong. So wrong to invade his mind. His privacy.

Trapped in the memory, she couldn't stop Dhalian's thoughts pouring freely into hers. Through his eyes, she saw her own fingers move deftly along the edges of Dunamai's Eye, a pattern they traced so often they'd memorized. Bright compassion shone in her eyes and the gentleness of her touch made his heart skip a beat. The aching hole that formed in his chest when he'd left River Hill.

Pain spread to every inch of Talullah's body. Fire again. Soon she'd be dead on the cold stone floor, just a pile of ashes lost in a memory.

Talullah's vision grew fuzzy. Dhal's voice faded, leaving her own confused thoughts. The pain receded as the room around her darkened into nothingness.

She hovered in the space between sleep and consciousness for a few moments.

"That's how she knew," Talullah whispered, groggily returning to the present. Her head throbbed in time with her heart, each pound a violent smash against her skull.

"Tules?" Dhalian's arms cradled her, now free of Zeri's spell.

Hazel supported her other side.

Talullah told him only what he needed to know. "She tortured you."

He nodded.

"Why didn't you tell me?"

"Because there's more you didn't see." Tears glistened in his eyes. "I had to make it stop. I couldn't handle it anymore. If I was stronger, maybe, but I'm not. I'm weak."

"What happened, Dhal?"

He buried his face in his hands. "I told her how to find River Hill. The raid was all my fault."

Chapter 30

Dhalian kept talking but Talullah didn't hear a word. It was as if someone had turned down her hearing so only faint mumbles filtered through her ears.

She identified the dark blurs in the background as the Mazuchawi's forest of trees, but the rest of the details escaped her.

There must be a mistake. Dhalian—her best friend since birth—never would have revealed the secret they'd all sworn to protect. The town's survival depended on the loyalty of its people and their shared commitment to each other. And yet, River Hill, the only home she'd ever known, lay in heaps of burning rubble. If she returned, would anything be left?

Her father was ill and missing. Renevelda held her sisters—her intelligent, innocent sisters—captive at Castle Terrapese. Now that Talullah had witnessed the sorceress's *methods* firsthand, she couldn't stop picturing Penny and Margot in Dhalian's place.

How? How could he do this to her? After everything they'd been through together.

Worse, he'd lied to her. Over and over and over. Dodged her questions about his wrist, offered little information about his time in the castle. And why? Because he feared she'd discover the truth.

Coward. Had it been her in Renevelda's clutches, she would have protected her loved ones all the way to her grave.

Deep down she knew Dhalian never wanted to hurt her, never meant to turn her world inside out. Maybe that's why his words pierced like arrows in her back. She owed her suffering to the only person who she'd trusted as much as herself. So, what did that say about her?

"Use this to stem the flow." Hazel's voice broke Talullah's reverie. She ripped off her tunic sleeve and wrapped it around Dhalian's wrist. Crimson blood tinged green seeped through the fabric.

"It won't stop," Zeri said. She sat with her legs crossed and drew shapes in the dirt with her finger. "Unless I make it. That's the problem with curses. Always act up at the most inconvenient times. Though I must say, this one has been quite useful to me. Not sure I would have been able to keep up with you, had Renevelda not laced Dhalian's scar with tracking magic."

Dhalian's brown skin turned ashen.

"Make it stop," cried Talullah. He had betrayed her, but she wouldn't do the same to him.

"He's losing too much blood." Hazel ripped off her other sleeve and added it to the makeshift bandage. Crimson coated her hands and arms.

"What do you want?" Talullah stalked toward Zeri, knife drawn.

"You can't hurt me with that. I'm a spirit, remember?" She batted her long lashes, the color of deception.

"Tell me how to make it stop or I'll rip every hair from your head, braid them into a noose, and hang you with it," Talullah growled.

"No need for hostility." Zeri stood and dusted off her fur vest. "My price is fair, I assure you. I'll save your friend's life in exchange for Renevelda's book."

"Anything but that." Though she tried, she couldn't mask her pleading tone. She couldn't. That book was her chance to save her family. But she couldn't let Dhalian die.

"Tick tock, Little Seer. The vine grows."

The first warning bolt flashed overhead.

Hell-damned spirits. Talullah's knuckles whitened, her grip on the book tightening.

"Hurry, Talullah," Hazel called.

"Promise to get us all out of the maze safely and save Dhalian, and we have a deal," Talullah said through gritted teeth.

"Are you really in the position to bargain? With your friend's life at stake?" Zeri cooed.

"Agree to my terms, or I take the book with me when the Mazuchawi goes. Don't think Renevelda would be pleased to know you failed her twice, do you?"

Bolt two streaked above them.

"Fine. I promise to do as you've asked. Now give me the book." Zeri held out her clawed hands.

"Dhalian first. Stop his bleeding."

Zeri stomped her foot but waved her hand. "This is why I avoid humans. Endless demands."

"It stopped," Hazel said.

"Now, the book."

With both hands, Talullah extended Renevelda's book. She'd figure out how to get it back. For now, she had to save Dhalian and get them all out of the maze. "How do I know you'll keep your promise?"

"Spirits are bound by their word. Even if I wanted to—and I want to—break my word, I can't." She took the book and waved her hand, a smile brightening her face. "Pleasure doing business with you, Talullah Bridgestone. I hope that boy was worth it."

As the third bolt struck, white light and smoke filled the maze.

"Please let this work." Talullah flung an arm around Dhalian and Hazel.

When the air cleared, grass tickled Talullah's arms. She lay on the ground with Dhalian and Hazel stirring awake beside her.

Zeri had kept her word. Dhalian lived, and they'd all escaped the maze.

Moonlight streamed down, but a curved shadow fell near Talullah's feet. She turned to see what had caused it and gasped.

After each previous round, it had disappeared to some unknown location. But the twisted archway whispered of rules recently changed.

No more wondering. No more waiting.

Because this time, the Mazuchawi stayed.

TALULLAH WASN'T READY to speak to Dhalian yet. Words eluded her every time she tried to articulate her feelings. Time. That's what she needed. And while he recovered at Hazel's, she took care of something else.

"Tea?" Mirella asked, leading Talullah into the kitchen. Whether or not her aunt knew the purpose of Talullah's visit, she didn't let on.

"Sure. Thanks." She sat at the table and searched the shelves of knick-knacks for answers. How to start? Her last attempt had lacked tact and had gotten a door slammed in her face. Maybe she needed to be less direct. Earn some sympathy first.

"So," said Mirella, setting two mugs on the table, "what can I do for you?"

Talullah told her about the Mazuchawi, Dhal's scar, and the deal she'd made with Zeri. She hadn't been able to talk to Dhalian or Hazel about it, so once she started, the words flowed in a steady stream of consciousness. Though not her original intention, the pressure in her neck and shoulders subsided as if she'd removed from her back a bag full of books. Sharing the burden eased her pain.

Mirella didn't interrupt. When Talullah had finished and finally took a sip of her now lukewarm tea, her aunt sighed with closed eyes. "You have endured so much, Talullah."

"Mirella, what do you know about Hazel? Not her memories, I mean. I know you don't want to—can't—tell me about those. But, was she here already when you arrived?"

A long silence stretched between them. Talullah almost gave up hope she'd get any answers. And then Mirella spoke in a strained voice.

"Yes, she was here already. I tried to convince her to leave with me. I noticed a few of the portals had closed, and I had a feeling the others would, too."

"But she refused? Why?"

"She said her path had been laid and she had to follow it." Mirella studied her tea as if pulling the words from it. "I couldn't let her stay alone."

"If you didn't know her, what obligation could you have had to her?" And then it hit her. "Unless you *did* know her before you arrived in Praeteriti."

Mirella nodded. "She's not a bad person, Talullah. And neither am I. We both have done things we wish we could change and know things we wish to forget. You don't yet understand why I gave her the Lethe potion, why doing so protected her, but you will soon. And when the time comes, I hope you'll have compassion. Facing our own truth is sometimes harder than we expect." She took her empty mug to the counter and rinsed it in the porcelain sink.

Talullah had been prepared for a verbal sparring match. Instead of anger or defensiveness, she'd received solemn admission. It threw her off balance. If her aunt had truly given Hazel the potion to protect her, could Talullah fault her? Could she have done the same thing to someone she cared about, knowing the cost? Doubt purred from its nest in her chest. Maybe she was she too selfish to do the right thing. Talullah stood, her restless mind powering her legs. She needed a distraction from all the thoughts vying for her attention. To clear her head. "Mirella, do you mind if I check on Mar and Penny?"

"Sure, dear. I think you know where to go."

Midnight blue smoke filled the mirror. Hundreds of Talullah's likeness reflected back at her from the other mirrors in the room, but she cared only about the image in the oval one framed in black. Seconds dragged on for hours as she waited for the shimmer to dissipate. Were they okay? She had to know. Needed to see them.

"Mar, Penny," she whispered, daring only to speak as loud as necessary to catch their attention.

Both her sisters cocked their heads. They had heard her. Good.

She assessed their appearances again, as she did every time they spoke. Each new scab or bruise poked a hole in her lungs. Six, today. Three each. Talullah's lip quivered.

Unsticking her tongue from the roof of her mouth, she licked her lips. "Are you okay?" Stupid question. Of course they weren't. But what else could she say? An apology would shatter her. She needed to be strong. As strong as they were.

Without glancing in her direction, they each nodded, almost imperceptibly. If she hadn't done this several times, she wouldn't have noticed.

Had she not given up Renevelda's book, mere days might have separated them. Phantom warmth mimicked their small arms hugging her.

She forced herself to keep going. "I'm so proud of you both. It won't be long now."

What if that was a lie? What if she'd sealed their fate?

Margot's eyes flicked up to the mirror, unknowingly meeting Talullah's gaze and holding it for so long Talullah wondered if her sister really could see her through it.

An abrupt clang broke Margot's eye contact.

"You two. I know you have it." The girlish voice punctured the air like a needle. A flash of bright red hair bled into Talullah's view.

Caprico's baritone contrasted with Zeri's squeal, shrinking her even more by comparison. "Zeri, how exactly do you think these two children stole something from your mistress's personal chambers? Something you put there only hours ago. Have you seen them anywhere near there?" Keys tinkled lightly followed by a click and the groan of old metal.

Caprico and Zeri both entered her sisters' cell. She held her breath, afraid of making any noise that could give her away. If anyone could sense her presence in a different world, it would be the Spirit Fox.

"Enough, Caprico. You know my orders and you know who they came from." Zeri stalked toward Margot and Penny, without a trace of the gentle innocence Talullah had seen when they'd first met. Baring pointed teeth, she hissed, "Where is it? Don't look at me like I'm an idiot. Where's the book?"

"W-we have lots of books, miss." Penny pointed at the pile in the corner of their cell.

Zeri stomped to the corner and picked up one of the books, checking the title. Dissatisfied, she hurled it at Caprico, missing his head by inches. She tugged at the black ribbon tied around her neck and rifled through the rest of the books. "I am so close. Nothing is going to ruin this."

Talullah flinched. Only one book would make Zeri's face pinch like that. Someone had already stolen Renevelda's book. Right from under her nose. And she thought Margot and Penny had taken it.

Bracing herself against the wall, Talullah rationalized. It couldn't be there. How could it be? Her sisters went nowhere without a guard, and Captain Caprico had slept outside their cell every night on Renevelda's orders. Plus, the book hadn't been in the castle long enough for them to figure out where it was, let alone steal it. And they'd never have known what it was in the first place.

"Please, miss, if you would tell us which book you're looking for we could help you find it." Margot blinked innocently, but the corners of her mouth turned up just slightly. A look Talullah had seen many times before, when she'd asked Margot if she'd really finished her arithmetic. Her sister lied.

A knot pressed against Talullah's windpipe. Everything about the situation reeked of botched plans. Had she never given Zeri the book, it wouldn't have been stolen. And the Spirit Fox wouldn't be interrogating her sisters.

Zeri huffed and spun around, swinging her fluffy hair. A grimace settled into her face, hardening her normally delicate features. "You're lucky Mistress has restricted my powers. Forced confessions are my specialty." She flashed her keen nails and returned to her search.

"This one feels different." Blowing her bangs out of her eyes she lifted a large volume and peered at its cover. "The letters have worn off."

Penny and Margot glanced at Caprico and he gave them a small nod, his jaw tense. What did that mean? If he'd done anything to put them in danger, she'd kill him on sight.

With two fingers, Zeri pushed open the book cover. Her eyes sparked, glowing like a freshly lit lamp. A sinister smile crept its way across her small mouth. "I knew it."

Goosebumps raised on Talullah's arms.

"Do you know what you've done? What she'll do to you for this?" Zeri pried the book from its hollow casing and held it out, far enough that even Talullah could read it.

RENEVELDA ANAIDEIA. Four threads braided together wound around the border.

A sour taste coated Talullah's tongue. No. They couldn't have. But Zeri held the evidence in her arms.

Talullah's baby sisters had stolen from the most powerful sorceress in the world.

Chapter 31

Curled in a ball in Mirella's mirror room, Talullah pressed her cheek against the cool wooden floor. Her muscles refused to move. How had she let this happen? Her one job was to protect her sisters. When their mother left, she'd vowed they would never feel the same abandonment that had shredded her heart like a dead leaf.

She'd failed them. Again. She never should have stopped running after Margot's horse. She should have killed Caprico in the forest when she'd had the chance. Instead, she'd let Zeri manipulate her into coming to Praeteriti, enabling Caprico to use her sisters for his own plan. Because he had to have a plan. Maybe he knew about the book's powers and the stone, too. Maybe he meant to use them for himself. Either way, her sisters would pay for his treason. And for her stupidity.

Would the sorceress kill them sooner? Or just torture them within a thread of death, prolonging their pain until it was time to enact her spell? From what Talullah had seen and heard, the sorceress favored a more sadistic style. Slow. Agonizing.

Silent sobs shook her body. What Renevelda wanted most was Dunamai's Eye. The soldiers had searched for her during the raid but had found her sisters instead. It should have been Talullah in that cell.

Mirella found Talullah an hour later and coaxed her into the sitting room. She'd lain awake while her tears evaporated, leaving salty scars in their place.

"Renevelda's book. It's gone." The squishy armchair cushion hugged her hips as she sank into it.

"Don't worry about that, dear. It's taken care of." Mirella set a mug of tea on the wicker side table.

A prickle of understanding raised the hairs on the back of her neck.

"Did you know?" Talullah snapped.

Her aunt sighed. "Dear, you must understand—"

"Did. You. Know?" she repeated, biting off each word. Though she didn't need a verbal response. Mirella's dark circles and rounded shoulders hinted her secrets weighed heavy.

Stern, her aunt said, "I am doing everything I can to help them."

Talullah stood. The mug of tea wobbled. "By almost getting them killed?" Her voice echoed off the ceiling, louder than she'd ever remembered it being. She quieted, each whispered word brimming with venom. "Do you understand what you've done?"

"When you relinquished the book, it ceased to be your decision." Mirella held up a hand to stop Talullah interrupting. "I am not chastising you for the choice you made. Other arrangements have been made to retrieve it. And they are going as planned." Her face softened. "I know you fear for your sisters, but I need you to trust me. They are taken care of."

"Have you seen them?" Talullah erupted.

Mirella nodded. "We all have made sacrifices and will continue to do so. Your focus must remain on finding the stone, Talullah. If you succeed, those sacrifices will not have been in vain. Now, if I'm not mistaken, you have a maze to finish."

"I thought you didn't want me to go in the Mazuchawi?"

"Before I understood its purpose, I didn't. But—"

A ringing sound cut off Mirella's thought.

"Hang on. This must be important." Mirella moved to the diamond-shaped mirror against the back wall and pressed the top corner.

When the blue smoke had dissipated, a blond woman stared through the glass. Wooden crates filled the field of view behind her. "It's time," she said.

Talullah joined Mirella. There was something familiar about the woman. Talullah seen her before somewhere. "Part two is beginning."

"Part two of what?" Talullah asked.

"Okay," Mirella said. "When we have the stone, I'll send the signal. Thanks, Gwen."

Gwen. *Gwen.* The name of the woman taking care of her father.

"Wait, miss," Talullah called. "Are you by chance—"

"Gwendolyn Caprico," the woman interjected.

"—taking care of Daniel Bridgestone?" Talullah finished at the same time.

"Cap-Caprico? As in Captain Caprico, the man responsible for endangering my sisters, Caprico?" Talullah's nails dug half-moons into her palms.

"He's a soldier in name only, I assure you. I can't explain everything. But I can let you talk to your father." She disappeared from view then reappeared in a cozy living area. A brick fireplace against the far wall housed crackling flames.

Once again Gwendolyn disappeared, but Talullah's father's face took her place. "My Talullah," he said, his voice shaking. His words embraced her. He buried his face in his hands. "My girls. I'm so sorry."

"Father. No. Shhh. It's okay. We're all okay. I've been so worried about you." She touched the glass, imagining she could tuck the peach-colored quilt around his bony shoulders. "That day we got separated and the soldiers took Margot and I thought you were with

Penny, but they got her, too." Her throat tightened with each word until the last one was barely audible. "What happened to you?"

"Had a run-in with one of Renevelda's men. Nasty fellow. He stole my cane and then my legs gave out. Luckily Gwendolyn's husband found me and brought me here. I'm alright now. Have you got it?"

"Got what?"

"I'm sorry, Daniel. We have to hurry. It's good to see you." At Mirella's interjection, her father's jaw clenched.

"It's okay, Father. We'll be together soon. All of us. Gwen?"

Gwendolyn reappeared in the frame.

"What's happening now? Where are my sisters?"

"Colfax—the Captain—is getting your sisters out of the castle. It won't be long before Renevelda realizes they—and her book—are missing. So, you need to find the stone."

"The book. But Zeri—?"

"Took a fake. She'll figure it out soon, but it should buy them enough time to clear the grounds. A messenger will bring the book to you after we've secured your sisters at the safe house. But he can't get it to you if the portal is closed. He'll use the tree portal from Nainehta Forest, the one you and your friend came through. You need to find the stone and open the door. Go, now. And pray that the blessed deities smile on us."

MIRELLA SENT WORD FOR Hazel and Dhalian to meet Talullah at the maze.

Talullah simply nodded at them when they arrived. She still couldn't bring herself to speak to Dhal. But she couldn't go inside the maze without him. He unfurled the map, his eyes asking questions Talullah didn't have answers to. Later. She'd make time to talk to him later.

She threaded her arms through Gillie's cloak and cinched the waist. Mirella had disabled the memory charm for her, so she could use it only as protection. Whatever external forces awaited, she could use all the help she could get.

The forest reappeared around them as they stepped through the first door. She had to believe this plan would work, that Zeri wouldn't realize her mistake. Talullah checked her heart-shaped compass, turned south, and took off at a brisk walk. Hazel and Dhalian trailed close behind, Hazel carrying Talullah's token. No one spoke. Tension clung to the air like dewdrops in a spiderweb. The air smelled like secrets.

Thirty minutes of silent walking led them to a clearing. Talullah's free hand hovered over her knife, just in case.

Saplings of all varieties filled the circular lawn, each secured to the ground by four colored threads. Talullah identified each one as she noticed it.

Elm. Oak. Walnut. Maple.

Hazelnut.

"What have trees got to do with anything?" Dhalian asked.

"Not just any trees," said Hazel.

Magic curled off the hazelnut tree in multicolored puffs. Talullah approached it and pocketed the compass. Its soft leaves reminded her of freshly washed cotton.

Dunamai's Eye warmed against her collarbone. Encouraging her.

"Tules, what is it?" Dhalian called.

"Magic. You don't see it?" she replied.

"All I see are branches and trunks. Hazel?"

"Yes," she said, barely audible. "I see it."

Kneeling, Talullah examined the trunk. Though still young, it stood straight and sturdy. A thread of a scene pushed its way into her consciousness, weaving a memory. Her own, this time.

She was five years old. Her mother planted trees in their yard, while she sat on the porch watching. Her mother tied string to the saplings' trunks and staked them to the ground. Talullah hadn't understood then why the trees needed help standing. She hadn't understood how she'd know when the trees were ready to stand on their own, without being able to see their roots. But her mother had said—

"We don't always see with our eyes, Talullah." Hazel's voice broke her concentration. "It's time to cut away the string."

And then Hazel smashed Talullah's token.

Chapter 32

Captain Caprico struggled to keep his eyebrow from twitching. Renevelda's red-haired pet made him uncomfortable. Her small stature and girlish voice didn't fool him. A storm brewed behind her yellow eyes, hinting at the powers trapped inside. A small vein on her neck throbbed beneath the black ribbon which signified her captivity. Energy infused with rage rolled off her in waves. How much longer could Renevelda's magic bind her?

Thinking about what the she-demon had to have done to ensnare and enslave the Spirit Fox sent shivers down his spine. No one else had ever done it. It was supposed to be impossible. And yet, there she was, licking her lips in anticipation of freedom.

"She will come soon," Zeri cooed, hopscotching across the stone floor, her hair swinging in her wake. "And Mistress will have what she wants. And then, so will I."

Caprico clenched his jaw. "Who?"

Zeri shot him a look. "The eldest one with hair like night, to save the young ones she will fight. My mistress knew and so did I, mirrors show more than meets the eye. Soon we'll know whose path is clearer, the sorceress or the Sezna Seer."

Cold sweat beaded on the back of his neck. He kept his face neutral as his brain digested Zeri's prediction. Could she really have known the mirror's true abilities? He never could tell what she knew and what she guessed. But how could she possibly have known? Regardless, it would be better to play dumb. Let her think he didn't have a clue what was going on. She'd already made that assumption about him and it had played to his favor so far. The puppet captain would perform again.

Zeri tugged on the ribbon at her neck and spat on Caprico's boots. "Don't ever make me do that despicable rhyme-speak again. Ah, but I shouldn't worry about prophesying for humans. Mistress will return this evening. She'll be so pleased to see this. And to begin the preparations. Don't be late bringing the sacrifice, Captain."

She caressed Renevelda's book and stalked out of the cell without a backward glance.

The older girl, Margot, stood in front of the younger with one with a hand on her hip and her chin pushed forward, glaring at Zeri's back. Defiant.

She reminded him of his youngest son, Palo. Brave. A fighter.

His heart swelled at the thought of his family. Two sons and his wife, all risking their lives at this very second.

Despite his order to deliver the Bridgestone sisters to their death, a cool calmness settled over him. "Do what you must, not what they want" played on repeat in his head, a refrain from his former life. That part of thievery had suited him, at least. The last few torturous years in Castle Terrapese had pushed him to the brink of his ability to serve someone else's plan. He'd never really liked following orders.

And now was the perfect time to stop.

CAPRICO PACED BACK and forth in front of his window. The last light of day dipped below the horizon, dragging his heart into his stomach, sinking it like the sun. It was almost time.

He'd been simultaneously dreading and anticipating this moment since he'd been summoned into Renevelda's service, his family threatened. Since that day five years ago he'd vowed to find a way out, and when he found it, he'd give up thieving for good and provide for his family in an honorable way.

The irony of his predicament drew a sarcastic laugh through his dry lips. Treason, kidnapping, and theft on a magnitude he'd never attempted paved his way to a life of honor and freedom.

His family would be successful in their individual missions. He knew it in his marrow. The rest was up to him.

He tightened the laces on his golden boots and grimaced. If everything went according to plan, he'd never have to wear the ridiculous things again.

THOUGH ONLY TWELVE, Palo had the finesse of an expert. If he'd been raised on the streets, he would have made a healthy living as a thief. Not that he liked stealing. Tonight, though, he buried his conscience.

He adjusted his apron, entered the kitchen, and plopped the residents' evening meal dishes in the sink. He scrubbed each one spotless and offered a smile and a wave to the other kitchen assistants as, one by one, they left for the night. When only he remained, he carefully dried and stowed the plates and silverware and wiped his hands on his apron. With care, he slipped behind the largest wooden storage chest and flipped a hidden switch. The secret compartment had come in handy over the past few years, holding scraps of food he'd saved and snuck down to the prisoners. Now, he removed the book, wrapped it in butcher paper, tucked it into his apron pocket, and returned the chest to normal.

Exiting the kitchen, he took one last look and slipped a sharp paring knife into the holster under his sleeve. Kitchen staff wasn't the worst job he could have been assigned. But being free would be better.

NOLAN FINISHED HIS duties in the stables and rubbed each horse on the nose as he passed their stalls, leaving the gates open. He'd miss them. But that was no reason to stay.

He tucked the bags his father had given him in a shadowed corner at the back of the stable and covered them with straw. Stepping back, he checked his work. Good. No one came to ride late at night, anyway.

Outside, he made his way to the edge of the pasture. That gate, too, he didn't latch. Carelessness of that sort would have earned him fifteen lashes, one for each year of his age. But it didn't matter. With any luck, Palo would have handed off the book by now.

He glanced shyly at the pale-skinned chambermaid as he rounded the corner to his room. Her auburn hair and green eyes had enchanted him for months, but they'd never exchanged words. Mouth dry, he parted his lips to speak. Now was his chance. His last chance. But what would be appropriate as a first introduction and final goodbye? Because he knew he'd never see her again.

She smiled and nodded at him as she passed. He smiled back, his face flushing. Two steps more and he'd gathered his nerve. But when he turned, she was already gone.

HOLLOW ECHOES RICOCHETED off the stone floor as Caprico crept down the stairs and wound through the corridors. But all who poked their heads into the hall shrank back into their chambers at the sight of his footwear. The she-devil's soldiers had the right to be anywhere they chose. Anyone who dared question them lost their tongue. Caprico rolled his shoulders. He needed to relax. This was the easy part.

The sisters—Margot and Pennilyn—feigned sleep in their cell as he approached. They stiffened at the clack of his boots against the floor. The poor girls, he thought. They may never sleep soundly again. He'd only done what he'd had to do to sell his performance. That and nothing more, hating himself all the while. Maybe one day they'd understand. He wouldn't hope for forgiveness. At least he finally had the chance to set them free. To fulfill the promise he'd made.

He tapped the toe of his boot three times and waited. One of Margot's eyes flicked open, and seconds later the other. She locked her gaze on his, blinked twice, then coughed.

Pennilyn stirred. "Now?"

"Yes, Penny," Margot whispered. "Like we practiced."

Caprico almost dropped the key his hands were so slick, but he recovered at the last second. Praying silently, he turned it in the lock and eased it open only enough for the girls to slip out. Luck was on their side. It didn't creak. He made a mental note to thank his brilliant little Palo for greasing the hinge with cooking oil that morning. The kid thought of everything.

He re-locked the door and led the girls down the corridor. Now came the difficult part. Staying hidden.

They reached the stables without incident, though Caprico was certain anyone within a mile could hear his heartbeat. Most of the horses still stood behind the gate, but a few had ventured beyond. Good. It would look less suspicious if they wandered away at different times.

He uncovered the packs with supplies Nolan had hidden in the hay. After confirming Renevelda's real book was in his, he handed the other to Margot. Praise the Fates Zeri was colorblind. He hadn't been able to find gold thread for the title on the cover of the fake one. Renevelda, however, saw color just fine. They had to move. Fast.

"Change your clothes and smear your faces and hair with dirt. Shove your dresses in the pack. We'll burn them when we get further away. I'll stand watch at the door." As he stared into the night, Caprico's senses absorbed every detail. The cool, fresh breeze meant rain was coming. Another good sign. Rantoul's horse was terrified of water, none of the others trusted him enough to let him ride, and Fallon was chickenshit of the dark.

They might be able to pull this off after all.

"Done," said Margot. She and Pennilyn drew level with him.

He scrutinized their faces. If he didn't know who they were, would he recognize them? "I think that's good."

"What about shoes?" Pennilyn asked.

Caprico checked their feet. Shit. He'd forgotten shoes. Too late now. "Just muddy them up a bit more. And Pennilyn, you're going to have to try to keep your eyes shut as much as possible."

"Why?" She cocked her head to the side.

"They're too recognizable. No one around here has eyes that color. Just pretend you're scared, okay? Margot, hold her hand."

Both girls nodded.

"Okay." He exhaled heavily. "Have your packs? Let's go." They walked in silence, following the dirt path from the pasture into the bordering forest.

Not five minutes later he felt a tug on his sleeve. "What, Pennilyn?"

"I don't have my dress."

"What dress? Gwen will have something for you."

"No. My old dress. The one I changed out of. It fell out of my bag."

Caprico's jaw clenched. He struggled to keep the anger out of his voice. She was only eight. But that dress could be a death sentence for all of them. "We have to find it. Otherwise the dogs will find us. Come on."

They retraced their steps, attempting to follow the exact line they'd walked.

Where the forest opened into fields, a sound made Caprico stop in his tracks. He grabbed the girls' packs to stop them moving and shushed them. They moved behind a tree and Caprico peeked out.

"What the hell's that thing?" Rantoul slurred, his thick brogue even more difficult to understand than usual.

"Dress," Fallon said, hiccupping.

His soldiers had been to town, had some drinks and fun, and now they were on their way back. Of course they'd take that route. It was the easiest to navigate in the dark and ran along the edge of the forest. His comrades couldn't find their way out of a linen sack after a few whiskeys. He should've known they'd go this way. Stupid.

"Could be Verita's, yeah?" Fallon said.

"Verita's a woman, you idiot. A well-developed one, at that. Curvy in all the right places, if you catch my drift. That doesn't even look big enough for your barely-adult what's-her-name."

"Katia is nineteen. And she's definitely a woman." Fallon burst out laughing. "This has got to be a kid's or something." He lifted the dress with one finger and Fallon and Rantoul's silhouettes leaned in to study it.

Caprico's brain whirred into overdrive, running through their options. Maybe they'd leave the dress and the storm would blow it away. Or maybe they'd bring it back to the castle, which was what they were supposed to do, and then the she-devil's hunting beasts would catch them. He couldn't take that chance.

"Looks kind of familiar," said Rantoul.

"Maybe a kid from town?" Fallon swayed and pointed vaguely in the direction they'd come from.

"They'd be fools to trespass here. Plus, doesn't look like anything they'd wear." Rantoul squinted at the fabric. "Don't make silk in Terrapese."

Fallon snapped his fingers. "I've seen girls that size in the castle. In that cell, remember?"

"Yeah...yeah...that might be right. But if they're in the castle, how'd this dress get all the way out here?"

A pause. Caprico held his breath. Maybe they were too drunk to put two and two together.

Margot and Pennilyn shifted their weight beside him.

"That doesn't make sense," Rantoul said.

Fallon clapped his hands once. "I've got it! Hear me out. What if...they escaped?"

Fallon was a wuss and a terrible fighter but damned if he wasn't logical, even drunk off his ass.

"Stay here," Caprico whispered. "Don't move. And whatever you do, don't make any sounds."

He walked a semi-circle to make it seem like he'd come from town and approached his soldiers. "Evening, gentlemen."

Rantoul let out a yell. "Shit, Cap'n. Where the hell'd you come from?"

"He's like a ghost," said Fallon, clutching his chest. "Thought you were going to steal our souls, Cap-hic-Cap-hic-Captain."

Caprico slackened his mouth to slur his speech. "Nope, just been for a drink."

"But we didn't see you. Had we seen you, we woulda had a pint with you, Captain," Fallon said.

"Seems you gentlemen had more than your share. Anyway, shouldn't you be getting back? Smells like rain. Storm's rolling in. Could hit any minute." Sweat trickled down Caprico's neck and he fought the urge to wipe it away.

"We were, Cap. And then we found this." Rantoul snatched the dress from Fallon and presented it. "Think maybe it belongs to one of those blond girls. Are they both blond, or just one of 'em? I can't remember. Either way, they're the right size."

"And it definitely can't be Verita's," added Fallon. "Already ruled her out."

Geniuses, his men.

"Hmm, must belong to a townsperson's kid. I saw the girls in their cell before I left." *Please let them buy this.* Caprico's hand twitched.

"But like Rantoul said, it's silk. We don't make silk in Terrapese, do we, Cap?"

"We don't mine rubies, either, but I seem to remember a certain lady wearing one around her neck last time I saw her."

"Ah, well, you see—" Rantoul fumbled.

"The Hidden Market draws many patrons, soldier. No need to explain. Just pointing out there are ways this silk could have made its way to Terrapese."

Rantoul sighed, visibly relieved. "Thought we were onto something there, Fallon. But the Cap is smarter than us, as usual."

"Just had a bit less whiskey, Rantoul. How about I check the area before I come up anyway just to be sure?"

"Ghost!" Fallon shrieked, pointing down the path. "Two ghosts!"

"Shut up, kid," Rantoul said.

"No, look!" Fallon grabbed Rantoul's cheeks and turned his face.

Adrenaline shot through Caprico's veins. Margot and Pennilyn peeked out from behind a tree less than ten feet away. He gritted his teeth. They'd moved.

Rantoul pulled away. "You idiot, it's just two little girls...wait a minute..."

"Her eyes. They're so green I can see them in the dark," Fallon said, bemused.

"Sorry for this," Caprico said. "You've been loyal to me. Maybe someday I can return the favor."

His fist connected with Rantoul's face first, then Fallon's. He didn't wait for them to hit the ground before he ripped the dress from Rantoul's hand and ran down the path toward the girls.

"It's okay, we're okay," he panted, shaking his hand. Hell and a half. It had been a while since he punched someone. He'd forgotten how much it hurt.

"Are they dead?" asked Pennilyn in a small voice.

"No, they're not dead. And they're going to wake up soon. We can't be here when they do. But I think we'll get a good enough head start, and with any luck they won't remember any of this. Let's all pray that Leda the barmaid's hand was heavy tonight."

Caprico stuffed Pennilyn's old dress into his pack and they took off running. Just as they reached the edge of the castle grounds, a screech split the air.

A stream of curses poured from Caprico's mouth.

Cleo, Renevelda's faithful servant, had found them.

Chapter 33

We don't always see with our eyes.

"Did you know my mother said that to me once, a long time ago?" Talullah asked.

Hazel approached her, eyes brimming with tears, and grasped Talullah's hands in her own. Her face flickered as if lit by candlelight. "When you first got here, I told you Praeteriti preserves people's appearance as they were when they first arrived. And that I didn't remember anything about myself before I got here. Both of those things were true. The first time I came here, I was sixteen. Please know that what I did, I did to protect you. Had I remembered anything, you wouldn't have succeeded. I didn't have enough time to teach you everything you needed to know. But you've done alright without me. You always were a fast learner." A tear escaped and slid down Hazel's cheek. "It had to be this way. I hope one day you will understand."

Talullah took in the picture of this crying girl she barely knew. But something had changed, or had she not noticed before? The way Hazel's mouth turned up just slightly at the corners in a sad smile. The way her eyes swallowed every detail of her surroundings, as if by seeing the world she could quench her thirst for adventure.

How her long dark hair cascaded down her back like a panel of the finest silk in Viltresor, the same way Talullah's used to.

The token's magic cleared the air, dissolving Talullah's confusion with it.

"Mother?" Talullah whispered. It couldn't be true. It had to be another one of the maze's tricks, designed to distract her.

But the warm hands holding hers spoke stories of trees planted in rich earth and weaving lessons. Of cinnamon pancakes, bows and arrows, and a thousand other memories Talullah had tried so hard to forget. Mostly, though, they spoke of love. Love shared and sacrificed. Love lost.

The teenage version of her mother nodded, her expression the fading last note of a song Talullah used to know.

This was the truth she'd sought for half her life. After so many years waiting and fearing and wishing and dreaming of this moment, Talullah's mind and heart warred, mixing emotions like ingredients in a potion. How was she supposed to feel? Relieved that her mother was alive? Angry that she had left in the first place? Deceived, elated, confused?

Yes. All of them. Her heart didn't know how fast to beat. Her hands wanted to both hold on and let go. She struggled to reconcile the memory of her adult mother and the teenage version, preserved by magic, who stood in front of her.

Why? How? When? So many questions rolled in her mouth, but her tongue couldn't form the words.

"Take the stone and get out of this place. Your sisters need you. I know you won't let them down."

"Wait a minute. This is your mother, Tules?" asked Dhalian, looking back and forth between the two women.

Talullah's voice cracked, addressing her mother. "You can't leave me again. Not now."

"The stone is the most important thing," said her mother, ignoring her plea. She squeezed Talullah's hands. "Believe you are strong enough. Now do what you came here to do, my brave girl. We are running out of time."

She needed to digest the information swirling inside her. But there wasn't time. Once she saved her sisters and located her father, they could be a full family again. She could ask all the questions and get all the answers. They would make up for the days when the Bridgestones totaled four instead of five. Time, then, would be on her side. For now, she answered to its demands.

Talullah unsheathed her knife. She glanced at Dhalian then her mother, who both nodded. One by one she sliced through the colored threads anchoring the hazelnut tree to the ground.

When she'd snapped the final one, an intense gust of wind blew in from nowhere and threatened to knock her off her feet.

Though she struggled for purchase, the tree stood strong. In the center of its trunk, a heart-shape glowed purple.

"It needs a key," Talullah shouted over the howling wind.

Use your heart, keep your mind, and what you seek, you shall find.

Use your heart.

She removed the compass from her pocket, squinting. It pulsed in her palm. She lined it up with the outline and pressed the gold metal against the trunk. Warmth spread from her fingers to her chest. When she removed the compass, a heart-shaped hole remained. Inside sparkled a small amethyst.

"Take it, Talullah," her mother yelled.

Talullah dropped the compass and grasped the gem between her thumb and forefinger, her short hair whipping her face.

A bolt of lightning cracked above the Mazuchawi. Sparks rained over them.

"Go now!" urged her mother, ringing a small silver bell that hung from the hazelnut tree.

"We can't get back to the entrance. There's no time!" Dhalian's panic raised his voice an octave.

"With the stone, you don't need to. Count backward from three," Talullah's mother said.

Talullah squeezed the stone in her fist and clasped Dhalian's hand in the other.

"Aren't you coming?" Dhalian shouted.

Talullah's mother shook her head.

"Are you crazy?" Dhalian continued.

"That is not my fate." Her square jaw hardened with decision.

Three.

"You'll die in here, Mama," said Talullah. "You can't leave. Not again. Not like this. What about Penny and Mar and Father? They need you. *I* need you."

"I'm proud of you, Talullah." She stroked Talullah's hair.

A spark ignited a branch of the hazelnut tree, but still it didn't budge.

Her mother stepped backward.

Talullah's heart froze. Her mother intended to stay. To abandon her family again. Talullah had let it happen once before. Not this time. "No! You can't!" She scrambled toward her mother, fighting the wind.

Her mother looked toward the sky. "This is only the beginning, Talullah."

An amethyst bolt streaked from the sky.

A deafening *crack*.

Two.

The lightning struck her mother and she crumpled to the ground.

"Mama!" Talullah hurled her body to her mother's side.

"Tules! It's collapsing!"

The shrub walls shook and tumbled around them. "I can't leave her, Dhal! Not after I just found her. She wanted to come back, but she couldn't. She couldn't leave but now she can, because I can save her!"

She covered her mother's body with her own, still grasping the stone in one fist.

"Wake up, Mama. We're getting out of here. Together."

Dhalian fell to his knees beside her. "It's going to be okay," he said, grabbing her free hand.

Heat radiated from the three huddled bodies. A ghost of a breath passed her mother's bluing lips.

"It's going to be fine, Mama. We're getting out of here."

Another bolt.

The faint smell of lavender.

Talullah's mother's body disintegrated, leaving only ash in her shaking hands.

One.

And then, darkness.

Chapter 34

Talullah coughed and opened her eyes. She lay in the field near Fisher's. A square of glowing embers marked where the Mazuchawi had been, but the maze itself was gone. Probably disappeared for the last time.

Every inch of her body ached. She sat up and noticed the dusty film coating her left palm.

Ashes.

From her mother's body.

Instinct made her fingers curl inward, preventing the ashes from blowing away. Keeping them safe.

She forced her thoughts elsewhere, coating her heart in liquid steel. If she focused on losing her mother—again—she'd lose herself, too. And right now, her sisters couldn't afford for her to fall apart. Not when she was so close.

Strong arms steadied her as she stood. "I know you're mad at me," Dhalian said. "But I want you to know I'm here."

She nodded once. An acknowledgment only. Not acceptance, not forgiveness. But as she did, her shoulders relaxed the slightest bit.

Ghosts moved around them in packs, chatting loudly. In all the time she'd spent in Praeteriti, Talullah had never seen the residents so animated. Normally reserved, they spoke in excited tones, their voices carrying down the streets.

A woman with a lace parasol and a hoop skirt caught Talullah staring. The woman placed her free hand on her hip and raised an eyebrow at Talullah. "It's rude to stare," she drawled.

"What's going on?" Dhalian asked.

She fluttered her eyelashes and offered a sugary smile. In the conspiratorial half-whisper of a skilled gossiper she said, "The Keeper of the Keys has found the gemstone. We felt the shift. As soon as the door opens, we'll be able to leave again."

The amethyst stone dug into the palm of Talullah's clenched fist. Should she put it in the necklace now? Should she go to Mirella first? "Keeper of the Keys?"

"Of course. The Keeper is a legend around the Four Worlds. No one quite knows who it is these days, but everyone's got their theories. I'd love to meet him or her someday. Wouldn't that just shut up my cousin Alice? She met a fallen Revolutionary War general once while traveling and she *still* talks about it. Makes me less sympathetic that she died from pneumonia. Horrible way to go, but God does work in mysterious ways."

"So, everyone here will be able to travel once the door is unlocked?" Dhalian asked.

"Most everyone. Not the Unforgiven, those poor souls. There's more than a locked door between them and freedom. I can't imagine what kind of terror they'd unleash if they could roam the Four Worlds, could you?"

"Well, we've got to go now, but thanks for the chat." Talullah steered Dhalian away from the ghost.

"I'm Cecile, by the way. Look me up some time, you tall, dark stranger." She giggled and sauntered away to join a group, twirling her parasol.

"There you are," Mirella said from behind them. She doubled over, panting, when they turned. "I came as soon as I Saw. Legs aren't quite as quick as they used to be. Follow me."

"Where are we going?" Talullah asked. She dropped her voice to a whisper. "What about the stone?"

"You haven't put it in yet, have you?" Mirella replied in kind.

"No."

"Good. Better to leave as little room for error as possible." She led them through the large library doors and to the closet through which Talullah and Dhalian had first arrived. "Gillie's meeting us at this entrance to bring Renevelda's book. And he should be here any minute."

Inside the closet, the books effused energy.

"Okay, Talullah. Now is the time."

Pinching the gem between her thumb and forefinger, Talullah used her other hand to move Dunamai's Eye away from her chest. "How do I know where it goes?"

"Looks like it's telling you." Dhalian pointed at the necklace. Each empty spot in the setting glowed a different color.

Talullah lined up the gem with the purple spot. Her fingers hovered over the necklace, tingling. Everything she'd gone through had been for this. She held her breath and clicked it into place. Warmth trickled from her collarbone through her limbs.

The room filled with a purple haze and a rush of fully-formed visions poured into Talullah's mind all at once. Conversations between people she didn't know. Buildings she'd never seen. Explosions in the distance. Children screaming. Parents running after them. Fire. Waterfalls. Snowcapped mountains and raging seas. Foreign tongues and clothes. War. Peace. Life. Death.

The whole of the past compacted into seconds.

When it ended, Talullah's eyes rolled back in her head. Her knees gave out, but she didn't hit the floor. Dhalian supported her weight.

"It will pass, dear," Mirella's voice soothed, stroking her hair. "And now, the portals reopen."

The tunnel passage appeared in the wall.

Cheers from outside suggested the others had opened as well.

Relief flooded her senses. She was free. They were all free. And now she would save her family.

From behind them, a horde of ghosts rushed past and through the passage, bumping both her shoulders in their haste. "Thank you, Keeper of the Keys," they chanted as they disappeared into the void. The woman with the lace parasol wiggled her fingers at Dhalian on her way out.

As soon as they'd passed, Gillie slid through the opening. "Take it," he said, thrusting the book at Talullah. "Hurry. Good luck. For all our sakes." When she'd relieved him of the book, he disappeared through the tunnel once more.

A sharp screech split the air. Seconds later a large hawk bolted through the door, clipping Talullah's ear with its talons.

She swore.

"Cleo," gasped Dhalian.

"No, not Cleo," said Mirella. "Another servant bird. Cleo's much larger. Brace yourselves."

The bird spread its wings and waved them. A gust of wind blew through the closet and knocked the books from their shelves. One by one they crashed to the ground, opening on impact. Wailing and howling filled the air. Was the screaming coming from the books or inside Talullah's head? She couldn't tell. She struggled toward the book nearest her and tried to shut it. It stuck to the floor.

Panic drained the color from Dhalian's face as he tried in vain to close another book. He recoiled as he touched it. Smoke billowed from the pages. The smell of singed flesh filled the air.

Translucent apparitions rose from each book, airing their grievances in sharp tones. They swirled around the room in a tornado of sadness and anger and hopelessness.

"Released but not free," they chorused. "Our debt must still be paid."

In one final gust, they, and the great bird, sped through the open portal.

As quickly as the cacophony had begun, it ceased. Talullah's ears rang.

Mirella peered at Talullah through her thick glasses, her eyes large as dinner plates. "Renevelda has released the Unforgiven. Founders help us all."

Chapter 35

Caprico shoved the girls to the ground and covered their bodies with his, hoping to shield them. The large hawk dove with full force.

He let out a yell as six-inch long talons dug into his shoulder. Hot blood seeped through his ripped tunic. Cleo screeched and pulled, trying to expose her true targets. The prisoners. The runaways.

The sacrifice.

Caprico resisted with all his strength. He imagined he weighed ten thousand pounds and nothing could move him. If Cleo wanted the children, she was going to have to go through him.

"I can't breathe," Penny wheezed.

"I'm sorry," he said through gritted teeth. "I'll think of something."

But what? If he reached for his knife Cleo would have a clean shot at Margot's face. And if he did nothing, the bird would rip his body to shreds and *then* take the Bridgestone girls back to a waiting—and undeniably seething—sorceress. He clenched his jaw against the pain in his shoulder. It stung from the inside out, like a million angry hornets digging their way through his flesh.

There had to be a third option.

Cleo released him and soared higher in the sky, no doubt plotting her next attack. The gashes weren't deep enough to kill him, but just imagining carrying extra weight made his stomach turn. He blinked the sweat from his eyes.

"Are you okay?" he asked, panting.

"Yes," said the girls together.

"Is it gone?" asked Margot.

"Not yet."

"What are we going to do?" asked Penny, her small voice breaking his heart with each word.

"Nainehta Forest," he said, stealing a glance upward.

Cleo circled above their heads.

"I can't carry you and fight off Cleo. You're going to have to run. Can you do that?"

"Yes," they said.

"Okay. I'm going to distract her. When I say 'go,' run straight until you can't run anymore. It's going to be very dark, but don't be scared. Take this." Eyes still locked on Cleo, he drew a small obsidian rock from his pocket. "Margot, move very slowly and pick up that stick in front of you."

Margot handed Caprico the stick and he banged it with the rock. Green flames appeared on its end. He handed the stick to Margot, careful to point the fire away from her.

"Cleo won't come near you as long as that's burning. She's afraid of the magic. It can also cast light in Nainehta Forest. One of the only things that can cut through that darkness. When I say so, take your sister's hand and run. I'll find you soon."

Caprico bent at the knees and grabbed three sticks from the ground. Cleo flapped her wings, holding position. She screeched.

With a quick swipe, Caprico ignited the ends of his branches with green flames. Cleo dove.

"Go!"

Margot and Pennilyn took off like a shot, the fire guiding their way. Caprico held the flaming torches with his injured arm. He couldn't tell whether the heat racing through his veins came from the fire, his wound, or both. Gritting his teeth, he used his other hand to hurl rocks at his incoming assailant.

One connected with the bird's right wing and she faltered. He took the opportunity to throw one of the torches. She screeched at him and retreated.

A smile crept across his face. "That's what I thought."

Holding a torch in each hand he stepped toward her. Emerald flames reflected in her beady eyes.

She dove. He ducked. But he wasn't fast enough. Talons sank into his injured arm, forcing him to drop the torch in that hand.

Caprico let out a guttural yell as Cleo lifted him off the ground. "Put me down, you demon-beast!" He swiped at the bird's belly with his remaining torch. She shrieked and clenched his forearm in her other foot, forcing his arm and the torch away from her body.

Don't drop it. Don't drop it. If he let it go, he was dead. Actually, if Cleo let go, he was also dead. They were now at least a hundred feet above the ground.

As if sensing his panic, the bird released his shoulder. He dangled by one arm and the great hawk's mercy.

A flash of blond caught his attention below.

"Hey, you big dumb bird. Bring him back!" Margot's voice carried upward.

Cleo stiffened at the sound.

Caprico registered the girl's empty hands waving in the air. The fire. She'd given Penny the fire. And now she was defenseless. "Margot, no!"

The great bird plunged toward her. Margot turned and ran.

The ground drew nearer, the wind making his eyes water. Gritting his teeth, he grabbed the knife at his waist with his free hand. They'd been too high up for him to consider using it before. But now, this was his only choice.

He waited until the last possible minute. Until he was almost positive they were low enough the impact wouldn't kill him. A slash, a spurt of blood, and the leathery leg released his arm.

His feet hit the ground first and he dropped the torch, forcing his body to roll.

Cleo hovered five feet above him. Margot was nowhere in sight. Good. She'd gotten away. His own panting breath filled his ears while he contemplated his next move.

The torch. Where was his torch?

He stood and combed the ground with his eyes. There. A faint green flame still burned on the end. Sidestepping, he moved toward it.

A snapping twig behind Cleo stole her attention just long enough so he could grab the torch. Holding it out, he backed toward the line of smoking trees. Nainehta wasn't the kind of place he ever wanted to go again, but at that moment he'd take the forest's unknowns over the six deadly talons threatening to rip his heart from his chest.

When he reached the tree line marking the entrance, he listened. No screams, no shuffling. He chose to believe that was a good sign. If the forest had harmed the girls, they would have screamed.

"This has been great, old girl. But I've got to go now. I'm taking the girls and you're not going to stop me." He launched the torch at Cleo, watched it connect with her wing and spark flames on her feathers, and ran. Normally he wouldn't turn his back on an enemy, but as soon as he entered the forest there were enemies all around. He couldn't face them all head-on.

His boots shuffled in the tall grass as he moved in a straight line, praying to every being he could think of that the girls had followed instructions. Every movement sent a sharp twinge down his arm. He sucked in a breath and pushed it out through clenched teeth. He would find them soon. They were young. They couldn't have gone too far.

A light rustling drew his gaze. Margot and Pennilyn sat huddled together under a tree, the torch held between them like they were sharing ghost stories. A relieved laugh bubbled up from his throat.

"You're alright," he said.

Margot's eyes widened, glowing eerily in the green light of the fire. Her mouth dropped open. Slowly she raised a hand and pointed over Caprico's shoulder. Pennilyn let out an *eek*.

Caprico whipped around, remembering his injury too late. Damn that bird. His eyes raked the darkness. "What is it? What do you see?"

"Ghosts," Pennilyn whispered.

"Where? I don't see—" But then he did. A few hundred yards away purple shapes came into view. Tension squeezed his lungs like a boa constrictor. The ghosts were heading right at them.

Thousands of screams spilled into his subconscious at once. He fell to his knees and shoved his hands over his ears. The girls did the same, agony ripping the innocence from their faces.

"We need to move," he said, not knowing if they could hear him. He beckoned the girls to follow. Tears streamed from their eyes, but they kept pace. They found a split tree large enough for the three of them and crawled inside, Caprico closest to the opening. "Extinguish the flames."

Margot's silent sobs made it impossible for her to blow out the fire. Caprico did it for her. They waited as the ghosts drew nearer and louder. Caprico watched with furrowed brows. Where had they come from? And why were they shrieking? All the ghosts he'd ever met in the forest had been pleasant.

"Released but not free," the ghosts intoned as they rushed by. "Our debts still must be paid."

Caprico swallowed hard. Whatever debts that crowd had accumulated, he felt sorry for the poor soul who'd have to reconcile them. Luck, it seemed, was on their side, though. The ghosts passed without any indication they knew three onlookers hid nearby, nor any inkling they cared.

At least one thing had gone right that night.

"I think it's clear," Caprico said, reaching in his pocket for the fire stone. His fingers felt only fabric. Panic flooded him. Without the stone they couldn't make fire. Without fire they couldn't see.

If they couldn't see…

Come on, Colfax. Get yourself together.

The thumping sound of an animal running broke his concentration. Four legs. Fast. Big.

He stood and braced himself. He may not be able to see, but he wasn't going down without a fight.

Impact never came. The animal halted directly in front of him. He felt its warm breath glide over his face in panting puffs. He forced his lungs not to breathe. Instinct must have told the girls to do the same because they stood, unmoving, behind him.

Bare feet shuffled through the fallen leaves and stopped next to the animal.

A gravelly voice punctured the silence. "Four Worlds, Kahu. You're goin' to give the poor kids a heart attack. And this brute, too, by the looks of him. Let's get one thing straight, Wrecker. The only reason I'm takin' you with me is 'cuz I owe your wife a favor. Lucky for you she thinks you're worthy of cashin' it in. Let's go."

Chapter 36

"Through the portal, quickly," urged Mirella. "The others will be restless now that the Unforgiven are free."

The first time Talullah and Dhalian had come through the portal, an invisible force had dragged them along the twists and turns. Now, endless stairs stretched ahead of them. Flame-tipped torches illuminated the woven murals she hadn't been able to identify before. Scenes of families sharing meals, life, war, and death. The whole of history.

Pain needled through her knees as she climbed the steep stones. Musty air filled her lungs with each inhale.

They moved too quickly for Talullah to ask Mirella what it meant that the Unforgiven had been released. Renevelda planned to use them somehow, but how?

And how many damn stairs did she have to climb?

Focus on the goal.

She'd found the stone. She had the book. Now she just needed to Alter the story.

Just ten more steps, she urged her aching body.

She'd see her sisters soon. She could smell their rosewater soap already.

Hold on for five more.

And her father. She'd nurse him back to health. When this all was over, they'd be a family again.

Almost there.

Thank the Founders, the door.

Legs heavy, she pressed down the handle and leaned against the wood. The rush of fresh air stole Talullah's breath.

She teetered out of the tree, using Dhalian's shoulder for balance. Frost blanketed the ground.

They'd made it back to Nainehta Forest.

Talullah's heart raced as she remembered the last time she'd stood in that spot. She'd sliced off her hair and slipped, literally, through Rantoul's hands.

Dunamai's Eye glowed, illuminating a small area in the otherwise pitch dark.

"Is it weird I'm happy to see this place?" Dhalian asked between gasps.

"I'm glad to be out of that underground prison as much as you are," Mirella said. "Now. We need to get to the safe house. Your sisters should be on their way." She pulled a palm-sized teardrop mirror from her pocket and gestured for Talullah to look.

In the mirror, Gillie and Kahu led a tall limping man through a thicket of trees. Atop Kahu's back sat two small figures. Tears pooled in Talullah's eyes. Penny and Margot. They were safe.

They were alive.

Caprico had done as Gwen promised.

"What about the hawk?" Dhalian asked, his scowling face pointed skyward.

"She'll have returned to Renevelda, I expect. But stay alert, just in case. Talullah, take my hand and I'll show you the way in case we get separated. If that happens, go directly to the safe house. Don't come looking for me."

She wanted to protest, but her aunt was right. She closed her eyes and reached out for Mirella's memory.

A hazy violet scene rippled into her consciousness. Mirella twisted and turned through the trees. Talullah noted landmarks she could use to navigate them to the safe house. When she'd replayed it three times, she felt confident enough.

"I've got it. Let's go."

Mirella led them through the gold- and silver-leafed trees in heavy silence, gesturing for them to turn one way or another.

Twice, Talullah stopped to assess noises, her knife drawn, but they were only squirrels playing chase.

The smell of wet earth and pine overwhelmed her senses as they neared the river. "This way. We're close, I think."

"Hang on," Mirella said.

"Do you need to rest?" asked Dhalian.

"No. Just because I'm older—that's not the point. Someone's trying to contact us." Mirella touched the corner of the mirror and Gwendolyn's face, framed in curls, appeared.

Worry lines creased her forehead as she squinted into the glass. "Mirella, thank goodness. I've been trying to get through for an hour."

Mirella stiffened. "What's happened?"

"Renevelda is coming." She locked eyes with Talullah. "There isn't time for you to reach the safe house. I was going to help with the Alteration, but that's not possible anymore."

"Use my house," said a gravelly voice. Gillie stepped into frame. "It's closer. And there's some extra protection she won't be expecting. Wood faerie magic. She'll work out how to disable it eventually, but it should buy you some time. I'll connect the spell to your cloak, so you'll be able to open the door."

Talullah clenched her jaw. "How much time do we have?"

"An hour. At most," Gwen said.

Only an hour to find Gillie's house, figure out which event to Alter, and actually Alter it. Not to mention the last time she'd tried Alteration she hadn't even done it right. She wasn't ready. But she had no other choice.

Gillie drew a symbol in the air with his pointer finger. The swirls on Talullah's cloak glowed.

"Good luck," said Gwendolyn. "We'll be waiting for you." Her image dissolved from the mirror.

"This way," said Mirella.

A bird screeched in the near distance.

Just a bird?

Or could it be Cleo?

Or Renevelda?

So much for an hour.

She broke into a run.

Staccato glances in every direction revealed no place to hide. They had to get to Gillie's house before Cleo got to them.

Dhalian wheezed but shot her a reassuring look. He'd never been good at running. Or maybe he never had proper motivation.

Now he did.

Despite Mirella's age, she kept up.

The large book thumped against Talullah's back as she ran. She gritted her teeth and pushed her legs to move faster.

The cloak's velvety fabric billowed out behind her as she ran.

"It's just...there..." Dhalian gasped.

"Thank the Founders," Talullah panted. An eerie silence fell over the sky. Void of flapping wings and screeches. Only the slight rustle of leaves indicated movement in the forest. Just the wind. All other life held frozen in time.

Talullah approached the triangular door. "How do I open it?" As the first time she visited, the door had no doorknob. Part of Gillie's security measures, of course. But he said the cloak would allow her to open the door. So why didn't the handle appear at her touch?

"What's wrong?" Dhalian asked, clutching a stitch in his side.

"I thought he said he fixed it." Talullah ran her hands along the frame. Nothing. She kicked the tree. "Why won't you open?

You're supposed to open. Mirella, can you call Gillie through the mirror...thing?"

"No connection. I can't get through."

"What does that mean? Are they okay?" Talullah paced in front of the tree.

"I don't know," said Mirella.

"What in the Founders' names are we going to do now?" Talullah scraped the bark with her fingernails.

"Should we just head for the safe house?" asked Dhalian.

"There isn't time," said Mirella.

"There has to be a way in." Talullah circled the tree. Hints of colors peeked through its bark. Like Igdrasil. She'd gotten inside that tree with Dunamai's Eye.

She leaned forward and pressed her necklace against the tree.

A rumble emanated from Gillie's house.

A symbol appeared in the wooden door, glowing as if drawn with embers. A soft *click* and then the door swung open.

"Thank the Founders," said Dhalian.

Talullah squeezed his hand. They walked through the door side-by-side. The way they'd always done everything.

Chapter 37

"Old magic, indeed," said Talullah.

The moment she sank into a kitchen chair, the weight of everything crashed down on her like a tidal wave when she'd forgotten to take a breath.

Inhale, exhale. Inhale, exhale.

For at least for a few moments, she could think and prepare herself for what she had to do. When had she last Altered anything? Days? Weeks?

Adrenaline heightened her senses. She could almost feel Cleo getting closer. It wouldn't be long before the bird, and then the sorceress, found them. "Hand me the book, Dhal."

"You can do it, Talullah." Dhalian's voice was soft yet strong.

Sure, she could do Alteration. It wasn't hard to ties knots in string. She'd been doing that since she could wiggle her fingers. Finding the correct event, however, was the difficult part. Too small an adjustment could change nothing. Too big of one could destroy her world.

And just because she had the power to Alter someone's story, did that give her the right to do so?

The weight of the tome mimicked the heaviness in her gut. Renevelda's past. Her future.

And everyone else's connected to sorceress. Talullah would change their course, too. What unintended consequences would come from Talullah's choice? Would innocent people die?

Her hand lay on the cover, its heartbeat pulsing through her fingertips.

Dhalian pulled her into a tight hug and squeezed. She breathed in his sweet scent.

"I know," he said. "I know you're scared. So am I. That's okay." He pulled back to look her in the eyes. "Remember that time when we were kids and we climbed the biggest tree on the riverbank. You dared me to jump off because you knew I was terrified of heights. You told me that if I didn't do it then, I never would. My legs shook, and my heart threatened to beat out of my chest. But you took my hand, looked me in the eye, and started to count. On two, we jumped. Together. You made me go before I was ready, and that's the only reason I went. It's time I repay that favor."

Warmth raced through her blood. He was right. This was one more challenge she had to conquer, but she wasn't doing it alone.

Talullah had to stop blaming Dhalian. He'd been at the wrong place at the wrong time. She couldn't fault him for telling Renevelda about Dunamai's Eye. The sorceress would have done anything to get it. Talullah had to count herself lucky Dhalian hadn't died in the castle, as Renevelda probably had planned. A lifetime of friendship shouldn't dissolve because of one mistake.

"Okay," she said. He deserved more than one word. Thousands of pages of words would never be enough to explain how much she appreciated him, how much she cared about him. But if she said anything else, she'd spill her entire heart.

It wasn't the time or the place. Maybe when it all was over. But for now, she had to focus. She had a timeline to Alter and a family to save.

The golden thread on the cover mocked her, shining as if inside it didn't hold terrors and tragedies.

"Mirella, can you talk me through it? I know I've done it before, but I'm not sure I can stay focused. I can barely hear myself think."

"Of course, dear. Close your eyes and feel for the memory you wish to change."

Her mouth went dry. "I don't know what I'm supposed to change. What do I do?"

"There may not be only one event that could give you the results you seek. Think about what you know about Renevelda. Her history, her relationships, her fears and desires. There is where you'll find the answer. You've Seen something of her past as well. Perhaps something in those memories is worth changing. Close your eyes and let your Gift take you."

Talullah obeyed. She wetted her lips. Dunamai's Eye warmed beneath her touch as her fingers traced the familiar pattern. She let her mind go blank in the hopes her Gift would fill it with the right memory.

What do I change?

Her other hand lay atop Renevelda's book, one finger curled under the cover, poised to turn pages. Snippets of memories in shades of purple raced behind her eyelids.

Renevelda as a small child sitting inside a white bassinet. Could something have happened to her at that age which made her into the monster she'd become? Would it be cruel to Alter the events of someone so young?

Flash.

A teenage Renevelda sitting in front of a vanity mirror. Talullah had seen this memory before. The day Renevelda's mother had decided to banish her from the Realm.

Another flash.

Renevelda wandering the streets of Viltresor. Rags hung loose on her thin frame as she crept through the street, stealing glances at the shops and stalls. Looking for something. Or someone. Was that the day she'd stumbled into the magical community and had begun her studies? If Talullah made it so she'd never found them, would it make a difference?

Stars winked in the corners of Talullah's vision. Keeping up with the memories was like trying to catch minnows with her bare hands.

A loud pecking at the door broke her concentration. Her eyes flew open. "Cleo? I haven't even picked the memory yet."

"Gillie's magic will hold her for a little while. Keep trying," Mirella urged.

Outside, the great bird let out a screech that stabbed Talullah's eardrums. Its wings thumped against the door.

Dhalian grabbed an umbrella, the closest thing to him that might be used as a weapon. Mirella armed herself with Gillie's butcher knife and pulled out her mirror.

"Do you See her? Is she coming?" asked Talullah.

"You don't need a mirror to see me," a silky voice said.

Renevelda.

"I've waited a long time to meet you, Talullah Bridgestone. But my patience has run out. If you ever want to see your darling sisters again, open the door."

Chapter 38

"Talullah, get to work on that memory. When she breaks through, I'll hold her off as long as possible." Mirella dropped the knife on the counter and motioned Dhalian to take it. "You'll have better luck with that."

"Does she have them? My sisters?" Talullah asked.

Mirella stole a glance at the mirror on the table. "No. They're still at the safe house. I've managed to get through."

"What about you?" asked Dhalian, grabbing the knife and clutching its handle so hard his knuckles turned white.

"Magic, of course. Not as strong as hers, but it might be enough." She drew a symbol in the air and waited. No one moved.

A faint rustling sound came from outside and Mirella smirked. "Gillie taught me a few tricks years ago. I'm a bit rusty, but I'll do what I can."

"What's that sound?" asked Dhalian.

"Trees."

Talullah focused on the page in front of her, willing her mind to ignore Cleo's screeches and Renevelda's orders. To not picture the tree roots snaking across the forest floor.

"Cleo, snap those twigs' roots. Ah, Mirella, of course. I thought we might meet again. But it's going to take more than bewitched trees to stop me from getting what I want. You want to play hide and seek? Fine."

The sound of cracking bark followed.

"Does anyone else smell smoke?" asked Dhalian.

Black clouds spilled under the door and through the window cracks. "The house is on fire," said Talullah. It filled the small space in a matter of seconds. They all dropped to the floor and covered their mouths, coughing.

For a second, she considered leaving Renevelda's book to burn. Maybe scorching it would kill the sorceress. Maybe it would be like she never existed. Mirella's warnings came to the forefront of Talullah's mind. If changing something small could leave giant scars on time, who knew what consequences would result from disappearing a person entirely. She couldn't take that chance. Her goal was to Alter Renevelda's path, not erase it. At least, not yet.

Talullah snatched Renevelda's book off the table.

She shoved it into the large pocket inside her cloak for safe keeping. The cloak would protect her from the heat, but it wouldn't prevent asphyxiation. They had to get out. Now.

"She's smoking us out like pests." Dhalian's hacking cough made Talullah cringe. Sweat trickled down her face.

"Plan B. We fight her head-on," said Mirella. She crawled to the door. Knowing there was no better option, Talullah followed. At least outside she'd be able to breathe for a few minutes more.

They spilled out onto the grass in a sooty heap, gasping for air.

"I knew you'd see it my way," said Renevelda in an icy voice.

With a wave of the sorceress's hand, bursts of green fire shot from Gillie's treehouse and landed in floating lanterns encircling the group. The rest of the flames dissipated in a blink, leaving the smell of charred wood in its wake.

"Please—" Talullah started, unsure what she was about to ask for.

"Cleo, secure the others."

"Wait!" yelled Talullah.

But Cleo sprang forward and pinned Dhalian and Mirella to the ground, each beneath one of her taloned feet.

Talullah dragged herself toward them.

"This is between us, Talullah."

Clenching her jaw, Talullah moved into a crouch.

Renevelda flicked her wrist. All of the breath left Talullah's lungs in an instant. A tight pressure prevented her inhaling or exhaling. Her mouth opened in a silent attempt to breathe.

A second later, crisp, cool air rushed through her nose and into her lungs, expanding them in a painful burst. Talullah coughed. Her chest burned as if she'd swallowed a handful of embers.

Renevelda paced back and forth in front of her. "There is a natural order to life, Talullah. Occasionally, something tips the balance. The Suditzas created Dunamai's Eye and its four stones to ensure none of them could emphasize her own Gifts over those of her sisters. And they entrusted their descendants to carry on their way, protecting the balance of life, writing destinies, and protecting time."

Talullah stayed silent but slipped a hand into her cloak's interior pocket. Renevelda's book was still there. She had to figure out a way to open it without Renevelda noticing.

"The Suditzas were wrong. They were foolish to divide their power. And even more so for giving it to mortals. They were the ancient magicians, masters of time and truth, and their trust led to their own demise. Did you know that? One of their earliest descendants turned on them."

"What does this have to do with me?" Talullah asked, although she knew perfectly well what Renevelda was after.

She needed to stall. To think of an escape plan.

"Our destinies, yours and mine, are entangled. I've spent a long time searching for Dunamai's Eye. The one thing that will allow me to return to my rightful place. Don't bother denying you have it. How dare you disrespect its power, wearing it like a junk store trinket?"

Renevelda stopped in front of Talullah, her eyes like lakes at midnight on a starless winter. A smile wound its way across her face like ivy on a trellis, a delicate curl that could strangle away life without the slightest hesitation.

"Get away from her!" yelled Dhalian.

Cleo pressed him further into the ground, her talons scraping his forehead open. Blood seeped from the wound and down his face.

Dhal uttered a sound between a groan and a growl.

"Pipe down, Messenger Boy." Renevelda turned back to Talullah. "I thought about killing you as soon as your friend here told me how to find River Hill. Unfortunately, the spell has strict rules not even my magic can break. The Suditzas protected their power from theft, both physical and magical. Clever, though not foolproof." Flame reflections danced around her irises. "Turns out this plan worked much better. You retrieved the stone for me and walked right into my waiting arms. It's time to hand it over."

So, Renevelda couldn't just take the necklace from her. Good. Whatever Renevelda did to her, she wouldn't give up Dunamai's Eye. Talullah's muscles clenched in anticipation of pain. She pushed her chin forward, and almost smiled at the memory of Margot doing the same when facing the soldiers.

"I thought that might be the case. I'm willing to offer a trade." Renevelda flicked both her wrists. Screams ripped from both Mirella and Dhalian's throats. Cleo had released her grip, but both stayed flat on their stomachs, pressing their hands over their ears.

"Stop! Let them be!" Lightning zapped her insides.

"That's your problem, Talullah. You're not creative. When your enemy has a weakness, you exploit it and compel them to do what you want. And mortals' weaknesses are always loved ones."

Mirella and Dhalian both fell silent and still.

"They're still alive. Give me the necklace and they go free." Renevelda's thin, pale eyebrows raised.

"Don't do it, Tules," groaned Dhalian.

"Remember, Talullah. Concentrate and use your strengths." Mirella's voice was hoarse, but the emphasis behind it was strong.

"I knew your mother, you know. Untalented. Weak." Renevelda made a *tsk-tsk* sound with her mouth. "You don't believe me? We met by chance in Viltresor, she and I, in the village I had made my home. She came to me seeking relief, but at the time I didn't have the skill to give her what she wanted. I didn't know about Dunamai's Eye and its power. Later I realized my mistake. Your mother had the Eye the whole time. I sent her away, and I didn't see her again for many years."

"My mother would never seek dark magic." Talullah shot the words like arrows nocked on her tongue.

"We'd all like to believe that, wouldn't we? But sometimes the people we put on pedestals do not deserve to be there. By the time I connected the Eye to your mother, many people had disappeared to River Hill to escape the war. I suspected your mother had gone—she seemed the traitorous type. But I was forced to be patient. I knew the Eye would show itself someday."

Talullah tried to block out Renevelda's words and focus on finding the memory she needed. The sorceress was trying to distract her. To break her down. It wouldn't work.

"Lucky for me, the opportunity wandered onto my doorstep. No one from Terrapese or Viltresor dares to enter the castle grounds uninvited. The intruder had to be from River Hill. Your friend had the answers I'd been seeking, and he led me right to you. Now he's going to help me once more."

She flicked her wrist again. Dhalian writhed on the ground. His shaking hands hovered over his ears.

"Dhalian!"

"Don't...give...to...her...Tules..." Gasps punctuated Dhalian's words.

"Tell me, Talullah. What do you value more? The lives of your long-lost aunt and closest friend, or the lives of your sisters?"

A burning sensation rubbed Talullah's wrists and ankles as she pulled against an invisible force, trying to get to Mirella and Dhalian. Renevelda's magic held her just far enough away she couldn't touch them but close enough to see the pain in their eyes. Tears blurred her own vision.

She wouldn't let Renevelda take anyone else from her. Her sisters were safe with the Capricos and she still had Renevelda's book. Destiny be damned. The whole world could rot for all she cared at that moment. The people she loved weren't going to die because of her.

"Okay!" she yelled. "Just stop. Stop hurting them and I'll give it to you."

"Fast learner." She flicked her wrist and the screaming stopped.

Dhalian and Mirella lay limp on the ground. Talullah's bindings released and she ran to their sides, crouching in between them.

"Pity. I didn't even get to the blade. Dhalian, as I recall, is acquainted with that one already." Renevelda stalked toward her. She held out a silk-gloved hand.

"Let them move," Talullah said, standing up.

Renevelda sighed and flicked her wrist as if shooing a bug.

Dhalian and Mirella both pushed themselves to a wobbly seated position.

"Go," Talullah said. "You both need to get out of here. Tell the others what's happened, that she's got it and they need to stop her."

"No, Talullah," croaked Mirella. "This is not the way."

"Please, Mirella. Someone's going to need to find her after she kills me." Talullah reached her stinging hands behind her neck and undid the clasp. The necklace weighed too heavy in her palm, as if it had absorbed her guilt.

"Tules!" Dhalian scrambled forward but Cleo caught his arm and squeezed. He cried out. "Don't do this."

"You have a choice, Talullah. Don't choose this." Mirella wheezed.

She couldn't beat Renevelda with magic, and she wouldn't let them die in front of her eyes when she had the chance to stop it. Alteration wasn't possible if she couldn't feel the threads. She wouldn't be able to find a memory and change it with their screams clawing at her heart.

"She's right," said Renevelda, waving her hand. "You do have a choice. And those choices have consequences. But with a power as splendid as encased in this necklace, choices can be changed, and consequences can be erased."

The necklace floated toward Renevelda, the gem sparkling in the firelight. Talullah watched it, dread pitting in her stomach. She'd altered their futures without even trying. But what fate had she decided for them all?

A twig snapped somewhere behind Renevelda. "Stealth is not your strong suit," the sorceress said.

"Stealth isn't the point," said a gruff voice, stepping into the ring of light. "I believe this belongs to you."

Gillie.

Talullah's heart soared. The wood faerie nudged a small figure into the light. Though gagged and bound with glowing rings, Zeri stood at full height.

The necklace hovered in mid-air halfway between Talullah and Renevelda. Maybe she could reach it while the sorceress was distracted.

"Azeria. How interesting of you to show up here like *that*."

Talullah took a step forward, then another.

She reached a hand out and—

A cool breeze grazed her palm as an arrow whizzed by. Dunamai's Eye snagged on its feathers. The arrow turned. It zipped through the air.

Talullah whipped her head around just in time to see a gloved hand pluck it from the sky.

Chapter 39

Gwendolyn brushed her messy golden curls out of her eyes with her free hand and tossed Dunamai's Eye to Talullah. "Don't ever do that again," she huffed.

Talullah gaped. She'd just seen Gwendolyn through the mirror. How had she gotten there so fast? And Gillie, too.

"Trees," said Gillie, reading her mind.

With shaking hands, Talullah secured the necklace around her neck.

Zeri spat, narrowly missing Gillie's bare feet. He tugged her glowing leash and she stumbled.

"I'll deal with you later," Renevelda said to Zeri, flipping her ice blond hair over her shoulder. "I'm too busy to scold naughty pets." She flicked her wrist, and though the necklace hovered above Talullah's chest, the clasp held firm.

Zeri smiled, showing her pointy teeth. "I've got a secret." She rocked back and forth on her heels. "Wanna know what it is?"

"No," said Renevelda, gritting her teeth and motioning with her other hand. A spark shot from Dunamai's Eye and landed in her open palm, singeing her glove. She recoiled and shook her hand. Her eyes darkened with malice and when she spoke to Talullah her voice was a poisonous whisper. "How dare you, you talentless mockery of magic."

An invisible fist punched Talullah in the stomach and she doubled over, wheezing. Her head whipped to the side as another blow hit her cheek. Gwendolyn rushed to her side. Out of the corner of her eye a giant white blur of fur moved behind Gillie.

"You're just like your mother. Weak. Scared. No imagination." A slash appeared on Talullah's arm with each of Renevelda's insults. Sizzling blood trickled from the wounds and slid to the ground.

"Gwen's arrow—" Talullah started.

"Broke the offer," Gillie finished. "She can't take it unless you offer again."

"You're clever for a wood troll." Renevelda's sharp eyes narrowed on him. "Trolls happen to be Cleo's favorite toy."

"Faerie, but who cares? The important thing is you can't use Dunamai's Eye unless Talullah gives it to you."

"Ah, but how or why she gives it is not specified."

"You'll want to know this, I promise," said Zeri. Mischief sparkled in her eyes. "Though I really should trade for it. It's valuable."

"If you know what's good for you, you'll shut your mouth," growled Gillie, yanking Zeri's leash.

"I'm tired of you all treating me like an animal. If only I could show you what I can really do…but I can't. Not yet, anyway. What do you say, Rennie? My freedom for my information."

"Fine. Say it and then shut up," Renevelda muttered, distracted.

Zeri tugged at the black ribbon she wore as a collar, and seeming satisfied, she smiled again. "Talullah has your storybook, too."

Renevelda's eyes flashed and for a fraction of a second, Talullah thought she saw fear hiding among the flecks of sapphire. The sorceress's mouth tightened as she smoothed her silk gown with calm hands. "You mean the book you were supposed to retrieve for me?"

Zeri hopped from one foot to the other, her red hair swinging. "Technically, I did as you asked. I brought it to the castle."

"And then you let her steal it? We'll deal with your punishment later. For now, Talullah, it's time you meet some of my friends."

A ring of fire burst in the sky, cascading like a waterfall. Screams ricocheted off the trees and pierced Talullah's eardrums. She pressed her hands to her head, but the harder she pressed, the louder the voices grew. Like they were trapped inside her head instead.

"The Unforgiven," Talullah said, though she didn't know if anyone could hear her.

"It was perfect timing. These poor, tortured souls lacked a purpose. I gave them one."

Wails turned to comprehensible voices.

I am guilt incarnate.

They'll never know the best of me.

I traded everything I loved for power.

Shame, despair, disgust.

Betrayal. Lust. Anger.

The flaming voices chanted their sins at peak volume.

And then a voice Talullah knew well crept in, softer than the rest but strong.

She was selfish and cruel and you're better off without her. She never loved you. How could she? What she did should be evidence enough. Coward. Liar. Weak. Like mother, like daughter.

The voice of her worst self. The one who painted her mother a villain to protect her from the pain. It wasn't true. She had seen her mother's sacrifice with her own eyes. Yet a part of her heart yearned to lean into the doubt she'd felt for so long.

Fear, regret, and blame raged in the swirling circle of fire. Her mind was so absorbed now, the fire was all she could see. Everything else had disappeared.

"Give me the necklace and it will stop," Renevelda said.

"Don't listen to them," said another voice in her head. "You have to focus. Do what you came here to do."

Whether by her command or its own volition, her fingers traced the Eye. She forced her mind to clear and sought a vision for what to do.

It came in an instant. A clear image she'd seen before, what seemed like a lifetime ago.

Smiling, Talullah covered her head with the cloak's hood. She moved closer to the Firefall and reached a hand toward it.

Angry voices screeched in her ears, unintelligible babbles once again.

From somewhere near, Dhalian said, "Tules, what are you doing?"

She ignored him. The steady rhythm of her heart and her even breathing confirmed it. This was what she had to do. Her body knew it. Her inner eye had Seen it. Just like her mother had no doubt Seen it years before. Had this been the event that set her mother down the path to Praeteriti, toward the stone?

Sweat trickled down her neck but her skin remained cool. She tucked her fists into her sleeves. Shoulders back and head held high, she walked straight into the fire.

Chapter 40

Outside the wall of flames, Renevelda laughed. "They'll consume her."

"And the necklace will be destroyed," said Gwen.

"That, Globe Witch, is where you're wrong. You think the Suditzas wouldn't protect their power from flames? No, the Unforgiven will convince Talullah to give the necklace and its power to me, its rightful owner. The only question is, how long will it take?"

"Tules, get out of there!" Dhalian screamed.

Talullah gritted her teeth against the pain in her ears and head. Somehow, in the middle of the chaos, her muscles had loosened.

She could do this. Her mother had believed it. Otherwise she wouldn't have sacrificed the years she spent trapped in Praeteriti. And now, Talullah had to believe it, too.

Voices assaulted her from every angle, trying to convince her to join them in the darkness of her past thoughts.

Your mother passed her burden to you because she loved you the least of her children.

The one who makes your heart sing will never return the chorus.

Plain.

Unoriginal.

Weave and sew, weave and sew. Forever, you will weave and sew.

She blocked the voices as best she could and knelt to the ground in the middle of the circle. All around her, flames made of ghosts plummeted from the sky and crashed into ash.

With sweaty palms, she pulled Renevelda's book from her cloak and rested it in front of her, careful not to touch any of the fire. She didn't know if the Firefall could burn her, but now wasn't the time to find out. And if Renevelda could come in after her, she needed to hurry.

Ashes swirled into her hair as she opened the cover and closed her eyes. Images formed in her mind with the turn of each page.

What memory should she change, and how should she change it?

The question played over and over, mixing with the onslaught of shrieks. Though the cloak protected her from external forces, her mind and emotions were still vulnerable.

Memories, memories, we all have them.

Dark and deep and troubled.

What we've done cannot be taken back.

No one mourns us.

Choose wrong, dear girl, and your loved ones will suffer.

You'll join us in our misery.

Forever in despair.

Forever Unforgiven.

"No!" Talullah shouted. "I won't!"

She flipped the pages faster. At Renevelda's whim, they tried to break her. She wouldn't give in. Not that easily.

A memory. She needed to latch onto a memory. Once she focused on that, it would be easier to block the voices.

About a third of the way through the book, her fingers grazed a thread with multiple knots. A jolt ran from her fingertip to her collarbone.

At once she stood in a room she recognized—Renevelda's mother's room. Renevelda, much younger than now, paced back and forth.

A woman dressed in fine silks and a long cloak entered the scene. The woman looked at Renevelda's bare shoulders. Seeing nothing, she raised her eyebrow and smirked. Renevelda burst into tears and approached the woman, begging and pleading. The woman shook her head and pointed toward a billowing curtain.

The scene dissipated in a flash of violet smoke, and another took its place.

A young Renevelda walking the streets of Viltresor.

"Having fun playing in my past?" Renevelda's icy voice sliced through the screams.

What do you know about Renevelda? Mirella had asked. This. Renevelda's strained relationship with her mother defined her.

"Do you really believe all of this will redeem you in her eyes?" Talullah asked, voice tinged with pity.

"You stupid girl," Renevelda said, venom dripping from her tongue. "You think all of this is to make my mother love me?" She let out a pained laughed. "This is to show my mother what I truly am. That I am greater now than she ever will be. Her rejection, though devastating at first, made me strong. It enabled me to make myself into whomever I wanted to be, and in the end, she will get what she deserves. And, so will you. Let's see how clever you truly are, Sezna Seer."

Images flashed by so quickly in her mind she didn't have time to orient in one before the next came and went. Renevelda used the Firefall to manipulate what Talullah could See.

Dizzy, she reached out with her mind, trying to grab any memory at all and stop the carousel from spinning around her.

A loud *thunk* from outside filtered in. "Arrows? You think arrows are a match for my magic?"

The sky lit up with a bolt of lightning and thunder rolled overhead.

"Keep going, Talullah. We'll keep her occupied," Gwendolyn encouraged.

Regardless of what the Unforgiven said, she was not alone. Her friends were here to help her. They were doing their part. She would do hers.

Through the growls and screeches, whizzes of magic, and voices, Talullah pressed on. The visions had slowed enough for her to understand the scenes, but she still couldn't control the rate at which they moved or how much she Saw.

Squeezing her eyes shut tight, she reached toward the memories, feeling each for authenticity. Her fingers danced across the book page, translating each knot's memory like a braille word to the blind.

Time was a language with structure and rules and individual parts that made up the whole. She hadn't understood before how to search it for meaning. But, in the middle of the chaos, she began to piece together the puzzle.

"Hurry, Tules," Dhalian croaked.

After dismissing the memories that didn't fit the pattern, two remained. Both she had Seen before. She played them back to back, feeling for anything that stood out. In one, Renevelda sat at her vanity in front of a broken mirror. In the other, she walked down the streets of Viltresor, eyeing the tables of trinkets.

Talullah's fingers sparked like flint meeting stone.

"Get on with it, Wrecker! We can't hold her any longer!"

In an instant, all sound ceased. The silence was almost as painful as the screams. The ghosts in the Firefall froze, open-mouthed, and a slit opened in the side of the ring.

Renevelda glided in and glanced down at Talullah. "Looks like I have to do this myself after all."

Chapter 41

Talullah's grip on Renevelda's book tightened, her thumb and forefinger still pinching a knot. Her breath hitched in her chest. Remembering Dhalian's encounter with the sorceress, Talullah refused to make eye contact.

Book or knife, book or knife. Which weapon would serve her best against this foe? She squeezed the book to her chest, as if Renevelda couldn't summon it at her will.

"I know you've Seen my past, Talullah Bridgestone. What do you plan to do about it?" Color rose on her sharp cheekbones, warming her porcelain skin.

Talullah scooted backward. Her back bumped up against the Firefall of the Unforgiven. She'd walked right through on her way in, but now the souls formed a solid barrier. Pushing her way out was not an option.

"I wouldn't touch them, if I were you."

With a snap of Renevelda's fingers, the Firefall roared to life once more, drowning out Talullah's thoughts. Her limbs were made of bricks. The book slipped in her arms. She couldn't press her hands to her ears without losing it. Echoes ricocheted inside her skull, the voices shrill and piercing. Too much to handle. They drained her energy by the second.

"How do you feel now?" The sorceress smirked.

Despite her best effort not to answer, the word leaked through her cracked lips. "Weak."

While hunting, her mother had taught her to look for the weak link in the group. "Look for the one with a limp or the one that can't quite keep up," she'd said. If they didn't catch it for food, something else would. The weak didn't survive in the wild. Nature made sure of it.

Thinking about it now she had to decide. Show her weakness and accept certain death, or tuck away her insecurities and physical pain and make Renevelda work for her reward?

Gripping the book in one hand, she clawed at the ground with the other. Damp earth collected under her fingernails. The Firefall held her in place. Memories that were not her own spilled into her consciousness. They drowned out her thoughts, beating upon her with the strong cadence of a war drum, until she could no longer separate her experiences from theirs.

"Their burdens are becoming yours. How kind you are to relieve them of their suffering. They have waited a long time for forgiveness."

Talullah's eyes fluttered. She struggled to reach one of Renevelda's memories while keeping hold of the book. The two visions tangoed in her mind, a choreographed dance of spinning and moving through the endless array of heart-wrenching experiences conjured by the Firefall.

The visions disappeared as Renevelda's book lurched from her hands and crossed toward the sorceress. "You should know, River girl, I always win."

Not this time.

Talullah drew her knife and flung it toward Renevelda. A sharp inhale told Talullah she'd struck her mark. She willed her eyes to uncross, to focus.

The spell on the book broke and it fell to the ground.

A drop of blood from Renevelda's bleeding side splashed onto the book's cover.

Talullah dragged herself to it. Pressure built up inside Talullah's head until she was sure it would burst.

Adrenaline turned her bloodstream into a raging river. Any number of things might kill her in the next few minutes or seconds. But before it did, she would to finish what she'd started.

She locked her fear and pain into the furthest corner of her heart. Renevelda was right. She *was* weak. She *was* afraid. She may not make it out alive.

But, by the Founders, she would do everything in her power to take Renevelda down with her. She wouldn't roll over and let the predator take her.

She refused to be easy prey.

Another arrow ripped through the air, narrowly missing Renevelda's arm. Kahu howled just outside the circle. The sorceress screamed.

It was now or never.

Clenching her jaw, Talullah flipped the book open and held each of the knots she'd been considering. Again, the memories played in her mind.

Teenage Renevelda pleaded with her mother to let her stay in the Realm of the Divine, despite her missing mark. Her half-sisters jeered and laughed. Renevelda's face tightened, her eyes darkening as she stalked through the curtain from her mother's room.

Could changing Renevelda's mother's decision be the answer?

The second vision showed Renevelda dressed in a torn dress walking the streets of Viltresor. She passed shops selling trinkets and women offering tarot readings. A portly man called to her from a shack at the end of the street. Nailed to its door, a sign advertised something in a foreign language. Renevelda smiled and disappeared behind it.

Maybe that was the place Renevelda had learned her sinister magic.

No matter how long she warred with herself and tried to rationalize one over the other, the truth remained that either choice could be wrong. Any choice was better than none.

Every inch of her ached and she could barely hold anything in her mind for longer than a few seconds.

It started low and slow, gaining strength as it played. Those familiar notes and words she'd called on so many times before.

Through the fire blazing bright

Trust yourself, harness your might.

Inner struggle blinds your eyes, let it go and win the prize.

Use your heart, keep your mind,

And what you seek...

"You shall find," she finished aloud.

Locking her mind on the memory of Renevelda in Viltresor, she let her fingers work their own kind of magic. The knot loosened.

Her hands shook as she retied it at a different point on the thread, making it so Renevelda never followed the man into the shop with the foreign sign. She tugged the thread to snap the end.

She'd done it.

She'd Altered someone's life.

Actually, she'd Altered everyone's.

Renevelda's head snapped up. "What have you done? You stupid girl, what have you done?" She stalked toward Talullah in a rage that matched the Firefall blazing around them. Sparks jumped from the sorceress's palms, narrowly missing Talullah. Her heart thumped wildly in her chest.

Talullah retrieved her bloodstained knife from the ground with shaky hands. The pain in her head receded enough that she could stand without falling. Ripples flowed through the wall of flaming souls.

Renevelda stopped inches from her.

"Something's happening," Gillie shouted.

"Get out of there, Tules!"

Another arrow whipped through the curtain of fire, but it missed its target.

"You did this. Remember that when we meet again." Renevelda disappeared in a blink, leaving Talullah alone to face the consequences of her actions.

The earth rumbled beneath her feet, throwing Talullah to her knees. She looked up. As if someone had detached its top from its place in the sky, the Firefall of the Unforgiven cascaded down in a wave of fiery souls.

What *had* she done?

"Tules!" Dhalian shouted.

She didn't have the energy to respond. Penny, Margot, and her father were safe. She'd done what she'd set out to do. If this was the price of her success, she welcomed it.

She tugged the hood of her cloak over her head and curled herself into a ball on the ground.

When the Firefall crashed down on her, she didn't feel a thing.

Chapter 42

Honeyed dew. The smell lifted her from sleep. Though she lay alone, her hand tingled as if it ached to hold something that had only just been there.

"Thank the Founders," Mirella squealed. "We didn't know..."

Bleary-eyed, Talullah looked around. Shapes took the forms of her allies standing in a semi-circle in a small sitting room. Mirella, Gwendolyn, Gillie, Dhalian. They'd all survived.

A large wet tongue slid across her face. Kahu danced in a circle, her fluffy white body coated in a layer of dark ash. The wolf whined and butted her head against Talullah's hand.

"Hi, there," she said. Her voice came out as a strained whisper.

"Praise the Suditzas," Gwendolyn said.

"Where is she?" Talullah asked.

"Gone," said Gillie. "We don't know where, but as long as she's not here I'd say whatever you did was an improvement."

"And Zeri?" She scooted so her back rested against the squishy arm of the sofa.

"Also gone," said Mirella. "Before she disappeared, she ripped the ribbon from her neck and said, 'Tell her foxes don't forget.' Then she shifted forms, into a small red fox, and ran off into the forest."

"My sisters and father?"

"In the kitchen," Mirella said. "I'll call them in soon. We wanted to make sure..."

Talullah nodded.

Dhalian gave her a once over, then said, "You look terrible." He picked a piece of ash out of her hair and tossed it to the floor. A smile cracked his lips and revealed his gleaming teeth.

"You're the picture of perfection, yourself," she replied, pulling him into tight embrace. "What happened to your arm?"

"Oh this? Talons. But, I'm aces. Gwendolyn's a B-plus medic, I'd say."

"B-plus?" Gwendolyn challenged.

"You're sloppy with the antiseptic."

Talullah rolled her eyes. "I'm glad you're okay."

Dhal's smile faded. "I think I speak for all of us when I say this. What in the Four Worlds were you thinking? We couldn't get in there to help you. We could barely see what was going on."

"My vision," she replied. "The red one with the girl in the cloak. It was always supposed to happen that way. The girl was me. I just figured it out a bit too late. But what happens now? I Altered one of her memories, but how do we know if it was the right one or if it worked?"

"We'll find out in time, dear," Mirella said.

Gillie interrupted. "You've retrieved one of the four stones. There are still three out there in the Worlds. Word will spread quickly that Renevelda has been stopped this time and that you were the one to do it. The few Sezna Seers who remain have been in hidin' for many years. The monsters who've hunted them will know you've got the Gift too, and they'll come for you, same as the rest. Even if you've Altered Renevelda's past enough to stop her seekin' the stones, others will take her place. As long as the stones are scattered, the stability of time is in danger."

"So, we have to keep searching," Talullah said.

"Yes. But not today. You've earned a bit of rest. Would you like to see your family?" Gwendolyn placed a gentle hand on Talullah's shoulder.

"More than anything."

The room emptied except for Talullah, who stood.

"Tuley!" squealed Penny. She ran full speed, only stopping when she collided with Talullah's legs. "Why are you so dirty?" she asked, wrinkling her nose.

"I am so happy to see you!" Talullah picked Penny up and squeezed her, twirling in a circle. She buried her face in her youngest sister's hair.

She smelled like rosewater soap and home.

How she'd dreamed of this moment. A happy reunion. And now it was here. She never wanted to leave again.

A second later, Talullah felt a tap on her back. She turned to see a wide-eyed Margot, her eyebrows drawn together.

"Hi, Mar."

Normally stoic, Margot burst into tears. Talullah set Penny back on her feet and bent down to Margot's level.

"Mar, what's wrong? I'm back. Just like I promised. Everything's going to be okay."

"I'm so sorry, Tuley. I'm so, so sorry for everything. I went to the pretzel cart even when you told me to just get a lemonade and then everything bad happened and you went away and I didn't know if I'd ever see you—"

Four Worlds, Margot blamed herself.

Talullah pulled her sister into a tight embrace, hoping her hug could convey the seriousness of her words. "Mar, listen to me. None of this was your fault. Do you hear me? Please don't ever think that. Sometimes bad things just happen."

She needed her sister to release her guilt. The howl of the Unforgiven had shown her the damage it could do.

Margot nodded.

Talullah stood and grabbed each of her sisters by the hand. They deserved to know their mother hadn't left them for lack of love, but because of how great her love had been. Talullah opened her mouth to tell them. The words caught in her throat like a fly in a spiderweb. At first, they rattled around in a feeble attempt to free themselves, but the more they struggled the more entangled they became. Finally, they stilled, accepting defeat.

She couldn't tell them. Not yet. Not now. There was still so much she didn't know herself. Like if their mother's story really had filled its last page, if she'd really died and gone onto whatever came next. Or, if she'd just traveled to a different of the Four Worlds where Talullah would find her safe and sound.

No, she couldn't risk telling her sisters either version until she'd verified the truth. Just for now, she'd keep it to herself. She'd tell them when the time was right.

When they entered the kitchen, Dhalian, Mirella, and Gwendolyn all sat at a small red table drinking mugs of tea. Gillie and Kahu lay in a corner, asleep.

And in the rocking chair next to the fireplace sat her father.

"My Talullah," he said softly as she approached. Dark circles had formed beneath his eyes. "I knew you could do it."

"What happened? Are you okay?" Concern replaced the relief she'd felt just moments before. She took his hand in hers. It was chillier than normal.

"Had a bit of an episode involving a poisoned sword, but before you get in a tizzy, Gwendolyn's fixed me up. I've made a good turn and will be good as new in a few weeks." His eyes sparkled, more alive than the rest of his body seemed.

"How long?" she whispered. "How long has it been since the Sunflower Festival?"

"Three months."

The breath left her lungs as if she'd been punched. Three months.

"Don't fret, Talullah. Soon it will be a distant memory." He smirked, pride amplifying his voice. "We watched it all through the mirror. You've got your mother's style."

Talullah cocked her head. "The sorceress mentioned..."

"That she knew your mother? Yes, I thought she might use that against you."

"It's true, then, what she said?"

"Some of it had roots in truth."

A connection formed in Talullah's mind. Her father's cane. That her mother had given him. And the vision. "Did you know?"

Her father sighed, his eyes fluttering as he fought sleep. "I knew she searched for the stones as a young girl. But I thought it was a hobby, a treasure hunt of sorts. Then, one day she gave me the cane and told me you'd see the vision in it one day. That it would help you understand. I don't have the Gift, so I never knew what it was or when you'd find it. But she said it was important, so I kept it. Grew to like it, even. It reminded me of her. I didn't know she planned to leave.

"Mirella wrote to me when she discovered your mother's plan to find one of the stones. I insisted Mirella stop your mother and send her home. Your aunt refused. Said it wasn't her place to decide."

"That's why we stopped visiting Mirella."

Her father nodded. "Your aunt did promise to protect your mother the best she could. I tried to contact Mirella not long after our disagreement, but she never answered. I figured she needed space, so I gave it to her."

"She was already in Praeteriti by that time. She'd followed Mother." Talullah paused. "I saw Mother, you know." She'd befriended her and suspected her. Had watched her disappear from view like a dream lost upon waking. Lost her for a second time.

"And you will again, I'm sure." Her father's eyes closed.

"It's the medicine," said a lower voice. "He comes and goes. But he's getting stronger." She recognized Captain Caprico as soon as he stepped into the room. It was strange seeing him in person again after their only other encounter in Nainehta Forest. "I'm sorry. I tried to keep them out of it from the beginning. I thought I could take them to your great-aunt's, but she was gone. Now I know why, obviously. But I couldn't leave them alone. And then the she-devil realized who they were."

She nodded, processing. "The note about going to see Mirella. That was from you, wasn't it?"

"Guilty." He paused, his jaw tight. "I need you to know I only did enough to convince Renevelda. If there had been another way—"

"I know," she said. She didn't really, never truly could. But something in his tone told her it was true. "Rantoul—"

He shook his head. "Only that first time. They were never alone with him."

Talullah exhaled through her nose. She could almost see the shame boiling inside him. "Thank you. For protecting them. And for getting them out."

"I couldn't leave them. I have two kids. Sons." His eyes looked wistful.

"Where are they now?"

"Preparing the next safe house. We'll meet up with them soon." His voice wavered as if trying to convince himself.

"Another safe house?"

"I've got friends in low places. Luckily, they don't have any hard feelings about me quitting the business. They're good people to know when you don't want to be found."

Talullah squashed her questions. It was probably better not to know too many details.

Silence fell.

"Actually, I need to go check on their progress. I'll just go do that..." Caprico trailed off as he left the room.

She silently acknowledged the sacrifices each person involved had made or would make in the future. These people, some of which she barely knew, had fought by her side. Had saved her.

Dhalian stepped up beside her and laced his fingers through hers.

She may not know what lay ahead, but she was starting to understand what had been. That was the real point of examining the past. Not to dwell on it, but to learn from it. To let it guide her.

As she wiped the ash from Dunamai's Eye, revealing the gleaming amethyst beneath, Talullah vowed, whatever came next, to do just that.

*WANT TO KNOW WHAT I'M working on, get exclusive updates on Talullah and friends' next adventure, and have first access to new content? Sign up for my mailing list! I promise never to spam your inbox or sell your data, because that ain't cool.

Click to join: Subscribe[1]

---

1. http://eepurl.com/cSQHuL

Acknowledgements

Writing this book is the most difficult thing I've ever done. Thank goodness I didn't have to do it alone.

I have to first thank God for answering my prayers in the least-expected of ways. Years ago I prayed for patience and to discover my true calling. Be warned, if this is your ask, He will give you the chance to practice.

This project has taken almost three full years from initial concept to final completion, and throughout that time has undergone countless rewrites. Never once did I consider giving it up. With each new draft I learned and grew. I sought out ways to make my writing better, even though it complicated and delayed my process. That's how I know writing is more than just a hobby. It might just be divine intervention.

To my parents, Christina and Jeff Manifold, you will never know how much your constant support means to me. From teaching me to read before kindergarten to going to a bookstore in Hawaii during a family vacation to buy *Harry Potter and the Deathly Hallows* when it first released, your enthusiasm for my love of books no doubt kindled my imagination and creative ambition. Thank you for being interested in my passion. Thank you for believing in me.

To my husband, Pat, thank you for helping me grow as a person every day. Thank you for reading a draft of this book I thought was ready to be seen and for encouraging me during the following two years as I ripped it apart and started over. Thank you for listening while I summarized countless podcast episodes about publishing. For sharing your creative spirit and inspiring me to use mine. For filling our home with music and laughter and joy. For walking the dog when it's cold and dark. For trusting me implicitly in all things. I couldn't have done this without you. Let's keep watering the tree.

Thank you to my developmental editor, Fiona McLaren. Without your input, Talullah would still be a cardboard cutout with no direction. Your enthusiasm for this story, even from our first conversation, helped drive me to finish when I'd tired of my own words. Thank you for pushing me to make this book better than I ever thought possible.

Thanks to Hampton Lamoureux for bringing this cover to life. It's more than I ever hoped for. You are a wizard.

Thank you to my first critique partner, Cassy Klisch. Though we parted ways before I completed the revised manuscript, your feedback on my early chapters made me realize I had so much more story to uncover. Thank you for helping me dig deeper.

To my first ever beta reader, Catherine Kopf, thank you for your kind words on a draft that did not deserve them. You gave me the confidence I needed to continue with a story I loved and the determination to fix what was broken.

To the mentors I've never met in real life and who probably have no idea who I am—Joanna Penn, K.M. Weiland, Kristen Kieffer, and Susan Dennard—without your blogs and newsletters and podcasts I would still be struggling blindly through my first draft. Thank you for giving freely your advice and time to those of us just getting started. What you do matters. This humble book is proof.

Thanks to all my friends and family members who have asked about this project. To be honest, that accountability truly helped me to see this project to completion. I'm so excited to finally be able to tell you it's ready.

Finally, thanks to you, whoever you are, for reading this book. Maybe you liked it, maybe you didn't. Whatever your opinion, thank you for having one. Thank you for spending some time in my head. I am eternally grateful.

About the Author

Kiersten Lillis is a lifelong bibliophile with a professional background in media production. She's spent many years building stories through audio and video while secretly coveting the written word and trying to bribe the muse. She loves sweet tea, libraries, and the Oxford comma. Originally from Indiana, she lives in Colorado with her family. *Amethyst in Ashes* is her first novel.

Read more at https://www.kierstenlillis.com/.